Why Women are Blamed for Everything

Exploring Victim Blaming of Women
Subjected to Violence and Trauma

Dr Jessica Taylor

Other works by Dr Jessica Taylor

Books

Taylor, J. (2020) Woman in Progress: The Reflective Journal for Women and Girls Subjected to Abuse and Trauma

Taylor, J. (2019) The Reflective Journal for Practitioners Working in Trauma and Abuse

Taylor, J. (2020) The Reflective Journal for Researchers and Academics

Eaton, J. & Paterson-Young, C. (2018) The Little Orange Book: Learning about abuse from the voice of a child

Reports

Taylor, J. (2020) Portrayals and Prevention Campaigns: Sexual Violence in the Media, VictimFocus

Eaton, J. (2019) Critical perspectives of child sexual exploitation practice and approaches, VictimFocus

Eaton, J. (2019) 'Logically, I know I am not to blame, but I still feel to blame': Exploring and measuring victim blaming and self-blame of women subjected to sexual violence and abuse, University of Birmingham

Eaton, J. (2019) The Human Rights of Girls Subjected to Child Sexual Exploitation in the UK, VictimFocus

Eaton, J. (2019) After CSE Films: Supporting children and families without traumatic imagery, VictimFocus

Eaton, J. (2018) Sexual Exploitation and Mental Health, Research in Practice for Adults, Dartington Press

Eaton, J. (2018) Can I tell you what it feels like? Exploring the harm caused by CSE films, VictimFocus

Eaton, J. & Holmes, D. (2017) Working effectively to address child sexual exploitation: An evidence scope, Research in Practice, Dartington Press

Why Women are Blamed for Everything

Exploring Victim Blaming of Women

Subjected to Violence and Trauma

Dr Jessica Taylor

Book cover design by Gemma Finn and Johnson Marketing.

First Printing: April 2020

ISBN 978-0-244-49834-4

Dr Jessica Taylor T/A VictimFocus

Derby, UK

www.victimfocus.org.uk

Email: Jessica@victimfocus.org.uk

Ordering Information:

Special discounts are available on quantity purchases by corporations, associations, educators, and others. For details, contact the publisher at the above listed address.

This book is dedicated to the millions of women and girls around the world who are routinely subjected to abuse, violence, torture, harassment, rape, forced marriage, mutilation and exploitation at the hands and minds of men and patriarchy.

The millions of women who are living their lives as best they can whilst trying to process the violence and misogyny committed against them, often without support or compassion.

You have my total respect, love and support. I commit myself to this cause and to doing everything I am capable of to continue to challenge.

I would like to thank Juliette McAleer for writing to me and letting me read her poetry. I have included one of her brilliant poems in this book because it demonstrates so accurately, the questions asked by so many women and girls who have been blamed for male violence.

My sincere thanks and respect to the radical feminist authors, activists, thinkers and practitioners who have come before me. Nothing I do or say today would have been possible without the effort, progress and ideas of incredibly brave women I look up to and aspire to be.

Thank you to all the professionals, volunteers and activists who work every single day to support women and girls subjected to violence, abuse and trauma.

As I finished this book during lockdown in 2020, I would like to thank Jaimi and Mandy for supporting me. Special thanks to Mandy for reading through my work, discussing it with me and motivating me when the world became a scary and uncertain place. I will forever argue with you both about the oxford comma. And about the 'pronunciation' of words I have written into this book but cannot say properly. All my love and thanks to you both.

Content

Foreword   8

'Chasing Redemption' by Juliette McAleer   11

Key terms explained   13

Key abbreviations explained   15

1. Introduction to violence against women   17

2. Introduction to women's trauma   28

3. What is victim blaming?   33

4. Examples of victim blaming of women   47

5. Prevalence of victim blaming attitudes   57

6. Why do we blame women?   92

7. How does our criminal justice system blame women?   111

8. How do our cultures and beliefs blame women?   119

9. How does the family and friend support network blame women?   136

10. How does the media blame women?   142

11. How does the education system teach us to blame women?   156

12. How do mental health services blame women?   163

13. An attack on the woman: All the other ways we blame her   173

14. Blaming the woman, blaming the girl   196

15. Talking to women about victim blaming   216

16. Talking to professionals about victim blaming   251

17. Discussions and considerations   275

18. Final thoughts   311

A foreword by Dr Jessica Taylor (PhD, FRSA)

Writing and releasing this book feels like such a huge task. It is the first book that attempts to bring together theories, research findings, case studies and real experiences from professional practice to explore why we blame women and girls for anything and everything we possibly can.

I named the book 'Why Women are Blamed for Everything' for a reason. This year, I have been working with and for women and girls subjected to male violence for 11 years – since I was 19 years old. I sometimes feel like no matter who the woman or girl is, what she did, what she said, where she's from – we will still find a way to blame her for everything that was done to her by an abusive man. I have heard women and girls held responsible for everything from being harassed in the street to being trafficked around the UK and sold to men.

This is to the point where women can be murdered by men, and as a society, and as professionals, we will still look for what the woman did wrong, what she could have done differently, and why she didn't tell someone what was being done to her.

I started my career in the criminal justice system supporting victims and witnesses of serious crime. The majority of my caseload was domestic and sexual violence. No matter how many women and girls I met, I was always fizzing with anger when I heard how they had been blamed or told to change something about themselves. It hurt me to listen to them say that they had changed all those things about themselves and they had blamed themselves – and yet the perpetrator had attacked them again. Much of my time was spent talking women and girls through their own self-blame and their experiences of being blamed by their parents, their partners, their friends, their community, the police, the social worker, the hospitals and even the professionals working in domestic and sexual violence support services.

When I moved into managing rape centres and sexual violence services, I hoped that I would be hearing considerably less victim blaming than I heard in my criminal justice jobs. What I found was that victim blaming was not less, it was just different. Instead of dealing with defence lawyers questioning what girls were wearing and why women were drinking – I was dealing with mental health teams telling women and girls they were mentally ill or had personality disorders because they 'still hadn't recovered' from being abused or raped. It was hard to hear women and girls aged from 13 years old talking about themselves as if they were broken, disordered and mentally ill. When I worked with them, they certainly didn't appear 'broken' or 'disordered' or 'mentally ill'. They instead appeared to me as completely normal, rational women and girls who were trying to cope with the trauma of being abused and violated.

Later on, I moved to work in child sexual abuse and exploitation. I remember thinking that there must be much less victim blaming within children's services – especially as so many children being sexually abused and exploited are under the age of consent and could not possibly be held responsible for anything at all. Every day, I was proven wrong. It was quickly apparent that even children who were being abused and exploited by adult men were being told to change something about themselves, to take responsibility and to take the blame for being raped and harmed. Talking to teenage girls who are convinced that they were sexually exploited is because, 'I keep putting myself at risk', is frankly soul destroying.

When women and girls have built up the courage to tell someone they had been raped or abused, the experience of being blamed or held responsible had stayed with them for years. It had changed the way they saw themselves. No matter how many times I heard it, I never became desensitized to hearing the impact of victim blaming on women and girls.

I decided to undertake a PhD which sought to explore the psychology underpinning the apparent need we have for blaming women and girls for the male violence committed against them. I wondered why we did this, how we came to these perspectives, where these biases came from and how this was all impacting women, girls – and the support they receive when they do disclose.

All my PhD research is contained within this book, in addition to other research projects I have undertaken in the last 10 years. I have written it to be accessible to as many people as possible and I have refrained from writing a traditional academic textbook based on my findings. However, I feel strongly that this book has brought together important and illuminating evidence of the way we blame women and girls in every way possible – and we do it globally and consistently.

My hope for this book is that it causes debate, discussion and forces us to ask some difficult questions of each other, our authorities, our governments, our services and systems. I would like it to provide a solid evidence base for women going forward – whether they are students, academics, practitioners or activists. This book contains evidence from hundreds of studies and authors, exploring the experiences of thousands of women and girls.

I am sick of hearing the endless reasons why women and girls are to blame for male violence. I am sick of not holding men responsible for their actions. I am sick of systems, risk assessments, policies and services being built to convince women and girls that they need to change who they are to stop male violence.

I have committed my life to challenging this disgusting misogyny and this book is my first offering to influence the world to change the way they think and talk about millions of women and girls subjected to male violence, abuse and oppression.

In love and solidarity,

Chasing Redemption
Juliette McAleer

Chasing redemption
In an endless quest
For equilibrium
And permission to feel ok

Salvation cannot be found
In social causes,
Academic success or
In being the very best little girl
(Or at least, pretending to be)

In pursuit of an answer
To the incessant 'why?'
Swimming around in my mind
Against an unrelenting tide of self-hatred
I cannot accept that these things are simply
Coincidence
Devoid of causal connection;
Unrelated to who I am.

Surely things happen for a reason
But then again,
Perhaps
I am irrelevant
After all
And believing that
I can control the universe
Is merely an egotistical occupation

So, who then, is to blame?
Karma?
Chaos?
Statistical probability?
Locked in perpetual struggle to understand
The universal law of cause and effect and
Where my part in all this
Begins and ends…

I cannot help but wonder if this is
Just another example of
Poetic justice?
Retribution for deeds I cannot remember
The justification for which
Is beyond the understanding of
The child protagonist
Who hears only
'I told you so'

So, unable to make
Head or tail of it,
We can flip a coin –
Take a chance

An exercise in semantics
A game of mental construct
Where winning is everything
And losing, the end.

Key terms explained

CSE – Child sexual exploitation. In the UK, this is defined as 'children who exchange things they want or need for sexual acts.' I reject this definition and write from the perspective that child sexual exploitation is child sexual abuse and there is no form of 'exchange'. Instead, I prefer to use the definition of CSA (below), however, lots of research uses 'CSE' specifically and so I will talk about this throughout the book and the way this has contributed to victim blaming of girls.

CSA – Child sexual abuse. In the UK, this is defined as 'forcing or enticing a child or young person to take part in sexual activities, not necessarily involving a high level of violence, whether or not the child is aware of what is happening. The activities may involve physical contact, including assault by penetration (for example, rape or oral sex) or non-penetrative acts such as masturbation, kissing, rubbing and touching outside of clothing. They may also include non-contact activities, such as involving children in looking at, or in the production of, sexual images, watching sexual activities, encouraging children to behave in sexually inappropriate ways, or grooming a child in preparation for abuse (including via the internet). Sexual abuse is not solely perpetrated by adult males. Women can also commit acts of sexual abuse, as can other children.' (Working Together, 2018)

Rape – In the UK, rape is defined in the Sexual Offences Act (2003) as an act by a man who intentionally penetrates the vagina, mouth or anus with a penis when the other person does not consent or cannot consent. Whilst anyone can be raped, only men can commit rape with a penis.

Misogyny – The hatred of women including prejudice and contempt for women and girls. Misogyny can also include the belief that females are inferior humans to males.

Oppression – A situation or active action in which people are governed or treated in a harmful discriminatory way which removes or restricts their rights, freedoms and opportunities.

Racism – The belief that people's qualities are influenced by their race and that the members of other races are not as good as the members of your own, or the resulting unfair treatment of members of other races. I use this term in conjunction with the understanding of White privilege. We live in a world in which White people are perceived (and perceive themselves) as superior to all other groups. Almost all racism is committed by White people towards people from other ethnicities and races. White people are not subjected to racism in day to day life and are likely to move through life without ever worrying that their skin would change the way individuals, systems and authorities would treat them. Racism therefore plays a powerful part in the victim blaming of Black women and girls being subjected to male violence.

Sexism – Actions based on the belief that the members of one sex are less intelligent, able, skillful, etc. than the members of the other sex, especially that women are less able than men.

Objectification – Treating people like tools or toys, as if they had no feelings, opinions, or rights of their own. According to Fredrickson and Roberts, sexual objectification is described as the valuing of a woman exclusively on the basis of her body and on her sexual parts, rather than on her full identity. When a woman is sexually objectified, her body becomes a mere instrument for satisfying sexual male desires.

Sexualisation – The act of sexualising someone or something, seeing someone or something in sexual terms.

Liberal Feminism – An individualistic form of feminist theory, which focuses on women's ability to maintain their equality through their own actions and choices. Liberal feminists argue that society holds the false belief that women are, by nature, less intellectually and physically capable than men; thus, it tends to discriminate against women in the academy, the forum, and the marketplace.

Liberal feminists believe that female subordination is rooted in a set of customary and legal constraints and therefore, like other liberal movements, they tend to work within the systems and within the laws to create change for women – to make them equal to men. Liberal feminists tend to lean towards supporting 'sex work', female sexuality as empowerment, pornography and Liberal feminism is contrasted with radical feminism.

Radical Feminism – Radical feminism is a perspective within feminism that calls for a radical reordering of society in which male supremacy is eliminated in all social and economic contexts. Radical feminists view society as a patriarchy in which men dominate and oppress women. Radical feminists seek to abolish the patriarchy in order to liberate everyone from an unjust society by challenging existing social norms and institutions. This includes opposing the sexual objectification of women, opposing the concept of 'sex work', opposing pornography, raising public awareness about such issues as rape and violence against women, and challenging the concept of gender roles.

Psychometric measures – Psychological tests which seek to measure attitudes, behaviours, abilities and cognitive skills in humans. Usually administered as questionnaires, multiple choice questions, scales or surveys (online or in person). Heavily used in psychological research, mental health and social research.

Key abbreviations explained

Abbreviation	Explanation
ACE	Adverse Childhood Experiences
AMMSA	Acceptance of Modern Myths about Sexual Aggression (Psychometric scale)
BJW or JWB	Belief in a Just World or Just World Belief
BOWSVA	Blame of Women Subjected to Sexual Violence and Abuse (Psychometric scale)
CSA	Child sexual abuse
CSE	Child sexual exploitation
FGM	Female genital mutilation
IRMAS	Illinois Rape Myth Acceptance Scale (Psychometric scale)
MRA	Men's rights activists
PVBS	Personal Victim Blaming Scale (Psychometric scale)
RMA	Rape myth acceptance
RMAS	Rape myth acceptance scale (Psychometric scale)
U-IRMAS	Updated Illinois Rape Myth Acceptance Scale (Psychometric scale)

1.

Introduction to violence against women

This book focusses on the way we blame women for being subjected to male violence. Within that term, I include all forms of misogynistic and oppressive violence perpetrated against women and girls, usually committed by men.

In my opinion, it is important to be clear about male violence and to refrain from simply calling this 'violence against women and girls' or 'VAWG'. This is because terms such as these erase the perpetrator of the offences by not mentioning them.

Male and patriarchal violence against women and girls is overwhelming.

Violence against women includes domestic violence, femicide, rape and sexual violence, corrective rape of lesbians, child sexual abuse and exploitation of girls, prostitution, trafficking, forced marriage, female genital mutilation, street harassment, online misogyny, forced abortions, ritual abuse, juju, acid attacks, public flogging of women, surrogacy and slavery.

According to prevalence statistics:

- 30-50% of women have been victims of domestic violence by male partners and ex partners
- 20-36% of girls are sexually abused in childhood
- 20% of women have been sexually assaulted or raped since the age of 16 in the UK
- 3 women per week were killed by men in the UK in 2019, up 10% on 2018
- Three times more sexual violence is perpetrated against girls in childhood than boys
- 700,000 – 2,000,000 women and girls are trafficked across the world every year for sex
- 7-40% of women report that their first sexual experience was forced (rape)
- Of women prostituted in the UK, 50% working outdoors and 26% working indoors had been subjected to violence

- 81% of women prostituted outdoors in the UK had been beaten, choked, raped, threatened with a weapon, slashed or stabbed

- Estimates show that hundreds of thousands of women are systematically raped during warfare, including rape as a tactic for ethnic cleansing through impregnation

- Estimates suggest that between 60 and 100 million women are missing from the global population due to sex-selective abortion, female infanticide and deliberate neglect of female newborn babies

(Femicide Census, 2020; CSEW, 2017; Watts and Zimmerman, 2002)

Acts of male violence committed against women occur in every country, every community, every religion, every time period and every language.

Whilst research tends to focus on working class communities as the sources of domestic and sexual violence, the reality couldn't be further from this stereotype. Women of all backgrounds and social classes are subjected to male violence and misogyny, hence why radical feminists position women as a class of oppressed people. Even in my individual experience of working with women and girls, I have supported women subjected to male violence who were powerful lawyers, chief executives, senior police officers, wealthy businesswomen and girls attending expensive, exclusive private education provisions. I've also spent time supporting hundreds of women and girls who were living in life threatening danger, poverty and oppression when they were subjected to male violence.

It would appear to many people that there is a 'type' of woman or girl who would be subjected to male violence – but this is not something I have ever seen in real life.

In fact, I would say that over a decade ago, I would have been one of those people. A quick and blunt way of learning that I was wrong was when I was working in the witness service, specialising in domestic and sexual violence. Every day, I met a new woman or new girl. I heard a new story. I saw new injuries. I heard of new assaults, new rapes, new exploitation and new oppression. Every time a woman walked into my room, she was a whole person, a completely new person, with a completely new story.

Women subjected to sexual violence and abuse are not a homogenous group. Where once I thought I knew 'which' women would be likely victims of male violence, years of working with those women taught me that there is no stereotype. There is no 'likely' victim. There is no set of characteristics, body types, ethnicities, backgrounds, age ranges or social class to look out for. The only thing all of these women had in common was that they were female, and their perpetrators were male. Other than that, it didn't look to me like male violence discriminated at all.

Prevalence and revictimisation of women

Prevalence statistics are likely to be underestimated. Not just because of the common arguments around underreporting, but also because of the normalisation of male violence. If male violence is successfully normalised in society, many women and girls subjected to it will not know what is happening to them. When a man shouts at a teenage girl as she walks to school, she will not think that his actions were illegal, misogynistic, objectifying and harassing – she will think that it is normal for men to sexualize teenage girls. When a woman is manipulated, derogated and abused by her partner, she will not blame him and recognise that he is a perpetrator of male violence for she has always been taught that she is to blame, she is pushing his buttons or that she should keep her relationship together 'for the sake of her children'.

One thing that always seems to surprise female professionals is when I suggest to them that it is very likely that all of us have been repeatedly victimised by men in our lives. Often, the behavioural response I notice is body language and facial expressions which suggest that those women do not accept this premise.

That is, until I ask them to quietly think about what their list would look like if I asked them to write down how many times since birth they have been sexually abused, raped, touched without consent, catcalled, harassed, beaten up, exploited, threatened, manipulated, coerced, trafficked, kicked, bit, spat at, bullied and oppressed by men in their lives. I ask them to consider how long it would take them to remember every single instance in which a man or boy harmed them, abused them, violated them or scared them into doing something they didn't want to do.

Every single instance through childhood, adolescence, early adulthood and womanhood (and for some women, into motherhood and older age too).

At that point, many women change their position. They consider that they have probably been subjected to male violence hundreds of times across their life spans. Thinking like this can be a shocking revelation for women who have always considered themselves 'not one of those women' – or have convinced themselves that they would never 'let themselves be a victim'.

In a misogynistic world, it is likely that most females have been subjected to male violence and misogyny.

This exercise directly challenges current theories and statistics around which types of women become victims of male violence – and how common so-called 'revictimisation' is.

There is a statistic that suggests that 2 in every 3 women who have been abused by men will be subjected to male violence again (Classen et al., 2005).

There are entire theories and fields of expertise that focus on explaining revictimization rates of women and girls. Most of those revictimization theories focus on vulnerability, behaviour or character of women and girls (Eaton, 2019). In line with traditional positivist perspectives of victimology, many theories suggest that there is something specific about certain women and girls which means they will be a repeated target of male violence.

Not surprisingly, there are few theories which argue that the reason for such high revictimization rates of women and girls is due to the sheer prevalence of male violence across the world. If each woman in a diverse room full of professionals can recount ten, thirty or fifty instances of when she was subjected to male violence, it is surely not something internal or specific to that woman that is causing or precipitating that revictimization.

Maybe, revictimization of women is so likely because male violence is so embedded into society.

Maybe all women are likely to be revictimised? Maybe it has nothing to do with our behaviours or upbringing or what we were wearing or how we walk down the street (as suggested by some researchers such as Kikue Sakaguchi et al.).

Maybe it has nothing to do with the women at all. Maybe revictimization theory needs to consider the scale on which male violence is being committed, endorsed, minimised, ignored or denied.

Violence against women and the embeddedness of misogyny has been present for millennia. It is rather surprising that we have spent such a considerable amount of time asking, 'what is wrong with these women who keep becoming victims of men?'

I guess that's misogyny for you, though.

Feminism and women's rights is taking something of a beating at the moment. Dale Spender wrote in 1980 that with every powerful wave of feminism comes a new wave of anti-feminist backlash. In current feminism, the backlash has included memes, social media posts, groups, podcasts, videos, news reports and forums that argue against the ideals and aims of feminism in all its forms.

This has included the denial of sex and sexism, denial of the sex pay gap, the conflation of sex and gender roles, denial of female oppression, the conflation of FGM with male circumcision, the anger and misogyny towards the #metoo movement, the increasing levels of victim blaming of women and girls being sexually exploited and abused, the plunging conviction rates of men committing acts of sexual violence and even the complete denial of a patriarchy.

Patriarchy

Whilst the concept of a patriarchy is sneered at in present day discussions, the reality of the power of male violence, male entitlement and male privilege is still very much real.

The word 'patriarch' or 'patriarchy' comes from two Greek words. 'Patria' which means 'family' and 'archein' which means 'to rule over'. 'Patriarch' therefore means the 'father/male who rules over the family'. This was slowly extended to mean communities and societies in which men ruled over other people. In more modern usage, 'patriarchy' is defined in the Cambridge Dictionary as 'a society in which the oldest male is the leader of the family, or a society controlled by men in which they use their power to their own advantage' (2020).

I was recently challenged during a lecture in which a student argued that the patriarchy didn't exist at all. When I asked them to explain their position, they suggested that the patriarchy didn't exist because issues of female oppression were being taken out of context. For example, they argued that men only dominate all of the major workplaces, industries and governments because women 'choose' to have children. The student argued that this is not true female oppression because women could 'choose' to focus on their career instead of having children. Seemingly, the student had forgotten that men also have children – and the women becoming pregnant and having children were not doing so via immaculate conception.

Before I could even answer, a female student shouted across the lecture hall, 'Funny how it's only women who have to 'choose' between having a career and having a child, isn't it?'

She was right of course.

Research not only shows that the pay gap is real and that men make up the majority of senior professional positions including 93% of business CEOs in the UK (Catalyst, 2019) but that when men become fathers, they are perceived as more reliable, more responsible and better employees. A far cry from the way women are perceived, where it is common for female academics to be warned not to get pregnant or have children if they want to achieve a PhD or be granted tenure. Whilst men are being celebrated for becoming a father in the workplace and are being given more rights and more flexibility in their working patterns to enable them to be an active parent, women are being told not to get pregnant or risk being demoted, having contracts and grants removed or not being accepted on to academic courses.

Outside of employment issues, the patriarchy is alive and well.

Globally, men are still the most powerful sex. They dominate governments, banks, courthouses, police forces and universities. Men make up 98% of presidents and world leaders. The majority of all female leaders have only taken up office in the last two decades. Men make up 75% of high court judges and 61% of lower court judges (The Guardian, 2019). 67% of UK MPs are men. 87.5% of police and crime commissioners are men (Home Office, 2016).

Whilst UCAS (2019) report that girls are a third more likely than boys to go to university, men go on to be the most powerful sex within higher education. They make up 75% of professors and 66% of senior lecturers (HESA, 2019).

In children's education, women dominate teaching – but get less and less visible in management. Whilst women make up 63% of teaching staff, they only make up a third of school leadership teams, including headteachers (Gov.uk, 2019).

Men are powerful in the management of the criminal justice system, but they also remain powerful when they are the offender within the criminal justice system. Men are becoming virtually untouchable within domestic and sexual violence prosecutions.

In recent years, we have seen court cases which do everything from blame 12-year-old girls for being trafficked by groups of men to using the underwear of teenagers to argue that they wanted to be raped. Our conviction rates for sexual violence offences committed by men are the lowest they have ever been, prompting legal activist groups such as the Centre for Women's Justice to begin lobbying and protesting 'the effective legalisation of rape'.

When the conviction rates for rape and sexual assault are so astonishingly low, it is arguable that we are sending a strong social message not only to women but to male perpetrators – that rape is not something we have an interest in stopping or challenging – and women are not worthy of justice.

The box below reports the CPS data being used by the Centre for Women's Justice as they compile their case for judicial review in the high court. Clearly, charging, pre-charge decisions, prosecutions and convictions fell significantly.

However, of the cases the CPS did decide to take to court, their conviction rate increased.

The Crown Prosecution Service published the 2018-19 Violence against Women and Girls report.

Data for rape and serious sexual offences shows that, compared to 2017-18, pre-charge decisions completed by the CPS fell by 14.9%, from 6,012 to 5,114.

The proportion of pre-charge decisions that led to a charge fell from 46.9% to 34.4%.

Completed prosecutions fell by 32.8% - from 4,517 to 3,034.

Convictions fell by 26.9% - from 2,635 to 1,925.

The proportion of cases where the police did not respond to CPS requests for additional evidence or reasonable lines of enquiry within three months increased from 21.7% to 28.6%.

But the conviction rate jumped from 58.3% to 63.4%.

The simplest way to interpret these statistics is to explore the idea that the CPS are deliberately dropping as many sexual violence cases as possible, whilst only taking forward the cases that they feel they have a very high chance of successful conviction. This means that thousands of women and girls are being told that their case does not warrant investigation, prosecution or conviction.

However, with some clever PR spin, the CPS can say that their conviction rate is higher than ever and that they are 'successfully convicting' 63% of cases*

*that they took to trial after dropping tens of thousands of other cases they remain silent on.

With a criminal justice system set on decriminalizing rape, new figures show that only 1.9% of reported rapes end in prosecution (Home Office, 2019). With the majority of all cases of rape being perpetrated against women and girls and 100% of rapists being male offenders – this does raise questions about why our society, institutions and government have such little interest in sexual crimes against women and girls.

Misogyny

Many feminists would answer with one word: misogyny.

Much like the language and concept of patriarchy, there has been a concerted effort to minimise and delegitimize the concept and language of 'misogyny'. When we discuss the reality and impact of misogyny, we are now met with accusations that misogyny is a myth dreamt up by feminist and 'social justice warriors'.

The word 'misogyny' comes from two words, too. 'Misos' meaning hatred and 'gune' meaning woman. In the mid-17th century, it began to be used as 'misogyny' to mean the hatred of women. 400 years later, the definition has not changed, and we continue to discuss the global phenomenon linked to sexism – the hatred of females.

To people who have never considered this before, the concept of people hating 51% of the global population probably seems unlikely or farfetched. However, as this book will and many other books about violence against women and girls already have shown, there are thousands of examples of the constant, enduring ways we hate, harm, control, abuse and kill women and girls all over the world and throughout history.

Misogyny is displayed in so many direct and indirect ways. Sometimes they are obvious, and sometimes they are hidden in seemingly benevolent messages and beliefs about women, men, and social roles.

Misogyny has existed in several forms for thousands of years. Aristotle wrote that women were 'inferior, incomplete, deformed versions of men' (Freeland, 1994). Ancient Greek mythology contains many examples of misogyny, in which stories are told that the world was a peaceful and balanced place until Gods created women. However, later Greek literature generally considered misogyny to be a disease, as it contradicted all natural and social aims and norms to hate women and girls.

Second wave feminists tend to argue that misogyny is both the cause and the result of patriarchal control. These feminists and others tend to suggest that misogyny has its roots in what is known as the 'Madonna-Whore Complex', in which women can either be perceived and regarded as mothers, or whores. They are therefore either nurturing, safe, selfless mothers or they are promiscuous, sexual, objectified whores. This is further suggested to be related to the 'Virgin-Whore Complex' in which women and girls are either seen as a virgin or a whore. Either pure, or sexual. In today's society in which we see even the youngest girls as sexual objects, it is hard to see where this line is drawn anymore. Once, where we thought it would be children who are seen as innocent, virginial females – it is becoming clearer that even young girls who are victims of male violence can be repositioned as 'whores' and 'child prostitutes' (See: Chapter 14).

In a society that has embedded and supported misogyny for so long, it is not hard to see why violence against women is commonplace, ignored, minimised and even supported. When we challenge the norms of violence against women, we are going up against thousands of years of misogynistic values, beliefs, faiths, rules, laws, control and abuse. It is so embedded in fact, that lots of studies have shown that women and girls apply misogynistic values to themselves and to other women (Ringrose, 2013; APA, 2007). Whilst some people may assume that men are the only ones to display misogyny, it is clear that women do, too.

One example of the way misogyny obscures the conversations and investigations into male violence is that talking about male violence becomes taboo, or irrelevant. This book will introduce you to the ways we talk about male violence as if women bring it upon themselves, or as if there is some sort of metaphorical violence that occurs to women naturally, without ever naming the perpetrators.

Instead of talking about the scale of male violence and the amount of men committing these crimes against women, we often see vague statistics about how many women will 'become' victims of 'rape' and 'abuse' and how many girls will be 'sexually exploited'.

By who? Men.

But we will get to that later in this book.

Whataboutery

One final point to end this chapter is that another symptom of a misogynistic society, in my opinion, is whataboutery. I first wrote about 'whataboutery' in 2018 in a blog that has been read around one million times since. I wrote about the way people would derail conversations about violence against women and girls by constantly asking, 'but what about men?'

This was particularly interesting to me as someone who already worked with men in another capacity. I noticed very quickly that when I spoke out about the abuse or suffering of men, people considered me to be a brilliant, authoritative, innovative thinker. But when I spoke about the abuse or suffering of women, I was just another hysterical, man-hating feminist bitch. I was relentlessly asked, 'but what about men?'

The same could not be said when I wrote about men. No one was emailing me aggressively asking, 'what about women?' No one was tweeting or messaging me telling me that I must hate women to work with men. No one was threatening me or sending me pictures of their vulva for talking about the abuse of men and boys.

Whataboutery is a deliberate way of derailing the conversation about misogyny. From the faux-concerned woke bros to the well-meaning commenters, it is still interesting to watch how quickly people will derail from topics such as FGM, forced marriage, rape, trafficking and CSE to simply say, 'but what about men, though?' or, 'why don't you care about male victims?'

Of course, most people who do this don't really care about men and boys at all. Whenever I respond with links to male support services, or reference lists containing journal articles or book chapters about the abuse of men – I never get a response.

Whataboutery has been successful, however. We now see large public campaigns kowtowing to pressure to include men in women's campaigns and women's services. We see academics, authors and speakers add in sections about how it 'happens to men, too' or 'we mustn't forget male victims'.

There is now a powerful counter-narrative to the issues of misogyny and male violence against women and girls:

That the same oppression and abuse is happening to men at the same rate, but they just don't tell us.

Whilst it is probable and acknowledged that men and boys do not disclose their oppression, abuse or trauma – this suggestion assumes that women and girls live in a society in which they can freely and safely disclose violence, abuse and harm. This is incorrect according to decades of research and theory on reporting and disclosure. It is on this basis that I do not accept the suggestion that men and boys are equally oppressed and discriminated against, I do not accept that men and boys are subjected to sex based oppression at the same rates and I do not accept that they simply talk about it less. The inevitable calls of 'misandry' are nothing more than whataboutery.

As Michael Flood describes, misandry does not have the 'systemic, trans-historic, institutionalized, and legislated antipathy of misogyny' (Flood, 2007). What he is saying is that whilst misandry exists as a concept, it has no power in a patriarchal world. The hatred of a ruling class by an oppressed class doesn't have as much power as when that hatred is expressed the other way around. The slave could hate the master, but the master would remain the master, so to speak.

As this book demonstrates, misogyny is a thread which continues throughout the social issue of victim blaming of women and girls. I have chosen to write about, talk to and support, women and girls. We are entitled to talk about and research the experiences of women and girls without relating them to, or including, boys and men. Women and girls are an entire group of humans who exist independently of males and as such, there is power, value and importance in topics that focus on and centre women and girls, unashamedly.

If you are looking for the section on men and boys, you have picked up the wrong book.

2.

Introduction to women's trauma

This book is written not only from a radical feminist perspective, but also from a trauma informed perspective.

This means that I think and write from the position that so-called 'mental illness' is a result of social, environmental and interpersonal pressures, abuses, oppressions and stressors. I endorse frameworks and theories such as Power, Threat, Meaning Framework (Johnstone and Boyle, 2018).

Adopting this perspective means that I work with, write, and speak about women and girls as whole people who have been traumatised and oppressed by others and are then displaying or experiencing completely normal trauma responses and coping mechanisms.

Instead of seeing women and girls as having mental health issues, or psychiatric disorders after being abused and violated, a trauma informed perspective would support those women and girls as being traumatised by the repeated acts of violence, and treat their trauma in the following ways:

- Their trauma is normal
- Their trauma is justified
- Their trauma is proportionate
- Their trauma is rational

Therefore, instead of seeing trauma responses as abnormal, disproportionate, unjustified and irrational behaviours and feelings, a trauma-informed perspective works from the belief that the many feelings, behaviours, symptoms and impacts of trauma are normal responses to acts of violence, oppression, and abuse.

It is normal for women to be traumatised after being subjected to male violence. Their feelings and reactions are justified.

Coping mechanisms and trauma responses are often pathologised by the medical model of mental health – and women are diagnosed with illnesses, disorders and psychoses. However, I write from the perspective that all coping mechanisms (such as self-harm or excessive drinking), and all trauma responses (such as panic attacks or sleep disturbances) are rational and normal.

Further, I argue that the reactions that women and girls have to male violence are proportionate, too. Whether those reactions are weeks, months or years long – they are normal and proportionate to the level of violence and oppression they were subjected to.

Much victim blaming focusses on the way women respond and react to being subjected to male violence – and this is why it was so important to include chapters in this book about the trauma of women and the way we blame women for their responses.

The prevalence of victim blaming within psychiatry and psychology should come as no surprise when we consider the history of the disciplines.

The medical model of mental health is so dominant that it is communicated as 'the' explanation of emotional and mental life. Many of us have been taught that mental health issues are genetic, neuropsychological/physiological, developmental or a combination of all. We are taught that medications can 'balance people out' or 'help them prepare for therapy'. We are taught that some people need to be locked up and sedated for their own safety.

As of September 2019, 7.3 million British adults (1 in 6 adults) were taking antidepressants and a further 3.9 million British adults are taking anxiety medications such as benzodiazepines, Z drugs and gabapentinoids (The Guardian, 2019).

But this monopoly on our mental life didn't happen overnight. Long before we started talking about 'mental health', we punished, killed, sacrificed, outcast and abused people who did not conform to our social norms of behaviour or character. Many feminists and historians now suggest that the death of up to 100,000 women who were murdered for being 'witches' between 1450 and 1750 were often women who were non-conforming, disabled, ill, intelligent, opinionated or had been abused and traumatised by men (Sollee, 2017; Horsley and Horsley, 1987).

History of mental health and trauma

In the European Middle Ages, mental health started to become mixed with religion. When someone was not conforming or was traumatised, it was proposed that they were possessed by demons or Satan. Most 'treatments' for mental health included religious ceremonies, exorcisms, torture or death of the person. In some cases, it was argued that the only way a demon could be stopped, would be to kill the 'host' person.

As time passed, mental health was proposed to be caused by imbalances of fluids in the body and brain. Excess bodily fluids such as bile, blood or choler were said to cause 'hysteria', 'melancholia' or 'mania'. However, the religious approach to mental health continued for a long time. Quakers set up many asylums and developed religious conversion treatments to 'cure' mental health issues.

Lieberman (2015) puts it well, 'The mentally ill were considered social deviants or moral misfits suffering divine punishment for some inexcusable transgression.'

Asylums multiplied across America and Europe during the 1700s and 1800s, and professionals from all different backgrounds became interested in working with the 'mentally ill'. Asylums became sites of experimental research, surgery, treatment, torture and death of patients – on which the 'science' of psychiatry was built.

Psychiatric experiments, tortures and surgeries included everything from holding patients under freezing cold water until they 'calmed down' (they passed out or drowned), to deliberately 'releasing humors' from the patient by bleeding them, blistering them, starving them, or purging them. In 1927, Wagner-Jauregg won the Nobel Prize for 'proving' you could treat schizophrenia by injecting malaria-infected blood into people with the diagnosis.

By 1941, insulin shock therapy was commonplace. In this 'treatment' for 'mental illness', people were injected with extremely high doses of insulin to cause seizures and coma, claiming that when they came around, they would be cured of madness.

By the 1940s, electroconvulsive shock therapy (ECT) and frontal lobotomies were common. Whilst frontal lobotomies stopped being used by the 1980s (although this did mean that over 100,000 people were subjected to them), ECT is still used today. In fact, it is making something of a comeback – and now being used to 'treat' autism in some clinics in North America.

I have personally worked with children who have been subjected to ECT in the Midlands in the UK, after they were abused and raped. One girl I worked with in 2013 was severely harmed by ECT sessions on the NHS, so much so that she used to come to my sessions and fall fast asleep on the sofa for hours, and then wake up confused and upset. She was being given ECT sessions for 'treatment resistant depression' because she had been sexually abused throughout childhood.

By 1955, psychiatric medications were a fairly common way of 'treating' madness. But it wasn't for many more decades that we stopped using language like 'hysteria', 'madness', 'retardation' and 'mental illness'. However, despite this seemingly positive shift in language, we are still using some of the same treatments, misconceptions, and oppressive practices we have used throughout history. We have moved towards the term 'mental health' which we now equate with 'physical health' – but we still use oppressive, dangerous and abusive practices to 'treat' the natural, normal distress of traumatised people.

The language got nicer but the practice, well, it didn't really evolve.

Throughout these years, the groups most significantly affected were Black people. Psychiatry is notoriously White, elitist, and racist. Always has been. Still is. For an excellent review of the oppression with psychiatry, I recommend reading Richard Bentall's books (Bentall, 2003; 2009).

Racism was (is) embedded into theory, practice and research. Psychiatrists believed that Black people had smaller brains than White people, were 'naturally' better at hard labour and slavery, were less psychologically developed, and were more aggressive, emotionally unstable and violent. These beliefs still have an enormous impact on mental health practice, in which people still believe that Black people are more likely to have 'mental health issues', more likely to have 'schizophrenia' and are more likely to be violent or commit crime (Bentall, 2003; 2009).

Women have been oppressed by mental health systems and theories for centuries. It was common for women to be sectioned and tortured after rape and abuse. Women were institutionalised and medicated for much less, too.

If women were gender non-conforming, lesbian, refused to have children, didn't want to marry, wouldn't smile and comply, were too educated, too politically active, or were seen in any way to be a threat to society, they were dealt with by the patriarchy.

For as long as we can remember, women have been blamed for their behavioural and emotional responses. Women were burned and drowned for being 'witches' (Horsley & Horsley, 1987). Women and girls were subject to exorcisms and religious rituals (Ussher, 2013). Later on, they were sectioned, medicated, tortured, abused, injured, and subjected to medical and psychiatric experiments. This will be explored later on in Chapter 12.

Women's mental health issues today are dealt with in much the same way – they are pathologised and medicated with little to no focus on the traumas women and girls face living in a patriarchy. Even women and girls who have been raped, abused, trafficked and oppressed are told that they are mentally ill or have personality disorders (Ussher, 2013).

Throughout this book and my other works, I frame this as a secondary form of victim blaming of women and girls. It is victim blaming because it blames the woman or girl for responding to being subjected to male violence. It blames her for being angry, sad, scared, betrayed, groomed, and harmed. Instead of validating her experiences, we tell her that she is mad. Women are told that their responses to being raped, abused, or attacked are excessive, incorrect, too long-lasting or too complex.

When they protest or refuse to be labelled, they are further pathologised and abused (Ussher, 2013). The more they claim they are not mad, the madder they are perceived to be. The more they refuse to take the medication or engage in the therapy, the more problematic they are perceived to be.

This has troubled me for several years now.

Having worked with women and girls subjected to sexual and domestic violence for over a decade at the time of writing this book, I have seen hundreds of cases of women and girls being diagnosed with poorly-defined, imaginative and downright offensive disorders and mental illnesses after they disclosed that they had been subjected to male violence.

I have talked to or worked with women and girls who have been medicated, sectioned, isolated, removed from their families, had their children removed from them, and have been coerced into termination of pregnancies.

This book therefore explores and discusses victim blaming of women who are subjected not only to male violence, but also to the oppressive systems and institutions that go on to blame women and girls for how they responded, or tried to cope with the violence and abuse.

3.

What is victim blaming and self-blame?

'Victim blaming', defined as the transference of blame from the perpetrator of a crime to the victim, was first coined by William Ryan in 1971.

Ryan used the original term 'blaming the victim' to argue that shifting blame towards Black people in the US was justifying racism and violence towards Black communities. This came after the Moynihan Report (1965) blamed poverty and racism on Black family life, stereotypes of single mothers, absent fathers, and lower levels of education. Ryan argued that Moynihan was blaming Black communities for being subjected to racism and oppression perpetrated against them by White people.

Victim blaming is therefore not unique to sexual violence or to women.

In sexual violence against women, victim blaming includes the blaming of the women's character, behaviour, appearance, decisions, or situation for being subjected to sexual violence, rather than the attribution of blame towards the male offender who committed the act (Burt, 1980).

Whilst victim blaming is not unique to sexual violence or to women, the way in which women are blamed for sexual violence perpetrated against them by men has become a central feature of victim blaming literature – and of wider cultures, media, religion, beliefs, justice and public health campaigns.

Simply put, victim blaming is the transference of blame for an act of sexual violence away from the perpetrator of the violence and back towards the victim of the violence.

Victim blaming is generally split into behavioural, characterological and situational blame; however, they often overlap.

Behavioural victim blaming, blames the behaviour of the woman as the reason for the sexual violence perpetrated against her.

Common behaviours we blame are:

- She was drinking
- She went out with her friends
- She walked home alone

- She got a taxi alone
- She was using a dating app
- She was flirting
- She was asking for it
- She wore revealing clothing

Characterological blaming blames her character or personality for the sexual violence perpetrated against her.

Common character or personality traits we blame are:
- She is promiscuous
- She is sexualised
- She is too trusting
- She is naïve
- She is vulnerable
- She makes poor choices
- She takes risks
- She is not very clever/wise/savvy

Situational blaming places the blame on the situation the woman or girl was in, rather than blaming the perpetrator for choosing to commit violence.

When the behaviour nor the character of the woman or girl can be blamed, we tend to blame the situation they were in. Situational blame is a curious approach, because it erases the offender from their own crime and blames something inanimate.

Common examples of situational blame:
- Parties like that can be dangerous
- Well, you know what happens at that park
- If you go to hotels like that, it might happen
- Walking home through parks is dangerous

- Going jogging alone is a risk factor for rape
- Carparks are a dangerous place for women

Often, victim blaming types occur simultaneously, such as when women are blamed for being promiscuous, walking home alone and being described as wearing revealing clothing. All victim blaming minimises or erases the actions and choices of the offender from their own offence.

Situational blame is particularly interesting because it is employed often by police forces, local authorities and safety campaigns. In posters which state 'alcohol is the leading cause of rape' or 'go out with your friends and have a good night, but do not take risks that might lead to rape' – the narrator is erasing the male offender from the offence.

In situational blame, the rape or abuse of the woman becomes almost metaphorical – as if the party or the carpark or the hotel is attacking her. There is no mention of how the rape or abuse happened, who perpetrated it or who caused it. Just a mention of it happening in a situation. Sometimes a direct causal link is suggested between the situation and the rape. What remains consistent however, is that the male rapists are never mentioned.

Language is important

Much of the way we communicate the blame of victims of sexual violence is through the use of language:

- Headlines and journalism
- Laws and legislation
- Conversation
- Advice
- Posters
- Awareness campaigns
- Messages
- Videos and films
- Lessons and education
- Social narratives and myths

Approaches influenced by relativism suggest that much of our knowledge and understanding is relative and subjective, based on where the knowledge came from, who gave it to us, how it was given to us, how it was explained and how we interpreted it.

Within this approach, some theorists argue that language constructs the world, and that the way we talk about social issues is not neutral, because every word we choose to say changes the meaning of what we say.

The words we use and the way we talk about sexual violence and victim blaming of women actively constructs, changes or influences the way we think about, talk about, and act on sexual violence and victim blaming of women.

There is debate surrounding the use of language and concepts of blame. Shaver and Drown (1986) argued that the concepts of blame, causality and responsibility have often been treated as the same thing or have been mixed. This may have been detrimental to the methodology and interpretation of findings in studies where the three concepts were not treated separately.

Shaver and Drown (1986) supported the arguments of Critchlow et al. (1985) and Heider (1958) by reporting that when participants were asked to attribute blame, responsibility, and causality to a variety of different actors and situations, responsibility was always attributed more than blame and causality.

Shaver (1985) argued that most self-blame research had not truly been measuring blame or self-blame and added that what Janoff-Bulman (1979) had previously categorised as characterological blame and behavioural blame were in fact attributions of causality and responsibility, respectively.

Finally, a comment made by Shaver and Drown (1986) shows consideration for the way language is used in the questions or stimuli with participants. It is posed that even when 'caused' and 'was responsible for' are held as equivalents, neither adequately describe blaming or self-blame, (p.698).

Consider the following statement about a woman who has been subjected to rape:

> *'I'm not saying it's her fault she was raped, I am just saying she needs to take more responsibility for her own actions or her own safety... and she needs to be held responsible for decisions which might have caused this to happen. She*

needs to learn from her mistakes, but she isn't to blame –
the perpetrator is always to blame.'

In this statement, the words 'fault', 'responsibility', 'caused' and 'blame' are used in contradictory ways. I tend to use this statement in training and speeches because narratives like this are so common in sexual violence, sexual abuse, policing, and child protection practice. I built the statement not only based on the types of things professionals and members of the public have said to me about women and girls; but also based on the research.

Studies showed that when people were asked who was to blame, they find the word 'blame' to be the most emotive and 'taking responsibility' to be the most socially acceptable way to talk about women subjected to sexual violence (Shaver & Drown, 1986; Shaver, 1985; Critchlow et al., 1985; Heider, 1958). This is important because we are seeing the cleansing of language around victim blaming. Where we may have historically said that a woman is 'to blame' for being raped or abused, we are now more likely to talk about all of the ways she should take responsibility for her own safety.

Positivism and victim blaming

These issues around language have their roots in positivist approaches to victimology and criminology. Whilst positivist criminology explores what differentiates those who commit crime from those who don't – positivist victimology has always tended to look for key characteristics or differences between those who are victims of crime and those who aren't. Key theorists in victimology as far back as 1948 argued that only certain types of people became victims of crime and often brought it upon themselves.

Hans Von Hentig wrote in Time Magazine (1948):

> *'Certain characteristics of law-abiding citizens arouse a*
> *counter reaction in the criminal. The inexperienced*
> *businessman, for example, invites embezzlement; the*
> *nagging wife is flirting with murder; the alcoholic is a natural*
> *for robbery. Thus, the victim becomes the tempter.'*

Later victimology theorists such as Benjamin Mendelsohn and Stephen Schafer also suggested that victims caused crime by being weak, vulnerable, female, old, disabled, or young. All three theorists suggested that victims precipitate crime by provoking offenders. Whilst this sounds somewhat outdated, these perspectives are alive and well. Many theories within psychology and criminology still rely on the assumption that women subjected to sexual and domestic violence either brought the offence on themselves, should have done something to protect themselves, should have behaved in a different way, or that their vulnerabilities led the offender to target and attack them.

To illustrate this point, consider the following passage in a national media outlet in 2014 which argues that blaming women for sexual or domestic violence is not the same as holding them responsible for their behaviour during or before they were attacked:

> *'With respect to prevention, understanding the conditions that lead to crime can facilitate safety. College women should not get drunk (or drink anything that was left unattended), not because it makes them morally contributory but because it's a sensible approach to personal safety. If a woman thinks there's a good chance of her getting hit during an argument, she should seriously consider leaving the relationship—but she should also avoid arguments until the issue has been clarified. Getting into an argument doesn't mean she would be blameworthy for getting hit; it just means she would be putting herself at risk. (…) when it comes to treatment of victims, they are often encouraged to take no responsibility at all for what happened.' (Karson, 2014)*

What is clear over an extended period is that influential thinkers and writers are still positioning women as the source and cause of male violence. Whilst they might not create lists of 'precipitating victims', they do clearly suggest that women should take responsibility for being subjected to domestic and sexual violence.

Victim blaming is rife, and it is backed up by problematic academic theory and language.

Victim blaming is not reducing, but it does seem to be getting more palatable and more socially (and professionally) acceptable.

How we explore the reasons for victim blaming

Over time, the reasoning behind victim blaming has been explored, with many researchers linking victim blaming with the acceptance of rape myths (RMA) and pro-sexism attitudes (Sleath, 2011).

Stemming from the feminist movement, Burt (1980) defined rape myths as being a set of inaccurate and harmful beliefs and myths about rape which contribute to hostility towards women.

From this point, many of the studies of victim blaming relied on RMA measurement and attitudinal scales of hostility to women or sexist beliefs. In 1999, Payne, Lonsway & Fitzgerald argued that rape myths tended to fit into seven categories, which have influenced many studies and psychometric measures of rape myths ever since. The seven categories of rape myth were:

Women asked for it

As one of the most common rape myths, this category comprises all the beliefs, comments and perspectives that suggest or directly argue that women did something to 'ask' to be raped, assaulted or abused.

1. A woman who dresses in skimpy clothes should not be surprised if a man tries to force her to have sex.
2. When women go around wearing low-cut tops or short skirts, they're just asking for trouble.
3. If a woman is raped while she is drunk, she is at least somewhat responsible for letting things get out of control.
4. If a woman goes home with a man she doesn't know, it is her own fault if she is raped.
5. A woman who "teases" men deserves anything that might happen.
6. When a woman is a sexual tease, eventually she is going to get into trouble.
7. A woman who goes home to the home or apartment of a man on the first date is implying that she wants to have sex.
8. When women are raped, it's often because the way they said "no" was ambiguous.

Women wanted it

This category contains the narrative myths that women actually want to be and enjoy being raped, abused, assaulted and harassed.

1. Many women secretly desire to be raped.
2. Some women prefer to have sex forced on them, so they don't have to feel guilty about it.
3. Many women actually enjoy sex after the guy uses a little force.
4. Many women find being forced to have sex very arousing.
5. Although most women wouldn't admit it, they generally find being physically forced into sex a real "turn-on."

Women lie about it

A self-explanatory category, this contains the myths and narratives that women lie about being raped and abused. This includes motives, including for revenge, to bully men and to cover up an affair.

1. A lot of women lead a man on and then they cry rape.
2. Rape accusations are often used as a way of getting back at men.
3. Many so-called rape victims are actually women who had sex and "changed their minds" afterwards.
4. Women who are caught having an illicit affair sometimes claim that it was rape.
5. A lot of times, women who claim they were raped just have emotional problems.

It wasn't really rape

This category contains myths and beliefs about rape that means it is often not seen as a 'real rape'. This includes beliefs that an assault or rape isn't really a rape if the offender doesn't use a weapon, there are no physical injuries on the woman, the woman does not go straight to a police station or the woman did not fight back.

1. If a woman doesn't physically fight back, you can't really say that it was rape.
2. If a woman doesn't physically resist sex – even when protesting verbally – it really can't be considered rape.

3. If the rapist doesn't have a weapon, you really can't call it a rape.

4. If a woman claims to have been raped but has no bruises or scrapes, she probably shouldn't be taken too seriously.

5. A rape probably didn't happen if the woman has no bruises or marks.

He didn't mean to rape

Rape myths were not just about women, there is also this category about the way men don't mean to rape women. Even in the present day, this usually comprises of myths about rape and abuse that blame the offences on men's uncontrollable sex drive or need for sex with women.

1. Men don't usually intend to force sex on a woman, but sometimes they get too sexually carried away.

2. When a man is very sexually aroused, hey may not even realize that the woman is resisting.

3. When men rape, it is because of their strong desire for sex.

4. Rape happens when a man's sex drive gets out of control.

5. Rapists are usually sexually frustrated individuals

Rape is a trivial event

This set of myths tend to position rape as something that feminists make up or exaggerate. Further, it can sometimes position the rape and assault of women as sex that doesn't really impact them the way they say it does. These myths still exist today in their original form as shown below.

1. Rape isn't as big a problem as some feminists would like people to think.

2. Women tend to exaggerate how much rape affects them.

3. Being raped isn't as bad as being mugged and beaten.

4. If a woman isn't a virgin, then it shouldn't be a big deal if her date forces her to have sex.

5. If a woman is willing to "make out" with a guy, then it's no big deal if he goes a little further and has sex.

Rape is a deviant event

The final set of rape myths include the narratives and beliefs that rape is only committed by deviant, dangerous men.

1. In reality, women are almost never raped by their boyfriends.
2. Men from nice middle-class homes almost never rape.
3. It is usually only women who dress suggestively that are raped.
4. Usually, it is only women who do things like hang out in bars and sleep around that are raped.
5. Rape mainly occurs on the "bad" side of town.
6. Rape almost never happens in the woman's own home.
7. Rape is unlikely to happen in the woman's own familiar neighborhood.

Sexism has also featured in many studies and theories of victim blaming including the critique of patriarchal systems oppressing women such as gender, the impact of the pornified society and sexual stereotypes that women are expected to conform to. The theories of sexism and gender roles will be discussed later on in Chapter 6.

Victim blaming can sound like lots of different things. Sometimes it sounds like misogyny, *'She went out looking like a slut, so it's no wonder she was raped'.*

Sometimes it sounds like logic, *'Women should keep themselves safe, they don't leave the house without locking the door in case they are burgled, so why is this any different?'*

Sometimes victim blaming can sound like concern or compassion, *'I hope she will be okay, and she learns from her mistakes and doesn't put herself in that situation again'.*

Victim blaming can even sound like ideology, religion or beliefs about justice and fairness, *'If this happened to her, she must have done something to deserve it'* or *'Life has a way of rewarding or punishing you for how you live your life – what goes around comes around.'*

Victim blaming is so diverse that it can also sound like personal safety advice that impedes on women and girls' lives, *'If you are going out tonight, remember not to leave your friends or drink too much. Always drink responsibly to protect yourself from sexual assault.'*

How people victim blame women and girls for sexual violence varies from person to person, and from authority to authority. Often, victim blaming is a mixture of misogyny, bias, stereotypes, attribution error, and beliefs about safety and justice.

Arguably, this could be why it is so hard to tackle and sometimes hard to recognise.

Women and girls can be blamed for sexual violence in the following ways:

- Being told to change the way they look or act
- Being told to stop going to everyday venues like pubs, bars, leisure centres, gyms or cafes
- Being told not to go out or walk anywhere at night
- Being told to take responsibility for the sexual desire and behaviour of men
- Being told that they are mentally ill or have a disorder after they are raped or assaulted
- Being told their actions and, or behaviours led to a rapist attacking them
- Being asked what they were wearing at the time of the offence (including underwear, clothing or makeup)
- Being asked why they didn't fight back, whether they asserted themselves enough or why they 'allowed' it to happen
- Being asked why they didn't report earlier or being blamed for risking other women and girls by not reporting earlier
- Being told their experiences are made up, fantasies, or malicious
- Being told they need to make better choices and decisions to stop themselves from being raped or abused

This is not an exhaustive list, of course. Women and girls can be blamed for anything from their body weight and ethnicity right the way through to drinking alcohol or staying with an abusive husband.

Women and girls who are subjected to sexual violence or abuse are likely to have heard many different forms of victim blaming, either directed at them or, women and girls in general.

The way they are blamed is important, because it may influence the way they feel about the rape or abuse. For example, if a woman or girl has been told that she was raped because she looks a certain way, she might start to cover her body or hate her own body. Whereas a woman or girl who has been told that she was raped because she didn't say no clearly enough or didn't fight the rapist off may conclude that she must have 'wanted it' or feel as if she colluded or encouraged the offender by staying still.

Messages of victim blaming have been found in the mass media, law, education, religion and cultural norms. This will be discussed in individual chapters as it comprises such a lot of evidence and points.

'Self-blame' is defined as a cognitive process of attribution that tends to be defined based on two categories: behavioural self-blame and characterological self-blame.

'Behavioural self-blame' is the attribution of deserved blame to self, based on behaviour or action. This type of self-blame leads to people considering how different behaviours or actions could have protected them or stopped the event from happening.

'Characterological self-blame' is the attribution of undeserved blame to self, based on internal character or personality. This type of self-blame leads to people believing that there is something internally or personally wrong with them that caused the event to happen.

Common examples of self-blame:

- I am a bad person
- I attract the wrong people
- I am stupid
- I should have seen it coming/figured out what was happening
- I should have been a better wife/girlfriend/daughter/mother

- I shouldn't have been drinking
- I should have said no clearer
- I should have tried to fight him off
- I should have left/escaped
- I should have reported the assault
- I deserved it
- I was being punished for something I have done wrong in life
- I shouldn't have led him on
- I shouldn't have gone to that place/met that person

Self-blame is also not unique to sexual violence, but studies have found that when women and girls experience victim blaming or negative reactions when they disclose sexual violence, they are more likely to blame themselves. Further, existing research suggests that women and girls use the messages they receive from society and support networks to measure whether they think someone will blame them for sexual violence, and to assess whether the rape, sexual assault or abuse was their fault.

Self-blame is seen by some to be adaptive rather than maladaptive. Whilst most would consider that blaming ourselves for being subjected to male violence would be a counterproductive and harmful way to treat ourselves, theorists and researchers have suggested since the seventies that women who blame themselves for being subjected to violence may have better psychological wellbeing than those who blame the perpetrator (Eaton, 2019).

Janoff-Bulman (1979, 1982) argued that behavioural self-blame was useful, in that women could identify the behaviours that led to the rape or abuse and then avoid them in future to protect themselves better. This suggestion still exists today, and I found it to be a common theme when I interviewed women and sexual violence support professionals in Chapters 15 and 6.

In 1982, Janoff-Bulman published research in which she argued that behavioural self-blame led to higher self-esteem in victims of trauma and abuse. This assertion did not go unnoticed, and there has been decades of research since that have unpicked and challenged her work.

Similarly, my own research did not confirm Janoff-Bulman's theories about self-blame, and instead found it to harm women.

Self-blame appears to be very common in women and girls subjected to male violence. However, self-blame does not naturally follow on from victim blaming. Many women blame themselves for being subjected to male violence having never been blamed by anyone else. They may never have told anyone else, and so no one else has ever judged or blamed them.

She may not even have been blamed by the perpetrator himself, which tends to be a common source of victim blaming in women and girls who are subjected to repeated attacks and abuse.

Rather, this book – and the work of others who inspired me, such as Dr Rebecca Campbell and Professor Sarah E. Ullman, has shown that self-blame of women subjected to male violence has its roots in much larger structures and social norms.

This means that before a woman or girl is ever blamed for being raped or abused – she is likely to already blame herself anyway. She is likely to have already started questioning her own behaviour, character and choices.

4.

Examples of victim blaming of women

Examples of victim blaming of women and girls subjected to abuse and violence are so common that entire websites have been developed to record and challenge the constant torrent of reporting and victim blaming narratives in our society (See EverydayVictimBlaming.com).

Over the years, I have found the use of specific examples to be useful and effective when demonstrating the impact and prevalence of victim blaming. When we discuss the victim blaming of women in terms of numbers or statistics, we can sometimes lose the important detail. If we are not careful, we can also lose the significance and the impact on women by talking so quantitatively. It is arguably much easier for someone to hear, and to disregard, a speaker or author stating '37% of people blame women' than it is to show them real examples of real women and girls who have been blamed for serious sexual offences, trafficking, child abuse or even their own murder.

For most of us working with women and girls in this sector, we have heard and seen thousands of real examples of victim blaming. For me, I have heard everything from blaming a small girl for crying too much during a police interview, through to blaming a grown woman for being raped because she wore headphones to listen to music. It is easy to find examples of victim blaming of women, because women can be blamed for absolutely anything that suits the person doing the blaming.

I am therefore using this space to discuss real examples of victim blaming of women and girls from sources such as the national and international press, reported court cases and public prevention campaigns.

Examples from the press

In 2015, ITV show 'Loose Women' ran a poll on afternoon television entitled, 'Is it ever a woman's fault if she is raped?'

It was argued that the poll was launched because singer Chrissie Hynde had been given an interview about being sexually assaulted when she was 21 years old. In the interview she had said that she took "full responsibility" for what happened and went on to say that women who dress provocatively while walking down the street drunk were also to blame if they were attacked. "If I'm walking around in my underwear and I'm drunk? Who else's fault can it be?" she said (The Guardian, 2015).

The poll ran as scheduled and resulted in 87.5% of viewers voting 'no' – that a woman could never be at fault for being raped. However, the panel discussion toyed with the idea of women being held responsible and being to blame when they are raped.

Rape Crisis England and Wales commented in the national press, calling the poll 'inappropriate' and further argued that legally, no woman is ever to blame for rape because it is a sexual offence committed by a rapist.

They were right, of course.

However, it is worth considering the impact of a female-led television programme hosted by an influential, authoritative group of women with a target audience of women – engaging in such a damaging discussion about women subjected to rape. It is highly likely that women in the live studio audience or in the national audience at home would have been raped, abused or assaulted. For women subjected to male violence, this particular show sent strong messages about culpability and responsibility for rape.

On breakfast talk show 'This Morning' in 2011, Eammon Holmes interviewed Hannah Cant (then just 20 years old) about being subjected to rape by convicted repeat rapist Jonathan Haynes. This example is problematic for two reasons: Hannah was being interviewed as a 'perfect' victim of rape because she was attacked on her way home by a stranger and had deliberately pulled her own hair out and left saliva at the scene to prove DNA evidence. Whilst she was being praised for being so resourceful whilst being raped, this did not stop Eammon Holmes from finishing the interview by saying 'I hope you take taxis home now?' and commenting, 'How many times do I tell people to take a taxi home?'

This particular example of victim blaming is striking because Eammon Holmes had gone from praising Hannah for her actions during the rape (which are extremely rare and not expected of any women subjected to rape) to criticising her for not taking a taxi home. Clearly, Eammon criticised her because he felt that she should have taken a taxi in order to protect herself from being raped. His question to Hannah is less of a question and more of a direction – or chastisement: 'I hope you take taxis home now' reeks of being 'told off' for being a stupid woman who should have known better and has now learned from her 'mistake'.

Again, Rape Crisis England and Wales played an important part in challenging this comment by Eammon Holmes and there was a flurry of news stories about the way he spoke to Hannah. However, just as they did with the Loose Women poll, ITV decided not to investigate or take any further action.

Newspapers and online news outlets have been found to play an important role in the narratives around victim blaming of women subjected to male violence (Franuik et al., 2008; Maier, 2008). Whilst many of the studies were conducted in the 1980s and 1990s, the way the national and international media write and talk about sexual violence has not changed much at all.

Consider this headline from The Sun newspaper on the 20th July 2016:

'Woman drank six jager bombs in ten minutes on the night she was raped and murdered'

This report was about the rape and brutal murder of 20-year-old India Chipchase who was attacked by 52-year-old Edward Tenniswood in Northampton. Tenniswood lured her into a taxi away from her friends before strangling her to death and raping her in his flat.

Notice the language of the headline, again. The reader does not even find out that India is dead until the final word. Instead, the reader is directed to her drinking behaviour (how much she drank, what beverage she drank, how fast she drank it). The headline positions the drinking as leading to the rape and murder of India – and there is no mention of the murderer.

It is clear that the headline was written to position India as drunk, irresponsible and stupid – before mentioning that she was raped and killed.

Examples are numerous and easy to find.

In 2018, Fox News Host Tucker Carlson argued live on air that women who do not report their rape or abuse are 'part of the problem' and are not 'fulfilling their obligation to protect the rest of us'. Whilst discussing Brett Kavanaugh, Carlson blamed women for 'not protecting the other 320 million people who live here'.

In this example, women are not necessarily being blamed for being raped or abused – but are being blamed for not reporting or disclosing what they were subjected to.

Carlson argued in September 2018:

> *'Sex offenders tend to commit serial sex crimes. Doesn't she have an obligation to tell someone? To stop him from doing that if he is, in fact, a sex criminal? Where's her obligation here? What about the rest of us? And I know it's hard, but why don't we have a right to know? If there's a rapist on the loose, if you don't tell anybody … if Bernie Madoff rips you off and you don't tell his other investors … you're part of the problem, are you not?'*

This narrative is deeply troubling in a society that generally disbelieves or attacks women who report sexual violence. Carlson blames systemic, continued male violence on the women who cannot report or disclose. This position completely ignores the number of women who do report and disclose – who are told nothing will happen, no investigation will take place and no arrests will be made. Further, it is yet another example of men not being held responsible for their own actions and their own offences against women.

Carlson could have argued that men were responsible for ending violence, making choices not to oppress and abuse or to seek help if they think they commit acts of abuse and violence. Instead, he becomes angry towards the women who find it difficult to disclose or report male violence and places the responsibility on women to protect millions of other people.

Examples from prevention campaigns

The impact of such twisted reporting and discussions of sexual violence against women and girls can be seen in the advice we give to women and girls to protect themselves from rape, violence, domestic abuse, sexual assault and even child sexual abuse.

This section will discuss sexual violence prevention campaign posters used in the last 10 years by authorities in the UK. A combination of social narratives about sexual violence, the sexualisation and objectification of women and girls, the consistent victim blaming of women and girls as the cause and solution of sexual violence and a tendency to suggest that women and girls should change something about themselves to prevent sexual violence is likely to have played a role in the development and publication of sexual violence prevention campaigns such as those discussed here.

Rape prevention posters tend to have clear slogans that encourage women not to 'be a victim'. Rather than rape prevention being aimed at rapists, all posters and adverts in the UK have been aimed at women and girls to shame them or scare them into protecting themselves from rape. South Wales Police (2011) launched a set of posters which advised women 'Don't be a victim' and Warwickshire Police (2013) advise women 'Avoid being a rape victim'. Both posters contain advice about alcohol consumption, with South Wales' poster written in what can only be assumed to be blood. The words 'Don't be a victim' are scrawled in halloweenesque red, dripping letters above a set of bullet points for women about not drinking too much alcohol. The poster does not once address rapists, male violence or mention men. In fact, you could be led to believe that alcohol causes rape, and that women are being attacked by bottles of their favourite wine.

As prevention campaigns, these posters were aimed at victims as if the women could prevent sexual violence by following some simple safety rules. The prevention message here, is that women are instrumental in preventing sexual violence by not drinking alcohol and remaining more vigilant. However, this of course does not prevent sexual violence, as preventing sexual violence would mean that campaigns should be aimed at the cause of sexual violence: sex offenders.

Interestingly, both posters contain vague, metaphorical language about 'being a victim', which erases the role and actions of the sex offender by omitting them completely. Language such as this positions the woman as the cause and solution to sexual violence – which she can avoid if she modifies her own behaviours and choices.

Rape and sexual assault prevention campaigns often focus on the behaviour of women who drink alcohol or go out to bars and clubs with their friends. Two further posters from Sussex Police (2015) and the NHS (2014) were displayed in town centres and women's toilets in bars, clubs and venues where they would be consuming alcohol.

They were both problematic due to positioning the prevention of sexual violence as being the responsibility of women to either stop drinking, stop socialising or protect their friends from sex offenders. Further, it is wholly unfair to blame friends of women subjected to sexual violence for not preventing rapes or sexual assaults committed by adults who chose to attack another person. Neither poster challenges the offender or potential offender to not commit offences or to think differently about women and girls.

In 2018, North Yorkshire Police launched a new child sexual exploitation campaign aimed at children, which positioned sexual violence as a poor choice. The poster collection asked children 'Which choice will you make?' about whether they will 'choose' to be exploited, raped and trafficked or whether they will choose to have nicer outcomes free from abuse. This prevention campaign was particularly problematic as it is aimed at child victims of serious sexual crimes and repositions their abuse as a free choice. In one example, there is an image of a small girl with a nice present on one side of the poster and the prospect of being raped and trafficked on the other. Along the bottom of the poster in large letters asks the children 'Which choice will you make?'

This is a clear example of victim blaming in which children are positioned as making an active choice to be trafficked, exploited and raped. It makes abuse sound like the result of poor decision making, and directly addresses children in a patronizing tone. It sends a strong message to abused children that they made a poor choice in life which led to them being raped and abused. Again, no perpetrator is mentioned. The posters never directly mention a rapist, trafficker or abuser. The fact that the child is a child with no power over an adult sex offender or abuser, is completely ignored, and these posters position children as the person with the power to end, prevent or exit child sexual abuse.

Whilst these examples are numerous and easy to find, I will include one more.

In 2009, Transport for London launched a rape prevention campaign. The poster was displayed around London transport links (train stations, tube stations and taxi ranks) and sent a clear message to women to stop taking unbooked taxis as they may be raped. The poster contains a large image of a screaming, crying young woman being attacked in the back of a car. Her face is poking out of a slightly open window as she looks directly at the camera lens. The poster is emblazoned with the words 'No, no, no, please. No! Please stop. Stop taking unbooked taxis.'

The language on the poster containing the protests of a woman being raped is problematic alone, without the additional image of the screaming, crying woman. It feels like a mockery of raped women. As if someone thought it would be witty to make a pun of a woman screaming for a rapist to stop attacking her.

The prevention message here is behavioural, again. Women should stop using unbooked taxis and in the smaller text, the poster tells women that 'you're putting yourself in danger'. As with the other prevention campaigns, there is no focus on the concern that unbooked taxi drivers were committing acts of rape and sexual assault – but the focus remains on women to prevent sexual violence by not putting themselves in danger.

This collection of posters is only a small proportion of the historic and current sexual violence prevention campaigns that have been published and promoted in the UK in recent years. They convey a strong message to women and girls that preventing sexual violence is their own responsibility and can be achieved by changing their lifestyles, choices and behaviours. Prevention campaigns, such as the ones discussed here, do not mention who commits the sexual violence and do not target potential offenders and abusers. Instead, they focus on women and girls as inevitable victims of sexual violence who must protect themselves from 'rape' and 'assault' (as the offenders, usually men, are never named in the prevention campaigns).

Examples of interventions

Reporting, discussions, imagery and words are not the only way we convey messages of victim blaming of women. Other real-world examples include interventions and support programmes that blame women or hold women responsible for the violence of men.

In Chapter 11 and 14, I discuss the way education programmes have led to professionals holding girls responsible for the abuse and harassment they face from boys and men. Further, Chapter 14 discusses the way girls subjected to child sexual exploitation have been routinely given 'healthy relationships work' and 'keeping yourself safe' programmes for over a decade in the UK.

It often comes as a surprise to professionals that I do not support these seemingly helpful programmes of work, in which girls who have been raped, exploited, trafficked and abused are given 6-8 weeks of lessons or support sessions about spotting the signs of an unhealthy relationship, understanding 'how to say no', understanding rape and abuse and learning how to 'reduce their own risk taking behaviours'.

Instead of supporting these programmes, I tend to teach professionals that there are better and more supportive ways of working with these girls that do not assume that they were abused because they lacked basic relationships education. In my opinion, this position is victim blaming. Worse still, these interventions are being given to children who cannot even consent to sexual relationships in the first place.

This means that girls who are being raped and abused by adult men, are given information and education about protecting themselves from dangerous and violent offenders. Providing these interventions are professionals who must believe that girls are being trafficked and exploited due to their lack of knowledge and information about male violence.

This approach is not unique to child sexual exploitation or to children, however. Important parallels can be drawn with the well-established and respected, Freedom Programme for women abused by men.

The Freedom Programme in itself is not oppressive or victim blaming. It is developed to 'examine the roles played by attitudes and beliefs on the actions of abusive men and the responses of victims and survivors. The aim is to help them to make sense of and understand what has happened to them, instead of the whole experience just feeling like a horrible mess' (Freedom Programme, 2020).

However, it is commonplace in UK practice for women to be directed to attend the Freedom Programme when they are living with abusive and dangerous men. In child and adult social work, it is common for women to be advised or ordered to complete the Freedom Programme for similar reasons to the girls being prescribed 6 sessions of 'healthy relationships' work when they are already being raped and abused.

In this way, an intervention which was built to be a voluntary, informative approach to understanding male violence can be used to blame women who are being oppressed by male violence. Women can be 'sent' on a Freedom Programme course by social workers or police officers in an effort to get her to 'protect herself' or 'realise what is happening'.

In my own practice, I have even heard professionals argue that a woman has been 'sent on the Freedom Programme several times and yet she is still being abused' – as if sending her on a training course will in some way protect her from a powerful abuser.

Sometimes I wonder whether these particular professionals know anything at all about abuse and oppression. It strikes me as ignorant and dangerous to assume that directing a woman living in abuse or violence to attend a training course on male violence would be enough to protect her from the man living in her house, controlling her life and committing violent crimes against her.

This again suggests that we hold a belief that all women need to protect themselves from male violence is some education.

This belief is something I strongly reject, especially as this further embeds the assumption that only 'certain types' of women and girls will be abused and raped: and in this case, it is the 'uneducated' women and girls.

This is not to say that education is unimportant or irrelevant because knowledge does make us more powerful in many circumstances. I do however reject the belief that in a power dynamic of oppression, education is the key to stopping male violence and protecting women and girls. Similarly, I would reject any argument that placed responsibility on oppressed groups of humans to become more educated on their own oppression in order to protect themselves from that oppression. The responsibility and blame sit squarely with the oppressor and the oppressive structures that allow the oppression to continue.

It is not on the shoulders of the victim of abuse and oppression to protect themselves from the oppressor.

Despite this, many academics and professionals would disagree with me. An example of who might disagree with me include those who believe that women and girls should train in martial arts and self-defence to protect themselves from male violence. A further example might be the academics who have developed entire bodies of work based on the concept of 'sexual assault refusal assertiveness'. For the intrigued reader, look up the work of Jennifer Livingston or Jennifer Katz, both of whom argue that women having 'low sexual assault refusal assertiveness' increases their likelihood of 'sexual revictimisation'.

Sexual assault refusal assertiveness is a concept discussed heavily in psychological literature since 2007, often with the narrative that women and girls who are not assertive enough have higher levels of 'sexual revictimisation' (Livingston et al., 2007; Morgan, 2018).

I do not accept this term in my own work, as I feel it erases the male from the offence, again. Women do not simply 'experience sexual revictimisation', they are deliberately attacked and subjugated by male violence, and so I reject the body of work which suggests that women and girls should be more assertive or develop 'sexual assault refusal assertiveness skills' in order to protect themselves from male violence and patriarchal dominance.

For me, it is another example of us aggressively swerving the global issue of male violence and instead forcing individual women and girls to consider whether they should be taking responsibility for being more assertive towards men who are abusive or harassing.

There are many issues with this approach, not least that we know women who do reject or assert their choice to say 'no' are usually subject to further violence and abuse by male perpetrators.

The literature around sexual assault refusal assertiveness has a tendency to believe that men would not attack women and girls if they just 'said no more assertively', which Payne et al. (1999) and McMahon and Farmer (2011) actually list as a common rape myth.

If it is generally accepted in forensic psychology that 'women should say no clearer and more assertively' is a rape myth, how has it developed an entire body of work within the same discipline which seeks to 'train' women and girls to become more assertive when being sexually abused and assaulted?

An example of the way sexual assault refusal assertiveness literature has become a victim blaming intervention is the way in which it has quickly been developed into training courses and interventions for women at college and university, and even adolescent girls. Morgan (2018) explores the effectiveness of sexual assault refusal assertiveness training with adolescent girls and found little to no change in their behaviours or body language.

Despite this, Morgan reviews literature by other researchers who have suggested that when women and girls use assertiveness, refusal makes the offender 'less aggressive or stops the offence'. This struck me as directly contradicting what thousands of women and girls tell us every year – that fighting back or trying to assert their 'no' was either completely ignored or made the perpetrator so angry that the violence escalated and the attacks worsened.

Wider than this, however, is the problematic assumption that we can 'train' adolescent girls to be more assertive when they are being groomed, abused and harmed by men they have no real control over in such a purposefully abusive power dynamic.

5.

Prevalence of victim blaming attitudes

The prevalence of victim blaming of women subjected to sexual violence has varied in studies that are situated in different points in time, locations and cultures. Historic studies found that over half of participants blamed rape on the woman being promiscuous or having a bad reputation (Burt, 1980), but more contemporary studies have not presented a change in victim blaming attitudes.

In 2011, McMahon and Farmer found that 53% of university students agreed that the actions of a woman led to her being raped and in 2017, the Fawcett Society conducted a large UK study of over 8000 adults and found that 34% of women and 38% of men agreed that women are at least partially to blame if they are raped or assaulted. As such, the prevalence of victim blaming is still a concern worthy of understanding.

In 2017, I was commissioned to explore the victim blaming attitudes of a police force in the UK. Senior leadership had identified that police officers were likely to blame children who were being sexually exploited and had very little empathy for girls in looked after care services. I was asked to design and implement new training for all officers at every rank, to challenge the misinformation and attitudes towards girls subjected to child sexual exploitation (CSE).

In responses, I asked whether I could test pre and post knowledge and attitudes of the officers to explore whether training programmes made any difference to the way police officers blamed children for being sexually exploited.

Officers received a confidential online questionnaire which included attitude Likert scales, open ended questions, a knowledge test and multiple-choice questions. This questionnaire was completed twice, once before training and once after. It had a 97% response rate.

There were 158 officers in this evaluation sample and in pre-testing, 100% of officers stated that they had no previous training in CSE. The majority of all officers rated their own knowledge as 'poor' or 'low'.

Module content delivered to all police officers

- Introduction to the topic
- Definitions of CSE and CSA
- Breaking down myths and misunderstandings (victims, perpetrators and crime)
- Exploring grooming and perpetrator approaches/'models of CSE'
- Constrained choices, consent and coercion
- Consent quiz (SOA 2003)
- Risk factors, vulnerabilities and risk assessment toolkits
- Trafficking quiz (scenarios)
- Safeguarding and reporting CSE concerns
- Child-centred approaches to working in CSE
- Conclusions and Q&A

Police officers were asked to respond to a set of Likert agreement items and to write about a 'typical CSE case'.

When officers were asked to write about a typical case in a free text box, most answered with stereotypical, misinformed descriptions.

Despite 37.5% of officers simply writing in the box 'I don't know what CSE is', the rest of the officers offered answers that contained common themes. The most common answer contained a description of a 'vulnerable' 'female' in a 'care home' who 'exchanges sex' for 'alcohol and drugs'.

One officer wrote:

> 'A female who is in care home, dressing in a sexual way and voluntarily performing sex acts on males for drugs/alcohol/somewhere to stay or party'

Another officer wrote:

> 'Female in care will perform sexual favours for men who promise to give them things such as alcohol or drugs.'

These responses were representative of the answers given by the 62.5% of officers who felt they knew what CSE was. Girls were being positioned as troubled and vulnerable but simultaneously with enough agency to choose to have sex with adult men in 'exchange' for alcohol and drugs.

At this point, I must make it clear that I do not endorse the concept of 'exchange' when discussing abuse or exploitation. This is thoroughly deconstructed in Chapter 14.

After officers wrote about a typical case of CSE, they were asked to respond to 34 items which were designed to test knowledge and attitudes to CSE practice, policy and theory.

Examples of items in the questionnaire

Knowledge based items

- CSE is a form of child sexual abuse
- Children can be sexually exploited up to 18 years old

Attitudes and perceptions of victims of CSE

- Children often make false allegations of CSA/E
- Girls who wear revealing clothing are the most likely to be sexually exploited

Attitudes and perceptions of offenders of CSE

- Most CSE perpetrators are Asian males
- Female sex offenders are very rare in CSE

Attitudes and perceptions of fault, blame and cause in CSE

- Most CSE could be prevented with better parenting methods
- Some children bring it on themselves by the way they act

Understanding of procedure, policy and child protection

- A child should be treated as such until they are 18
- Once children reach the age of consent, there is little we can do to protect them from CSE

The findings to the questionnaire item were originally perplexing and rather depressing.

Pre-training, police officers answered in ways that demonstrated the prejudice they held about girls subjected to CSE. However, after police officers completed training and received the questionnaire again, the findings were not what we had hoped for.

Questionnaire item	Before training	After training
Some children make bad choices and take risks which lead to CSE	70% agreement	88% agreement
Some children bring it upon themselves by the way they act	85% agreement	84% agreement
Children are sexually exploited because they want something, and they know how to get it	45% agreement	66% agreement

All police officers scored significantly better on the knowledge and fact tests which included items about the age of consent, the nature of the law and local safeguarding policies. Officers went from stating they didn't know the answers to most of those items to knowing the answers over 90% of the time.

Clearly, knowledge had been received and retained.

What was concerning was that the attitudes were not only unchanged but were getting worse in some cases. It appeared that training was unlikely to change the values of professionals but may be able to increase basic factual knowledge of abuse and violence. Training did not seem able to create major change in victim blaming of children who are subjected to child sexual abuse.

Whilst these findings were disheartening, I was determined to use them to educate other providers and educators. Very often, we assume that we can reduce the prevalence of victim blaming by educating professionals. This study and two others I have conducted with professionals has shown that this is not strictly true.

Instead of seeing the exercise as a failure, I gave speeches and seminars about what these findings could mean.

It made me wonder why we ever thought that we could change the embedded, complex and socially supported victim blaming views with one day – or half a day – of classroom training. It made me wonder how we ever got to a place in which we thought we could simply 'educate' oppressive beliefs and prejudices out of people who hold them.

These studies changed the way I understood the prevalence of victim blaming – and forced me to consider how we understand, theorise about, and challenge such deeply held views about women and girls.

Understanding the measurement of victim blaming attitudes

Psychological research treats victim blaming as a set of attitudes. Therefore, most studies exploring these attitudes use psychometric measures with large numbers of people to gather data for exploratory and correlational studies (Anderson, 1999). The most common measures used to assess victim blaming have been the Rape Myth Acceptance Scale (RMAS) (Burt, 1980) the AMMSA, (Gerger et al., 2013) and the IRMAS (Payne et al. 1999). Whilst these measures have been shown to be valid and reliable in measuring rape myth acceptance (RMA) and sexual aggression myth acceptance – there are issues to consider when discussing how they are currently used in the topic of victim blaming. Briefly, the three core issues include the way the items are written and affected by socially desirable responses, the language used to describe the action of 'blame', and the way the scales have been used to draw conclusions about victim blaming without measuring blame attribution at all.

Whilst it is logical to suggest that people who accept common rape myths are likely to blame victims of sexual violence, the current scales do not seek to measure whether or how people blame the victims of sexual violence, they seek to measure the acceptance of myths and stereotypes about women, rape, sex and gender roles – which whilst arguably related, are separate concepts (Dawtry et al., 2019, p.2). Rape myths are common societal myths about rape, sex offenders and their victims whilst victim blaming is about how much blame is assigned to an individual victim of sexual violence. To draw conclusions about the prevalence and type of victim blaming in a sample, the psychometric measure would require valid items pertaining to the blame of sexual violence victims, which presents important questions about previous studies which have used RMA and attitudinal scales to theorise or hypothesise about victim blaming in sexual violence. Have previous studies conflated RMA with victim blaming?

Some of the RMA measures contain items or subscales that blame the woman for sexual violence. In the IRMAS, subscales 'she asked for it' and 'she lied' both focus on the character of the woman. However, whilst a woman 'asking for it' would be perceived as victim blaming, asking participants about items that positioned women as lying about sexual violence is more about rape denial than victim blaming. Accusing a woman of lying about rape happening is not the same as blaming her for being raped.

Burt's RMAS (1980) includes several rape myth items that relate to the behavioural and characterological blame of the woman. In a similar way, asking participants whether they believe rape myths about the blame of women is not the same as asking participants whether they *blame* women for being subjected to sexual violence. Items about agreeing to rape myths or sexist beliefs may be related to the attribution of blame to a woman but these are concepts which should be measured separately (Dawtry et al., 2019). I read this research with great interest, and this influenced me to separate the issues of rape myth acceptance and victim blaming of women. I considered that people could believe and accept rape myths without directly blaming a woman or girl for being sexually abused – and that people who blame women and girls for being subjected to sexual violence may not use any myths at all.

The second issue is the way the items in previous and existing scales are written, which includes problems with scales having outdated language. In Burt's RMAS there was outdated and colloquial language in the items such as 'necking', that was no longer used to mean kissing by the time Lonsway & Fitzgerald (1995) started to study RMA. Issues with item structure and type were suggested, as Burt's RMAS utilised agreement items and other open ended or multiple-choice questions of prevalence and attitudes within the same scale (Xue et al., 2016). Critiques about language and item meaning contributed to the development and testing of the IRMAS (Payne et al., 1999), which included considerations of item linguistics, colloquial words and phrases and item clarity during validation (Xue et al., 2016).

The original IRMAS was a 40-item, seven factor measure that was used widely after validation. The seven factors included (1) she asked for it, (2) it wasn't really rape, (3) he didn't mean to, (4) she wanted it, (5) she lied, (6) rape is a trivial event and (7) rape is a deviant event. The scales therefore sought to measure specific beliefs about the woman and her culpability, beliefs about the perpetrator of the rape and wider societal beliefs about rape as an event.

Later, McMahon & Farmer (2011) also recognised that issues with language were important to psychometric measurement of RMA. By engaging an undergraduate sample to seek their perceptions of the items, the authors redeveloped the IRMAS and named it the Updated IRMAS. McMahon & Farmer (2011) found that the most overt sub-scales including 'she wanted it' and 'rape is a trivial event' were so unlikely to be answered honestly, that they removed them from the U-IRMAS. This followed comments from the undergraduate participants that no one would ever agree with the items even if they really did agree with them (McMahon & Farmer, 2011). There were also changes in language between the publication date of the IRMAS (1999) and the year of study (2011) which led the researchers to replace the words 'woman' and 'man' with the terms 'girls' and 'boys' more often used to describe young adults; and the addition of the words 'slut' and 'slutty' to the items to reflect feedback from the undergraduate students that this was now the most common way of describing women's sexual behaviours.

This study provided evidence for concerns that the items written in scales must be updated as the population changes and must consider the way socially desirable responses may also change over time and between different populations.

For example, whilst the group of undergraduates eliminated three sub-scales because they felt they were too overt – they chose to add the words 'slut' and 'slutty' in place of 'a woman who wears a low cut top' which could be seen as contradictory changes to eliminate the overt statements in one sub-scale but to then add in more overt, misogynistic language elsewhere. This may also suggest that words like 'slut' and 'slutty' have become normalised sexual slurs over the decade. The findings from this study suggest that undergraduates are now more aware of giving socially acceptable responses to self-report measures and attitude questionnaires, even when anonymous.

Cause, fault, responsibility and blame

The third issue to be considered is about the language used to discuss the act of blaming victims of sexual violence and the impact this has on measurement and research methodology. Researchers have been using 'fault', 'blame', 'cause' and 'responsibility' interchangeably. For example, studies showed that participants were asked who was to blame but the conclusions were about who was responsible – despite other authors finding that people perceive and employ blame, cause and responsibility differently (Shaver & Drown, 1986) – often with 'blame' being the most emotive and 'taking responsibility' being the most socially acceptable terms used about victims of sexual violence (Shaver & Drown, 1986; Shaver, 1985; Critchlow et al., 1985; Heider, 1958).

To illustrate this point, consider the following passage in a national media outlet which argues that blaming women for sexual or domestic violence is not the same as holding them responsible for their behaviour during or before they were attacked:

> 'With respect to prevention, understanding the conditions that lead to crime can facilitate safety. College women should not get drunk (or drink anything that was left unattended), not because it makes them morally contributory but because it's a sensible approach to personal safety. If a woman thinks there's a good chance of her getting hit during an argument, she should seriously consider leaving the relationship—but she should also avoid arguments until the issue has been clarified. Getting into an argument doesn't mean she would be blameworthy for getting hit; it just means she would be putting herself at risk. (…) when it comes to treatment of victims, they are often encouraged to take no responsibility at all for what happened. (Karson, 2014)

This frequent conflation and contradiction of the terms in discourse means that even when research participants have been asked about blame, some researchers have written discussions about responsibility or causal reasoning (Shaver et al., 1979). For this reason, the third consideration of psychometric measures of victim blaming must be linguistics. If participants are asked questions about victim blame, the term 'blame' must be used consistently. As an extension to the argument of linguistics, the same can be said for the way the word 'rape' is perceived by participants in contrast to the term 'sexual assault' or 'non-consensual sex' – or even 'forced to have sex'. Studies have shown that even when participants have been raped, less than half of them say yes when asked directly in questionnaires (Donde et al., 2018). Studies find that women who have been raped or sexually assaulted respond differently to the language used in the item (Donde et al., 2018). Considering the issues of linguistics in sexual violence and blame, psychometricians must remain vigilant to the way technically correct words may affect the way respondents answer items. It may therefore be of use to look at blame and myth acceptance for a range of sexual offences, using diverse language to describe the offences to explore how the words may affect responses from groups of participants.

The original aim of this study was to utilise existing, validated psychometric measures to explore how much blame would be assigned to women subjected to sexual violence. However, due to the problems with existing measures as discussed above, and lack of specificity (to victim blaming of women rather than broader attitudes to women, sexual aggression or rape myths), I decided to do something different.

I decided that a new psychometric tool should be built and tested to specifically measure the assignment of blame of women subjected to all different forms of sexual violence in the modern world. This was no mean feat and I was worried that I would be adding another ineffective psychometric to the long list of not-so-good-methods-of-psychological-measurement.

Mapping the ways we measure victim blaming of women

In order to explore the requirement for a new psychometric measure, examination and mapping of all existing items was conducted on the following psychometric measures:

- Updated Illinois Rape Myth Acceptance Scale (U-IRMAS)
- Acceptance of Modern Myths about Sexual Aggression (AMMSA)
- Rape Myth Acceptance Scale (RMAS)
- Personal Victim Blaming Scale (PVBS)

The items from each measure were first explored to look for overlapping items, language use and the meaning of items. The U-IRMAS and AMMSA had an overlap of 8 items which map directly on to each other, three of which also map directly on to items from the RMAS. The wording of these items were similar and were likely to be measuring the same concepts.

The language of blame was also of interest whilst exploring the existing measures. U-IRMAS uses the words 'responsible' and 'fault' in one item each but the word 'blame' is not used in any of the items. In the U-IRMAS, items 1-5 from subscale 'she asked for it' are statements of victim blaming which could be used to test for one type of victim blaming attitude, that women ask to be raped. However, the other items pertain to a range of rape myths and not victim blaming. Similarly, Burt's RMAS items are based on hostile sexism, violence against women and rape myths rather than direct victim blame attribution. The AMMSA measures attitudes and rape myths. It uses the phrases 'partly to blame' in one item, but the rest of the items do not contain any of the words, 'blame', 'responsibility', 'fault' or 'cause'.

The PVBS is different from the other measures due to being vignette-based and the items asking participants about the character of the victim (Rayburn et al., 2003). Three items on the PVBS are related to blame. One item asks about whether the victim is blameless or blameworthy, a second item asks whether the victim is at fault or faultless and a third item asks whether the victim is responsible or irresponsible. All others ask the participant about other perceptions of the victim including whether they think they are kind, hurtful, harmless, good-natured and reliable.

Content analysis of all items of the U-IRMAS, AMMSA, RMAS, PVBS and Burt's Sex roles and Interpersonal Violence Scale revealed the following themes of victim blaming of women in sexual violence:

1. Women engage in behaviours that cause or encourage rape – behavioural blame

2. Men cannot or should not control their sexual desires and women must accept their lack of restraint towards them

3. Stereotypical gender role and sex role assumptions that imply a 'norm' of misogyny

4. There is something about the woman (character, attitudes, mental state, motivations) that causes rape or enables women to use sex/rape as a weapon – characterological blame

5. Women and society overreact to sexual advances

6. Rape is not as prevalent or important an issue as it is being perceived (rape denial)

7. Other items that are not related to blame, rape myths or other attitudes

The analysis found that scales that are used to draw conclusions about victim blaming of women do not measure the blame of women specifically. In some cases, such as the AMMSA, the scale focusses much more on perpetrator excusing and social narratives of sexism and attitudes towards sex. Burt's sex roles and interpersonal violence scale was mainly made up of items which measured the wider social narratives of sexism and misogyny with only a 1/5th of items directly measuring the blame of women. Half of the items on the U-IRMAS and on Burt's original RMAS (1980) directly measured the blame of the woman or girl. The PVBS focusses solely on the victim and asks participants to read a scenario and then to decide on characteristics of the person based on what they read. Whilst only one of the items is about blame, two more include 'fault' and 'responsibility', seemingly presented as individual and unrelated concepts. The rest of the items are characterological but are not related to blame.

However, whilst this scale did focus on the victim, it requires scenarios, which does not lend itself well to attitude measurement as scenarios can be interpreted differently by different participants. Scenarios often contain numerous salient factors that may influence the answers, and it may be difficult to know which factor in the scenario contributed to the responses of the participants.

When developing the current measure, the scenario method was initially considered. However, the use of scenarios was deemed inappropriate given the primary aim of the research, which was to obtain highly specific, quantitative measures of the apportioning of blame towards women subjected to sexual violence. The scenario method would have entailed presenting each participant with detailed passages of sexual violence examples (such as those used in Abrams et al. (2003) and Dawtry et al. (2019)) which may have made it more difficult to draw conclusions about why participants apportioned blame in the way they did due to the number of salient factors within a detailed scenario. However, shorter items used in psychometric measures could encounter the same difficulties that arise from the linguistics used in the items;

but answers arising from short, controlled items were considered easier to analyse and interpret than detailed scenarios.

Developing the items

As discussed by Clark & Watson (1995), language and item construction can make or break a psychometric measure with poor wording, biased or emotive language and item complexity influencing the way respondents interpret and answer items. Despite this, item development processes and face validity are not consistently reported in the literature, with one review study finding that only 66% of 114 scale development articles had conducted or reported face validity processes to evidence the items used in the new scales (Anthoine et al., 2014). Furthermore, the same study found that most scale development articles did not give descriptive information about individual items or score distributions. These criticisms are important to the transparency of item development and so this section provides thorough details of how the items of the BOWSVA were developed and tested.

At an early stage, items were developed to represent as many different scenarios of male-perpetrated sexual violence against women as possible which resulted in over 60 items describing sexual violence ranging from sexual harassment in the street from a stranger through to rape in a long-term relationship due to emotional blackmail. Items were initially developed to cover the offences in the Sexual Offences Act (2003). This decision was made in order to reduce ambiguity about whether the item described a real sexual offence and further, to increase validity of the measure by ensuring that all items correctly described an illegal sexual act. The descriptions of sexual offences according to the law were then manipulated to include different male and female characters and language to describe these items in different ways – in order to make them as diverse as possible for the research.

It was intended that one set of items would be specific scenarios such as 'A woman makes a sex tape with her husband. Years later when they divorce, he posts it all over the internet' in which participants would answer whether they thought the woman was to blame using a Likert-type scale. In addition to this, the original plan was to include a second set of items containing general statements of victim blaming in society such as 'Women sometimes bring rape upon themselves by the way they act' in which participants would respond with their agreement or disagreement with the statement on a Likert-type scale.

During the process it was decided that the general statements items bore too much resemblance to the U-IRMAS and AMMSA so all items were deleted and focus remained on the specific items exploring how much participants would blame the woman in each scenario of sexual violence. Instead, it was decided that when the items were ready for testing with a large sample, they would be tested with the U-IRMAS to look for concurrent validity with the more general statements of RMA.

The items then went through three stages of critique, amendment and feedback with an expert group of 12 academics and professionals specialising in sexual violence; who agreed to examine and give feedback on items, scale structure and measurement. Due to the complexity of the items and the development of the scale, this process occurred seven times in total, until the final items were agreed upon for testing with a general public sample.

The process of critique, amendment and feedback

With the initial 55 items developed, linguistic analysis of item content was undertaken to ensure that the items were not weighted heavily one way, such as having too many items that include descriptions of vulnerable women. This task was highly valuable to the process to ensure that the scale and items are as valid as possible.

Content was explored for overt/subtle, stereotypical/non-stereotypical, stranger perpetrator/familiar perpetrator, vulnerable/non-vulnerable woman, woman choice/constrained choice and behavioural/characterological descriptors.

It was important to develop a new measure of victim blaming that equally used a range of scenarios. Especially as previous psychological studies had used highly stereotypical scenarios of sexual violence against women, which runs the risk of further confirming rape myths (Eaton, 2019).

The questions I used to develop the items are here:

1. Is the scenario used overt? (Does the scenario contain the use of words such as 'rape', 'attack', 'assault', 'force' or 'threaten' and the use of scenarios that would be easily perceived to be an offence by general participants?)

2. Is the scenario used more subtle? (Does the scenario contain the use of the words 'persuaded', 'touched' and the

use of scenarios that might not be easily perceived as an offence by general participants?)

3. Stereotypical versus non-stereotypical sexual violence (Does the scenario conform to common rape myths in the literature? Is the scenario outside of common rape myths and societal myths about sexual violence, perpetrators or victims?)

4. Stranger perpetrator versus familiar perpetrator (Does the scenario describe a sexual offence in which the perpetrator is a stranger (passer-by, person in a bar, person they have just met, person on train) or someone familiar to the woman (work colleague, boyfriend, husband, brother in law, friend, boss)?)

5. Vulnerable woman versus non-vulnerable woman (Does the scenario present the woman as stereotypically vulnerable (homeless, drunk, scared, threatened, in poverty, drug-dependent) or does the scenario present the woman as stereotypically non-vulnerable (a CEO of a company, strong, confident, feeling safe, having fun, with her friends)?

6. Woman had perceived choices versus woman forced or constrained (Does the scenario present a situation where the woman might be perceived as having a choice (being offered a place to stay in return for sex with strangers, being told to have sex to pay her debts off, being too scared to say no to a partner) or does the scenario present a situation where the woman was clearly forced (weapon, threatened, attacked, beaten, trapped, unconscious, asleep)?

7. Victim behavioural detail versus victim character detail (Does the scenario comment on the victim's behaviour in some way (she walked home alone, she went out to a bar, she got a new job) or does the scenario comment on the victim's character in some way (she is flirty, sexy, happy, embarrassed, scared, ashamed)?

I also considered the language surrounding the offence itself. As a significant proportion of the general public subscribe to rape myths and beliefs that obscure the real definitions of rape, sexual assault and abuse, I thought it best to include many different ways of describing sexual violence against women. I had the added interest of whether calling a rape a 'rape' or describing it as 'forced sex' would have any impact on whether the general public blamed the woman.

Instead, I decided to construct scenarios of sexual violence which contained the descriptors:

Rape, sexually assaulted, sexually abused, forced to, touched, manipulated into, threatened to, coerced etc.

I also included some scenarios that described the offence in more subtle terms to explore whether this had an impact on how much the woman would be blamed. Items were refined and checked by an expert group to ensure that every item clearly described a sexual offence under the SOA (2003).

Once the items were balanced and linguistic issues had been addressed, a private questionnaire was sent to 12 experts in sexual violence for them to respond to. The purpose of the questionnaire was to check whether professionals working in sexual violence felt that the items were easy to read, were realistic scenarios of sexual violence and whether they felt the item may elicit victim blaming from a general public sample.

The expert group was comprised of 7 females and 5 males working in social care, psychology, education, prison, policing and sexual violence charities.

Each professional was able to provide feedback on any of the items they felt were inappropriate, unsuitable or unrealistic. However, 99% of items were found to be clear and realistic.

Some items caused more comments than others, with some of the expert group being concerned that item language like 'a woman with no class' or 'known for being a slag' or 'she doesn't act like a decent woman' were so unrealistic that no one would answer the item.

This was an interesting observation as it was similar to the results from McMahon & Farmer (2011). Some also commented that they hoped that items which presented clear scenarios of rape and violent assault would cause no one to blame the victim at all, but they accepted that some people probably would blame the woman.

When the questionnaire was finally delivered to participants, there were a total of 55 scenarios of sexual violence being committed against women by men. As the study was specifically about the prevalence of victim blaming, each participant read the scenario and were then asked how much they blamed the woman for being subjected to the sexual offence by a man.

Initially, the items were to be accompanied by a single 4-option forced Likert-type scale which asked how much the woman was to blame for the sexual offence occurring. It was decided to deliberately remove a 'middle' or 'I don't know' option in such a controversial topic in case participants chose to 'sit on the fence' for difficult items. It was also consciously decided not to use the word 'victim' in the measurement question and instead to refer to the victim of the sexual offences as 'the woman' to avoid leading respondents who might not feel she was a victim of an offence at all.

Example of response options for each scenario

How much is the woman to blame for what happened?			
Definitely not to blame	Probably not to blame	Probably to blame	Definitely to blame
Score 0	Score 1	Score 2	Score 3
How much is the man to blame for what happened?			
Definitely not to blame	Probably not to blame	Probably to blame	Definitely to blame
Score 0	Score 1	Score 2	Score 3

Despite the participants of this study being anonymous computer users (which is linked to more honest responses in self-report measures (Gribble et al., 1999)), socially desirable responses are still common in self-report measures assessing sensitive topics (Mann & Hollin, 2010). It was considered that presenting a scenario describing a sexual offence and then only asking participants how much the woman is to blame would result in significant socially desirable responding.

It is also common to hear people excuse perpetrators or apportion blame to both the victim and the perpetrator of a sexual offence. Due to this, it was suggested that offering two options to apportion blame may reduce socially desirable responses such as self-deceptive positivity and impression management (Mann & Hollin, 2010), especially for those participants who feel both parties are to blame in sexual offences. As some participants may blame both the woman and the man in certain scenarios, two sets of response items were chosen to explore whether there is any relationship between the amount of blame apportioned to the man and the woman in each scenario.

The measure was named the Blame of Women Subjected to Sexual Violence and Abuse Scale (BOWSVA Scale).

Participants were recruited from the general public using an open call for adult participants (18 years and over) to take part in an online, anonymous study about the perceptions of sexual offences. Adverts for the study were placed on three social media platforms (Facebook, LinkedIn and Twitter), on the research participant platform 'Call for Participants' and in social media groups to aim for the most diverse sample possible.

There were 997 people who consented to take part, but only 456 people completed the study (i.e., answered all of the items), resulting in a completion rate of 45%. In 55% of cases, participants began to fill in the demographic questions but did not complete any of the scale items, and therefore all were deleted listwise.

Participants

Of the 456 people who completed the study, 247 (54%) were female, 205 (45%) were male and 4 (1%) identified as transgender. This does present a slight over representation of female participants as the ONS (2019) shows the current UK population is 51% female and 49% male. All participants were aged 18-75 years old. Of all participants, 366 were White British (80%), 33 were White Other (7%), 16 were Mixed/Multiple Ethnicity (4%), 13 were White Irish (3%), 7 were Asian Indian (2%), 4 were Asian Pakistani, 4 were Black British, 3 were other Asian heritage, 2 were Black African, 1 was Asian Bangladeshi, 1 was Black Caribbean, 1 was Arab and 5 selected 'other ethnicity'. This data represents a diverse sample which is more diverse than the general population of the UK. According to the ONS (2019) 86% of the population is White British.

Participants also had a range of educational levels with 78 participants educated up to the end of high school education (17%), 79 achieving a college or vocational qualification (17%), 139 educated up to and including a Bachelor's Degree (30%), 102 achieving post graduate certificates or Masters Degrees (22%), 26 achieving a PhD or Doctorate (6%) and 32 people preferred not to say (7%). When compared against the NOMIS (2012) and Census

(2011) data, this sample has an over-representation of people with higher education degrees which national data reports to be between 27-40%.

Participants were also asked about their job roles to check for diversity of respondents and so job roles were listed as taken from national recruitment and employer website 'Indeed.com'. It was important to check this in case participants were found to be overwhelmingly from one sector that may have confounded the results. Participants had a wide range of job roles, and 61% had two or more job roles. This is significantly higher than current national statistics which report that around 20% of adults have two or more jobs (Coople, 2018).

Participants also had a range of religious affiliations and beliefs. The majority reported having no religion (53%) which is the same as the most recent national social attitudes surveys (BSA, 2017). In addition, 36% identified as Christian, 5% as Other, 2% as Buddhist and all other religions were less than 1.5%, which is very similar to the findings from the BSA (2017).

Recent research suggests that about 30-40% of the British public blame women for rape (Fawcett Society, 2017). Therefore, it was expected that the distribution of responses would not be normally distributed, and this is considered throughout the interpretation of results.

Results

There were seven components of victim blaming that were derived from conducting a factor analysis on the data:

1.   Subscale 1 – She was asking for it
2.   Subscale 2 – She was in a dangerous situation
3.   Subscale 3 – She should have been more assertive
4.   Subscale 4 – He was entitled to her body
5.   Subscale 5 – The non-stereotypical sex offender
6.   Subscale 6 – The stereotypical rape myth
7.   Subscale 7 – She was a sexually active woman

Factor 1 'She was asking for it'

The results from principal components analysis grouped these six items together, all of which position the woman as doing something that would be considered 'asking for it'. All items described women who took some form of action or made a decision that could be perceived as causing or encouraging sexual violence from men. All items positioned women as sexual, alluring or taking some form of perceived 'risk'. This factor is strongly supported by previous evidence from the literature, and items are similar in nature to AMMSA and U-IRMAS in places. From a linguistic perspective, it is also interesting to note the way items that describe women as sexy or talk about sex have grouped together in this component.

Asking for it

The maximum score any participant could achieve from consistently and totally blaming the woman for every act of sexual violence was 27. 58.1% of participants blamed the woman, with a small number of participants blaming the woman almost totally for every item, scoring 26 out of 27.

The blame assigned by the group of 456 participants varied considerably depending on the content of the items. Item 13 (below) resulted in 42% of participants assigning blame to the woman for being raped whilst drunk, this is likely to be related to rape myths and victim blaming when women drink alcohol (Romero-Sanchez et al., 2017).

Item 19 and 22 both reference the way the woman is dressed and resulted in high levels of victim blaming of the woman with 30% and 32% blaming the woman, respectively.

All women described in this subscale were assigned some blame and were all described to be dressed in revealing clothing, dancing in clubs, walking alone or drinking. None of the items resulted in zero blaming of women.

08 *A woman chooses to walk home alone through a dangerous area because her bus failed to turn up. While doing so, she is sexually assaulted*

Result: 18% blamed the woman

10 *A woman goes out for the night wearing a sexy dress. While out she is touched on her breast as she walks past a man*

Result: 14% blamed the woman

13 *A woman gets so drunk that she keeps blacking out in a guy's flat. She wakes up the next morning naked and he tells her they had sex during the night*

Result: 42% blamed the woman

15 *A woman in a nightclub is twerking on the dancefloor and kissing different men who she doesn't know. When she goes to the toilet, a man forces her into the cubicle and rapes her*

Result: 25% blamed the woman

19 *A woman who is wearing revealing clothing is catcalled in the street by men who tell her to take her top off*

Result: 30% blamed the woman

22 *A woman who likes to dress sexily because it makes her feel good about herself is constantly sexually harassed by the men she works with*

Result: 31% blamed the woman

Factor 2 'She was in a dangerous situation'

This factor appears to group together items in which the woman is in a situation that could be perceived as dangerous or risky for her. Items loaded without any overlap with others and this subscale required no deletion of cross loading items. As many of the items were situational, this presents a problem for explaining victim blaming in which the type of blame is not necessarily characterological or behavioural, but relates to the environment the woman was in, or the actions of others. This factor includes items in which the language is overt. Words such as 'forced', 'raped', 'assaulted', 'threatened' and 'violent' are used in these items and may have influenced the way participants responded to the scenarios. Despite there being overt mention of violence, rape and threat to the woman, participants still attributed blame to the women in the items.

Subscale 2: She was in a dangerous situation

The maximum score any participant could achieve from consistently and totally blaming the woman for every act of sexual violence was 24. 29% of participants blamed the woman, with the majority of participants assigning little blame to women in these scenarios. There were a small number of participants with scores of 20 and 21, out of a total of 24, indicating that they blamed the woman wholly or partially in every scenario on this subscale. Generally, however, items on this subscale saw much lower levels of blame than subscale 1 and tended to contain more stranger attacks, violent rapes and stereotypical examples of assault. All items describe a situation in which women may be asked 'what did you expect to happen?' or would be questioned about why they were in a risky or dangerous situation or environment alone. The three items that resulted in the most blame of women despite the stereotypical attacks were all items in which the woman was described negatively as having no class, cheating on her partner or doing nothing to stop the assaults.

06 *A woman who has no class is sexually assaulted on a number of occasions by a friend*

Result: 12% blamed the woman

09 *A cheating woman is set up by her secret lover to be raped by one of his friends*

Result: 12% blamed the woman

28 *A bar maid who is very attractive, is slapped on her bottom whenever she walks past the door staff*

Result: 10% blamed the woman

39 *A woman who leaves her friends after an argument on a night out is raped on her way home*

Result: 9% blamed the woman

41 *A woman is raped by her brother in law. He threatens to shame her to her family and the community if she says anything*

Result: 7.5% blamed the woman

45 *A woman is on a deserted train home and a stranger pushes her into the corner of the train and forces her hand into his trousers. She doesn't say anything or do anything to stop him.*

Result: 17% blamed the woman

47 *A woman was walking her dog in the park when she is violently assaulted by a stranger and then raped multiple times behind some trees*

Result: 5% blamed the woman

49 *A woman is walking back from her local shop when she is held at knife point and forced to give oral sex to the perpetrator*

Result: 6% blamed the woman

Factor 3 'She should have been more assertive'

The eight items in this component all relate to whether the woman said no, asserted herself or stopped the offences from happening. In every item that was grouped together in the analysis, the woman is positioned as submissive, trapped, unable to say no, manipulated or exploited. There is therefore a possibility that participants viewed these women as making free choices rather than being raped and assaulted. From a linguistic perspective, it is interesting to note that the words 'rape', 'assault', 'violent' or 'force' are absent from all items, and in every item, the woman is described as scared or submissive.

She should have been more assertive

The maximum score any participant could achieve from consistently and totally blaming the woman for every act of sexual violence was 24. 80% of participants blamed the women and items on this subscale resulted in some of the highest and most consistent victim blaming of the woman. All items on this subscale position the woman as submissive, unable to say no or trapped in a situation or assault that she cannot escape.

Items also include manipulation, blackmail and intimidation of women to perform sex acts or to be continually sexually assaulted. These features appear to have elicited much higher levels of blame from the participant group with over 75% of items in this subscale scoring high levels of blame of women. In this subscale, the issue appears to be about the woman's agency and lack of power in the sexual offence, which increased the amount she was blamed; because she did not assert herself or stop the offences, she was blamed by the participants.

01 *A woman performs unpleasant sexual acts that her husband has seen in porn films because he threatens to leave her if she doesn't*

Result: 30% blamed the woman

29 *A woman keeps receiving naked pictures from her work colleague but is too scared to tell him that she is not interested so he keeps sending them*

Result: 30% blamed the woman

30 *A woman has sexual comments made to her every morning by her neighbour. She feels there is nothing she can do about it and so has no choice but to accept his comments*

Result: 27% blamed the woman

31 *A woman who has never worked and therefore has no savings of her own stays with her sexually abusive husband*

Result: 33% blamed the woman

33 *A woman who has been homeless for months is offered somewhere to live if she performs sex acts on a number of men each night, so she moves in*

Result: 46% blamed the woman

35 *A woman really admires and loves her husband but when he's drunk he tells her she must have sex with him even if she doesn't want to because she's his wife*

Result: 13% blamed the woman

43 *A woman is groped by her boss but doesn't tell anyone because she's worried about losing her job*

Result: 17% blamed the woman

44 *A woman who is too scared to say no to her boyfriend lies still and closes her eyes until he has finished having sex with her*

Result: 32% blamed the woman

Factor 4 'He was entitled to her body'

The three items in this component relate to sleeping or unconscious women. Participants tended to respond in similar ways to these items and they were grouped together in the analysis. Possibly, this is because there is a perceived 'grey area' around having sex with a long-term partner who is sleeping, unwell or not aroused. All items talked about husbands, boyfriends or partners explicitly, which also may have influenced the way participants responded to the item because the perpetrator was their partner.

He was entitled to her body

This subscale only has three items, but they did not load onto any other factor and all contained the description of a sleeping or non-consenting woman. The maximum score any participant could achieve from consistently and totally blaming the woman for every act of sexual violence was 9. Whilst 63% of participants assigned no blame to the woman in any of the scenarios 37% of participants assigned blame to the woman, despite her being asleep or not being aroused enough to have sex. A small number of participants (5%) assigned full or almost full blame to the women in all three scenarios. As the woman is asleep or clearly non-consenting, it is not reasonable to assume behaviour or characterological blame – but that 37.1% of participants blamed her for some other reason. The items appear to describe a partner who is not concerned about the woman, but feels they are able to sexually abuse or rape their partner even if they do not want sex or are unable to have conscious or consensual sex. These items appear to be about male entitlement to sex with their partners or to touching her body even when she does not want it or cannot consent to it.

14 *A woman tells her boyfriend that she wants to have sex with him, but she starts to feel unwell and falls asleep on the sofa. She wakes up to find him performing oral sex on her*

Result: 22% blamed the woman

24 *A woman is having sex with her partner and wants to stop because she is no longer aroused but her partner forces her to continue*

Result: 23% blamed the woman

25 *A woman wakes up to find her husband very turned on and touching her vagina whilst she was asleep*

Result: 20% blamed the woman

Factor 5 'The non-stereotypical sex offender'

These items were deliberately designed to test whether participants responded differently to victim blaming when the male offender was described as handsome or vulnerable. This presents the offender in a non-stereotypical way and could have therefore influenced the way participants responded and caused the items to be grouped together in the component analysis. However, whilst the description of the man was manipulated to be non-stereotypical by describing him as vulnerable, upset, handsome or in need of support, the language used to describe the offence still contained overt words such as 'force', 'threaten', 'rape', 'assault'. Nonetheless, the description of the man as non-stereotypical seemed to group these items together, meaning that victim blaming of women may be affected when the male perpetrator does not fit the stereotype of the sex offender.

The non-stereotypical sex offender

The items in this subscale appear to have been grouped based on the behaviour and character of the offender, rather than the behaviour or character of the woman. The maximum score any participant could achieve from consistently and totally blaming the woman for every act of sexual violence was 12.

83.1% of participants assigned no blame to the woman and scored zero. 16.9% of participants assigned partial blame to the woman, with none of the participants assigning full blame to the woman.

These items were designed to explore whether victim blaming would change if the offender in the scenario was described in a non-stereotypical way, for example as vulnerable, helpless or handsome. Despite the offender being described as non-stereotypical, the blame of the woman remained low. It is of interest that whilst the description of the offender had been manipulated to elicit sympathy or understanding, the items still contained overt language about the offence such as 'threaten', 'held down', 'raped', 'assault' and 'forced'.

It is interesting that the items that were designed to explore the perception of the non-stereotypical offender grouped together in the analysis, but more research is needed to understand how this links to the blame of the woman.

34 *A woman goes out for a date with a really attractive man from college. He threatens to tell everyone at college that she's had sex with him if she doesn't give him a blowjob*

Result: 11% blamed the woman

51 *A woman was the last person getting off the bus at night when the bus driver, who had just received the news that he was being made redundant, held her down and groped her*

Result: 7.5% blamed the woman

53 *A woman was at a house party when she realised she had been drugged. She went to seek help but was pulled into a bedroom and raped by a male friend who was also high on drugs*

Result: 7% blamed the woman

54 *A woman was in the unisex showers at her new gym when a man who had been talking to her about his marriage breakdown walks in. He obstructs her only exit and sexually assaults her*

Result: 8% blamed the woman

55 *A woman was studying in the library when a man starts to tell her about how depressed he is since his business went bust. She listens to him and he asks her if she is single and when she tells him that she is not interested, he forces his hand up her top*

Result: 7% blamed the woman

Factor 6 The stereotypical rape myth

In this component, items that represented the stereotypical rape myth appeared to group together in the analysis. In all items presented below, the women were described as outside of their homes, alone and feminine or sexual. All men were strangers or acquaintances and all offences were public, forced or overtly violent. When these factors are added together, they represent the 'classic rape' as suggested by Williams, (1984). These items appeared to group together because they elicited low levels of blame and many participants responded in the same way to these items.

The stereotypical rape myth

Items that grouped together to form subscale 6 appear to be related to the classic rape stereotype. In these items, the woman was either alone or described as sexual. All of the women were attacked outside of the home environment and all of the offences were violent, forceful or public in nature. None of the offenders were partners or family members, with most being strangers or acquaintances. Therefore, the items contain many of the rape myths arising from the classic rape stereotype. The maximum score any participant could achieve from consistently and totally blaming the woman for every act of sexual violence was 15.

78.1% of participants assigned no blame to the woman and scored zero, causing another mode and mean of zero. However, 21.9% of participants assigned blame to the woman, despite the items conforming to the stereotypical rape myth. It is interesting to note that all women in the scenarios were travelling somewhere or were away from home, as if this was a salient factor, it would mean that women living independent lives was a factor in victim blaming of women.

23 *A beautiful woman with a curvaceous figure is on the tube when a man rubs his groin up against her*

Result: 7% blamed the woman

27 *A woman who was wearing a clingy dress instead of the appropriate clothing in her community is raped on her way to a family gathering*

Result: 10% blamed the woman

37 *A woman who makes a real effort with her appearance is suddenly pushed against a wall by a work colleague at a party who then kisses her*

Result: 11% blamed the woman

46 *A woman is outside of her home when she is approached by a man in a car who stops to ask her for directions. As she gives the directions, she is dragged into the car by the man and then raped*

Result: 7% blamed the woman

50 *A woman had just finished an evening board meeting when she is knocked unconscious in a multi-story carpark and is sexually assaulted*

Result: 6% blamed the woman

Factor 7 'She was a sexually active woman'

The final factor appears to group all items in which the woman is described or positioned as sexually active or sexually liberal. These items elicited some of the highest amounts of blame and many participants answered these items in the same way. From a linguistic perspective, there is no mention of the words rape, assault, threaten or violent – but the word or concept of being forced is frequent. However, this appears to be negated by the sexual descriptions of the women who are described as flirting, working in a brothel, sending naked selfies, being sexually exploited for drugs, making sex tapes, working as glamour models or reality TV stars. These items are grouped together because the women are positioned as sexually active and this may have caused judgement or lack of empathy from participants; with between a fifth and a half of participants attributed blame to the woman in all of these items.

Sexually active woman

The final subscale relates to women who are sexually active or sexually liberal. The maximum score any participant could achieve from consistently and totally blaming the woman for every act of sexual violence was 27. 64% of participants blamed the woman in these items either partially or fully.

In items in this subscale, women were described as enjoying or engaging in sex acts, taking sexual images, making sex tapes or being sexually exploited. This subscale also contains the item which resulted in the most blame (item 17) due to the woman taking selfies that were subsequently used to blackmail her.

Despite the clear description of the blackmail, over half of the participants still assigned blame to the woman in the item.

Due to the way these items grouped together in analysis, it is probable that the component relates to blaming women for being sexually active, ultimately blaming the woman for being 'easy' or 'promiscuous' and therefore to blame for any sexual violence perpetrated against her.

04 *A woman has been flirting with a man all night long. She is groped by him against her will as she tries to leave the club*
Result: 32% blamed the woman

12 *A woman chooses to go back to the hotel bar with a man she just met while out for the night. In the taxi on the way to the hotel, he forces his hand up her skirt even though she asked him not to*
Result: 20% blamed the woman

16 *A woman working in a brothel as a sex worker is forced to have anal sex by a client*

Result: 26% blamed the woman

17 *A woman sends a lot of naked pictures and videos of herself to a guy she is dating from work. Using the pictures, he then blackmails her into kissing and masturbating him*

Result: 56% blamed the woman

18 *A woman is forced to have sex with lots of men to pay off her drug debts*

Result: 32.5% blamed the woman

20 *A woman who enjoys the attention she gets as a famous glamour model has her skirt lifted up and her vagina touched by a man in a restaurant*

Result: 16% blamed the woman

21 *A woman who shot to fame as a reality TV star finds that the paparazzi have published up-skirt photos of her at an event*

Result: 24% blamed the woman

36 *A woman makes a sex tape with her boyfriend but then finds out he's shared it with his mates without her knowing*

Result: 34% blamed the woman

38 *A sex worker who only offers her clients a "hand job" or a "blow job" is forced to have vaginal sex with a client*

Result: 21% blamed the woman

These new suggested factors of victim blaming present a new way of understanding the reasons why participants might assign blame to women subjected to sexual violence.

Despite all the items describing illegal sexual offences against women, none of the items resulted in zero blame being apportioned to the female victim.

The factors also demonstrate the diversity of possible reasons for victim blaming which include scales about the woman's behaviour and character hailing from gender role stereotypes, sexism and misogyny (she was asking for it, she was not assertive enough and she was sexually active or sexually liberal), scales about the situation the woman was in, (the situation was dangerous or risky), stereotypes and rape myths already established in the literature (the offender was non-stereotypical and the rape conforms to rape myths) and finally, male entitlement to women's bodies when in relationships which supports work on token resistance, sexualization and objectification of women and feminist approaches to male violence (he was entitled to her body).

This factor structure appears to bring together many of the prevailing theories of victim blaming.

Whilst there is a common belief that women tend to victim blame other women less than men do, my study was one of many which found no significant difference between male and female attitudes towards victim blaming of women (Viki & Abrams, 2002; Gerber et al., 2004).

This means that male and female participants did not differ in their attribution of blame towards the female victims of sexual offences, despite many people expecting women to have higher empathy and therefore lower victim blaming towards other women.

Further testing on the mean summed scores for subscales of the BOWSVA returned no significant differences between sexes, except for on subscale 4 'He was entitled to her body' in which male and female participants did respond differently to the items describing women who were asleep, unwell or unconscious.

On this subscale, men did blame women more than women did – but much more research would be required for me to comment on why that might be (especially considering how many participants left confused comments about their own experiences of having sex with sleeping women or being women who often awoke to their partners having sex with them).

Other statistical tests confirmed previous theories that rape myth acceptance was strongly positively related to victim blaming attitudes. This meant that the stronger the belief in rape myths, the more the participant tended to blame women for being subjected to sexual violence. Specifically, the stronger their beliefs in rape myths and rape stereotypes, the more they blamed women for asking for it, for not being assertive enough and for being sexually active.

Interestingly, those who held strong victim blaming beliefs on my scale also tended to hold strong beliefs that women lie about being raped.

This suggests that rape myth acceptance may strongly correlate with these three assumptions or beliefs about women subjected to sexual violence: that she asked for it, that she should have been more assertive or that she is promiscuous for being previously sexually active. However, it shows that rape myth acceptance alone cannot explain why so many women will be blamed for being subjected to sexual violence.

For this reason, it was vital to conduct interviews with women who had been blamed for sexual violence to explore the other reasons this might happen and how it feels to be blamed in these ways. The interviews are reported in Chapter 15 and 16.

Participant feedback about the BOWSVA study

At the end of the study, all participants were invited to give feedback on the experience of taking part and to give any thoughts about the method, topic and their own personal experience of answering the questions.

The reason I offered all participants the option to leave anonymous feedback was to learn from their comments and experiences of taking the study and reading about so many scenarios of sexual violence. I wanted to review the study methodology too, in case participants told me that they had found the study too distressing, too long, too difficult or too repetitive. This is not just about the experience of the participant, but issues like this can be detrimental to psychological and attitudinal studies. When participants get bored, annoyed, distressed or distracted – results will be affected and can sometimes become too impacted to analyse effectively or ethically.

Out of a total of 456 participants, 281 left anonymous feedback which varied considerably. A thematic analysis of the comments was conducted, exploring the frequency of phrases and words used by participants.

24% of participants left positive comments about taking part in which they described the study as 'important', 'eye-opening' and wrote that they felt happy about taking part. However, 15% left negative comments about their experience such as that the study was 'too long' or 'depressing'. A further 9% of participants left mixed comments, 'It is a really good study, but it took ages to complete and was small on the screen.'

Whilst this data was important, I was interested in the 26% of participants who wrote that it was hard to decide who was to blame in each of the scenarios:

> 'It really forced me to think about who was to blame. I struggled with some where I thought they were both to blame.'

These comments from just over a quarter of the participants were important not only to the study but to all other studies of this nature. Only by offering a free text comment box at the end of the study did I learn that a quarter of the participants found it hard to answer the victim blaming questions because they felt both the perpetrator and the woman was to blame for sexual violence.

Comments such as this have implications not only for other studies, but for criminal justice and professional practice. It is important that participants were able to reflect and report that they found the study hard to complete – especially as so many of them felt that both women and men were to blame for men committing sexual violence against women.

Some comments (7%) included rape myths within their answer. In these answers, people wrote about rape myths that they believed to be true:

> 'I chose this answer because women do actually lie about rape often.'

Whilst only 7% of participants left comments like this, it is important to consider that having taken part in such an overt study about the victim blaming of women and the issues around rape myth acceptance – they still left comments strongly endorsing rape myths and arguing that they answered the questions based on their belief of rape myths, which they thought were true.

Finally, a further 17% of comments in the free text box were either abuse towards me, whataboutery comments or misguided accusations of bias.

These comments are also important to consider and analyse.

3% of participants left explicit personal abuse towards me:

'The researcher is an (several expletives) and I hope she fails her PhD.'

Slurs included 'bitch', 'stupid', and 'misandrist' among others I will not write into this book. One academic wrote that his undergraduate students could produce a better PhD than me and he looked forward to seeing me fail. He left his name and some kisses at the end of his comment.

6% of participants accused me of being biased because I chose to study the victim blaming of women and suggested that my work would be better if I included men or focused more on men. A further 8% of participants left comments asking, 'what about men?' and 'what about male victims of abuse?' This was despite the introduction to the study explicitly linking to the work of Dr Emma Sleath on the victim blaming of men subjected to sexual violence.

Together, most of these comments were based on the misunderstanding that feminist research ignores or minimises the harm and abuse of men and boys, which caused some participants to leave angry comments about feminism, me as a person and the concept of a study that only explored the victim blaming of women.

Despite some of the negative feedback and comments, I still found this to be an important and illuminating exercise. It is such a loss to quantitative psychological and sociological research that we do not ask participants for their experiences of taking our studies. Because of the assumptions made about qualitative and quantitative research, students and academics often assume that reflection belongs in the realm of the qualitative. However, as this study has shown, I learned a lot about the way my participants were answering a quantitative, anonymous study by asking them a simple question at the end.

Further to this, a concerning number of participants had used this space to ask an important question that had been raised by my study:

Is sex with a sleeping woman rape?

The free-text box had been utilised by both men and women asking this question. Women wrote that they often woke up to their male partners having penetrative sex with them or performing sex acts on them – and they thought it was normal. Men wrote that they liked having sex with their female partners whilst they were asleep and were offended at the suggestion that this was a sexual offence.

Clearly then, there is significant work to do here around implied consent and – more obviously – the issue around sex with sleeping or semi-conscious women.

It was this anonymous free-text box which allowed over 60 men and women to write that they thought sex whilst asleep was normal and that this study was the first time they had ever been forced to consider whether it was indeed, normal.

If anyone reading this is looking for a dissertation or thesis topic to explore – explore that!

6.

Why do we blame women?

There are several prominent theories which attempt to explain why we blame women for being raped, abused and attacked by men. Whilst much of the work tends to lean towards one or another theory, the more I read, the more I thought that all of the theories of victim blaming were correct. Instead of presenting them as standalone theories, the best way to read this chapter is to consider all theories as intersecting with each other or building upon each other.

I am going to discuss six key theories of victim blaming women and girls before then considering all of the other factors and institutions in society that encourage and uphold those victim blaming narratives in the next few chapters.

The six key theories to be discussed here are rape myth acceptance, sexism and gender role stereotypes, belief in a just world, individualism and self-preservation, attribution theories, counterfactual thinking and perceived control.

Rape myth acceptance (RMA)

As previously discussed, Brownmiller (1975) and Burt (1980) defined a rape myth as a set of persistent and widespread beliefs and attitudes held about rape, despite them being false, that contribute to the hostility towards victims and ultimately, victim blaming. Rape myths include beliefs about the victim's character, appearance and behaviour, the motivations and behaviour of the offender and the situational factors surrounding the offence such as the time of day, area, method and impact on the victim (Burt, 1980; Brownmiller, 1975; Sleath, 2011). In early work, Burt (1980) presented that over half of respondents agreed with the item 'In the majority of rapes, the victim was promiscuous or had a bad reputation'. The same proportion of respondents agreed that '50% or more of rapes are only reported as rape because the woman is trying to get back at the man she was angry with or was trying to cover up an illegitimate pregnancy'.

As the measurement of rape myth acceptance (RMA) developed, Payne, Lonsway, & Fitzgerald (1999) presented the Illinois Rape Myth Acceptance Scale (IRMAS) which further categorized rape myths into seven main types of female rape myth: 1) 'she asked for it'; 2) 'it wasn't really rape'; 3) 'he didn't mean to'; 4) 'she wanted it'; 5) 'she liked it'; 6) 'rape is a trivial event'; and 7) 'rape is a deviant event'. In 2011, McMahon & Farmer updated the IRMAS to present four types of rape myths about women: 1) 'she asked for it'; 2) 'he didn't mean to'; 3) 'it wasn't really rape' and 4) 'she lied'.

The acceptance of societal myths surrounding rape has been shown to increase blaming of the victim for their experiences, by positioning women as the cause of rape (Frese et al., 2004; Golge et al., 2003; Sleath, 2011).

Johnson (1997) found that a significantly higher proportion of men than women endorsed rape myths that stated that most rapes could be prevented if women didn't provoke them and if women didn't secretly want to be raped (Sleath, 2011).

More recent studies found that a third of the UK general public sample believed a woman was to blame if she was raped whilst drunk, believed that a woman behaving in a flirtatious way was responsible for being raped and believed that a woman was responsible for being raped if she failed to say 'no' clearly enough (Amnesty International, 2005).

A drop from a half to a third could be presented as a significant decrease in acceptance from the eighties and Vonderhaar & Carmody (2015) have suggested that such a drop is due to an increase in education and an increase in awareness of rape and sexual assault. However, in a study in which undergraduate students gave feedback on the IRMAS items and suggested changes to update the items and make them more realistic, McMahon and Farmer (2011) found that 53% of the students agreed that the actions of the woman led to her being raped. In the UK, The Fawcett Society (2017) found that 34% of women and 38% of men agreed that women are at least partially to blame for rape.

When a number of rape myths come together (such as the victim should have injuries, the victim was attacked by a stranger, the victim did not do anything to cause the assault, the victim was not drunk and was dressed modestly, the victim immediately reported the incident) they form a false stereotypical rape against which the general public, authorities and victims themselves, compare their experiences (Kahn, Mathie, & Torgler, 1994; Ryan, 1988; Sleath, 2011). When a rape or sexual assault experience falls outside of this stereotypical rape, it can lead to the victim being blamed or not believed at all. In fact, the greater the stereotypical belief of the observer, the more responsibility attributed to the victim and less responsibility to the perpetrator (Koppelaar, Lange, & van de Velde, 1997). This effect is also seen in women who have been subjected to rape, who use the same set of rape stereotypes to compare their own experiences to make a decision about whether to report (Campbell et al., 2011; Mont et al., 2003).

Evidence suggests that rape myths operate in different ways for different people. Men tend to use rape myths to excuse or minimise sexual violence, but women tend to use rape myths to deny their personal vulnerability (Heath et al., 2011; Sleath, 2011). Whilst many rape myths include direct victim blaming about the appearance, behaviour or character of the victim – others are based on broader attitudes to sexual violence, attitudes towards women as a class of people or attitudes and beliefs that excuse or sympathise with the perpetrator (Payne et al., 1999; Sleath, 2011). Therefore, not all rape myths are related to blaming women for rape.

One of the weaknesses of RMA as a theory of victim blaming has been the way RMA has been conflated with victim blaming. Whilst RMA and victim blaming of women has been shown to be strongly linked (Donde et al., 2018; Sleath, 2011), the act of attributing blame to a woman subjected to rape is not the same as accepting societal myths about rape and should not be used as a singular explanation of victim blaming (Buddy & Miller, 2011). Another weakness lies in the specificity of rape myths being only about the act of rape, whilst the victim blaming of women and girls is seen in elder abuse, child sexual abuse, child sexual exploitation, adult sexual exploitation, rape, sexual assault and sexual harassment (Bows, 2016; Eaton, 2018; Eaton & Holmes, 2017; Fawcett Society, 2017; Ullman, 2010). The assertion that similar victim blaming messages are used against girls being sexually abused in childhood or older women being subjected to cat calling suggests that there are larger influences than rape myths that cause and maintain the victim blaming of women and girls.

Sexism and Gender Role Stereotypes

Sexism is defined as prejudice, stereotyping or discrimination based on gender (Oxford Dictionary, 2016). In addition, gender roles are defined as a set of socially constructed norms, generally derived from sexism, that dictate which behaviours and characteristics are considered acceptable or desirable based on gender (Alsop et al., 2002; Levant & Alto, 2017; West & Zimmerman, 2002). These messages and norms contribute to victim blaming and self-blame by communicating a set of expected or accepted characteristics, behaviours and stereotypes of women and of victims of rape and sexual assault (Ben-David & Schneider, 2005).

Hostile sexism is defined as overt misogynistic stereotypes and attitudes that position women as inferior to men, and used for sexual pleasure (Glick & Fiske, 1996; Lee, Fiske, & Glick, 2010). Hostile sexism contributes to victim blaming by justifying the global exploitation of women as sexual objects and men's greater tolerance of sexual harassment of women (Abrams et al., 2003; Kunst et al., 2018; Masser et al., 2006; Page et al., 2016; Russell & Trigg, 2004).

Benevolent sexism is defined as sexism which appears positive or traditional, but patronises women using traditional gender role stereotypes to position women as weaker, helpless, cherished and vulnerable (Glick & Fiske, 1996). This form of sexism has been found to elicit protection of traditional, gender role conforming women but hostility towards non-traditional, non-gender conforming women (Bareket et al., 2018; Fowers & Fowers, 2010; Sakallı-Uğurlu, 2010, Kunst et al., 2018).

Victim blaming increases when the woman is seen as not conforming to the perceived appropriate characteristics and behaviours of a woman (Viki & Abrams, 2002; Harrison, Howerton, Secarea, & Nguyen, 2008; Kunst et al., 2018). For example, Viki & Abrams (2002) found that when the characteristics of a woman were manipulated to describe her as contradicting gender role stereotypes of a woman, she was blamed for the rape significantly more than when no information was given about her gender roles, marital or family status.

It has been recognised that some of traditional gender role characteristics of 'femininity' are contradictory. Women are expected to be submissive or passive in sex and yet simultaneously expected to control and preserve sexual activity (Simonson & Subich, 1999). Women are socialised to be emotional, nurturing and submissive to men but also responsible for limiting, causing and controlling men's sexual behaviours (Bem, 1993; Worell & Remer, 2003).

Women can therefore be blamed for being submissive or passive, controlling or preserving in sex depending on the situation. Females are expected to perform an identity that is 'sexy but not a slut' (Ringrose, 2013). Duschinksy (2013) agree that desirability is acceptable in sexist society but being perceived as a 'slut' means that the woman is positioned as deserving of her rape, exploitation and commodification (Duschinsky, 2013; Klein, 2013).

Dichotomous gender roles and sexism provide a foundation for victim blaming beliefs about women 'asking for it' by what they were wearing or how they were acting. Gender roles are therefore instrumental in reinforcing a male-constructed, male-serving stereotype of a woman. When these strict social, cultural and behavioural boundaries are not conformed to, women can be positioned as to blame for sexual violence and harassment.

An example of a sexist prescription of female behaviour is the way in which women are expected to engage in 'token resistance' to sex due to the expectation that women are submissive and are not supposed to express interest in sexual activity (Frese et al. 2004; Sleath, 2011).

Resistance is seen as a positive action on the part of the woman which contributes to a reduction in victim blaming by others (Garcia, 1998). Conversely, a woman who does not resist or fight back in a rape or sexual assault is positioned as enjoying or wanting it. Garcia (1998) conducted research to explore the perceptions of 'token resistance' to unwanted sexual contact. It is argued that men are socialised to believe that women who show resistance to sex are 'playing hard to get' (Garcia, 1998).

The findings from Garcia's study bore similarity to the victim blaming messages that insist that a woman must fight back against a perpetrator during a sexual assault or rape and that resistance increases the credibility and reduces the blame of the woman. However, the study showed that only the most extreme responses from a woman who was sexually assaulted (slapping, screaming and crying) were deemed to be 'genuine' resistance by men, whilst body language, non-verbal cues and saying no repeatedly was not considered to be resistance (Garcia, 1998).

Now is the time to consider quite how common token resistance is in our media. After I had read about Garcia's work, I started to notice how embedded token resistance was. I wrote some blogs about this, which were received with moderate discomfort by thousands of readers.

I discussed famous and well-loved films and books that tell the story of a woman who is not interested in a male character, until he badgers her for weeks or months until she gives in and dates/marries/sleeps with him.

Take a moment to consider the films I am discussing. How many romantic comedies, sitcoms, chick flicks and love stories are based on a plot in which a man harasses a woman for 90 minutes until she gives in and 'gives him a chance'?

How many of these films minimise and romanticise harassment from men and frame women's resistance, rejection and refusal as irrelevant? Many of the films I have watched include obsessive behaviours from the man, in which he turns up at her door, her place of work, her parent's house, her holiday abroad, her pottery class or her gym to persuade her to be with him. He sends her flowers, letters, gifts and messages. He sets up grand gestures in public to guilt trip her into dating him or taking him back.

Her 'no' is ignored. Her 'no' means nothing.

Her 'no' simply means, try harder.

It is fairly obvious how this translates into victim blaming of women and girls subjected to male violence. Much victim blaming focusses on whether, and how, a woman or girl has said 'no'. Entire criminal trials can become arguments about whether she was assertive enough, or whether she said no clearly enough. Surely media such as those I have discussed here would suggest that it doesn't particularly matter whether she has said no or not, because it is going to be ignored and mocked anyway.

I often hear professionals and academics suggesting the women and girls needs to learn how to say 'no' and remain assertive when men harass or push them into sex. This perspective seemingly misses the point: a sex offender doesn't care whether she has said no or not – and media celebrating and confirming the concept of token resistance is not helping.

Recent research has shown that victim blaming, sexual violence tolerance and hostility towards the '#metoo' movement are all correlated with hostile sexism (Abrams et al., 2003; Kunst et al., 2018; Masser et al., 2006; Page et al., 2016; Russell & Trigg, 2004). Gender roles and sexism as theories of victim blaming of women are not only consistent and significant but should be seen as underpinning RMA. Indeed, many of the rape myths are supported by both hostile and benevolent sexism, with gender role stereotypes and cultural pressures providing a fertile environment for rape myths to be developed, nurtured and communicated. Rape myths contain gender role stereotypes and sexism; and gender role stereotypes and sexism reinforce RMA (Sleath, 2011).

Examples of common misogynistic beliefs that cause and encourage victim blaming of women:

- Women and girls are sexual objects to be enjoyed
- Women and girls should look a certain way
- Women and girls should act sexy, but not slutty
- Women and girls should be sexually available but also engage in token resistance and be coy
- Women and girls should simultaneously be domesticated and sexually available at all times
- Women and girls should submit to sex with a partner to please them

When women and girls are positioned in society as sexual objects to be enjoyed by men and boys, there is fertile ground for victim blaming. They are treated as mere toys or ornaments for men and boys to play with, use, exploit and look at. In a society in which everyone is groomed to perceive and treat women and girls like this, it is always the fault of the woman or girl when they are then raped, abused or killed. The most obvious form of victim blaming that this causes is the 'she asked for it' or 'she led him on' or 'she wanted it'.

As twisted as the gender role stereotype can possibly get, women are expected to be 'a lady in the streets, but a freak in the bed', to quote numerous songwriters from the noughties.

What this means is that women are expected to be sexually available to men, to give them sex when and as they want it – but to also remain demure, domesticated and compliant in public and in the home. They are therefore the perfect, male-serving woman. She is the cook, the cleaner, the caregiver, the supporter, the personal secretary, the mother, the lady, the arm candy, the trophy – and the whore, the sex object, the 'hole to be filled' as Julia Long would put it. But only on his terms, and only when he says.

The reason this dichotomous expectation leads to victim blaming is then clear: if women step outside of these roles at any time, they are to blame for whatever is done to them. If they are not domesticated enough, they were not a good enough woman. If they are not demure enough, they were asking for it. If they were not giving him enough sex, they were being unfair and 'withholding sex' he assumes he is entitled to.

Linked to this is the misogynistic belief that women and girls should give sex to a boyfriend or husband whenever he wants it, in order to keep him satisfied. Whilst rape within marriage was outlawed in the early 90s in the UK and confirmed in the Sexual Offences Act (2003), more recent research has suggested that an alarming proportion of the British public believe that there is no such thing as rape within a relationship. A YouGov survey in 2018 found that 16% of people aged 16-24 years old do not consider forced sex within marriage or relationships, a rape. Over a third of people aged 65 years old and over responded in the same way.

This view has roots in 18th and 19th century laws of marriage. Traditionally (and globally) the concept of marriage is the transfer of ownership of a woman from one man (the father) to another man (the husband). Therefore, the father 'gives his daughter away' by walking her down the aisle, and the woman is expected to take on the surname of the new husband. This is also why the marriage certificate only asks for the occupation and details of the father of the bride and groom. Marriage is the transfer of property between two male owners: the woman is the property of her Dad, and then becomes the property of her new husband and his family.

Throughout history, marriage was positioned as whole, unending, unconditional consent to sex. Sex was seen as 'wifely duties' to the man, in which the woman should perform sex whenever her male partner wanted it. Within this construction of marriage then, it was impossible for a woman to be raped because she had already given her never-ending consent by marrying him.

It is important to consider how narratives, beliefs and social norms like this contribute to the victim blaming of women subjected to male violence, especially as some of these norms are so well embedded that most people do not notice we are supporting them. I know that when I got married the first time around, I had absolutely no concept of why my father 'gave me away' and why I couldn't put my mother's details on my marriage certificate. In a similar way, I had never considered that saying no to a man I didn't have any interest in might be perceived as 'playing hard to get'.

Belief in a Just World (BJW)

Lerner's (1980) Belief in a Just World (BJW) theorises that people hold beliefs that the world is a just place in which good things happen to good people, and bad things happen to bad people – meaning everyone gets what they deserve. Whilst heavily cited in the victim blaming literature, it has contributed contradictory findings when applying the theory to sexual assault and rape victims (Kunst et al, 2018; Pinciotti & Orcutt, 2017; Sleath, 2011; Sleath & Woodhams, 2014). Despite there being some cultural differences across the world in the endorsement of BJW, this type of reasoning is present in many cultures and religions.

The benefit of employing the BJW in everyday life relates directly to sexual violence. The belief buffers against the reality that horrible things can happen to anybody at any given time, without reason or logic (Furnham, 2003). It is suggested that this benefit transforms from a psychological, protective 'buffer' to a path of non-rational reasoning that when applied to real life events like the rape of a person, the observer may conclude that they must have done something to deserve or prompt the event for it to have happened to them (Correia, Vala & Aguiar, 2001).

The second benefit, is that this reassures the observer with the BJW that it is highly unlikely to happen to them if they just keep living a good life and do not do anything to 'invite' the rape or sexual assault (which is arguably where this theory comfortably interlinks with rape myths about characteristics and circumstances causing or encouraging rape and sexual assault).

Whilst this reasoning seems over-simplified or even 'astonishingly crude' as Williams (2003, p.463) describes it, this reasoning is embedded in societal discourse. Examples from language could include 'karma will get them in the end', 'what goes around comes around', 'you reap what you sow', 'they didn't deserve that to happen to them', 'why does the worst always happen to the best people?' 'they'll get their just deserts'.

It appears that these examples of popular discourse are easily applied to victims of sexual violence in a way that would allow the observer to assume that events that happen in a person's life are either deserved or undeserved and this may prompt the observer to look for factors that would contribute to that reasoning process.

BJW examples from everyday language:

'Karma will get them in the end'

'What goes around comes around'

'You reap what you sow'

'They didn't deserve that to happen to them'

'Why does the worst always happen to the best people?'

'They'll get their just deserts'

'You'll get your due'

'You got what you deserved'

'You'll get what's coming to you'

Correia et al. (2001) suggest that observers will initially focus on the victim's behaviour as an explanation for the situation. In sexual violence, this could be the act of walking home alone or drinking with friends. Where this reasoning fails, and the responsibility cannot be attributed towards the victim's behaviour, then the responsibility is attributed towards the victim's character, which bears resemblance to the theory of fundamental attribution error (Ross, 1977).

In line with common rape myths, this could be the victim's sexual history or their prior communication/relationship with the perpetrator. The point of this attribution of responsibility is supposedly to create balance and to affirm their BJW by reinterpreting the situation to make it appear just and fair. It is argued by Lerner (1980) that this is because when a 'bad thing' happens to a 'good person' it threatens the observers' BJW.

Therefore, where a victim was shown to be innocent, the observers with BJW engaged in much higher levels of victim derogation in order to restore their BJW (Correia & Vala, 2003; Crome & McCabe, 1995; Hafer, 2000; Pinciotti & Orcutt, 2017; Sleath, 2011).

Importantly, Lerner (1997) proposed that people will reason backwards when they learn that a woman has been raped and will then make assumptions or guesses about her behaviour or character to provide reasons for why she was subjected to sexual violence.

Whilst BJW has been included as a theory of victim blaming for some time, the results from psychometric measures are often inconsistent and have shown strongly correlated positive, negative and inverse relationships with victim blaming and RMA. Therefore, there appears to be a link, but how much this influences the victim blaming of women subjected to sexual violence is still unclear. It may be that BJW is not a singular explanation of victim blaming of women; it instead may be linked to other biases and values about women, sexual violence and social justice.

Individualism and self-preservation

Individualism has links to victim blaming due to the way that it encourages individual responsibility for actions and decisions. In contrast to collectivism, in which the person is viewed and views themselves as part of a larger group or collective; individualism is defined as the social theory that the person takes priority over any group or collective. They are free to act in an independent way, make their own choices and are responsible for those choices and decisions (Triandis, 1995).

The theory that we are all responsible for our own safety is an extension of this (as personal safety is an action and a choice). However, the argument that all people are responsible for their own safety from harm seems to run counter to the argument that we are all responsible for our own actions.

Generally, in individualistic societies, we are taught that we are all responsible for our own actions (Inglehart, 1997; Sampson, 2001; Oyserman et al., 2002). Yet with rape, the individual responsibility of choice and decision making is shifted away from the perpetrator being responsible for their actions and towards the counter-argument, which is 'the victim is responsible for their own safety'. This approach has recently been found to increase victim blaming and does not improve the safety of women (Jago and Christenfeld, 2018).

In a dyad conversation study about a rape of a woman on university campus, Anderson et al. (2001) found that participants said that the woman should have kept herself safer and known about the previous rapes, commenting that she was irresponsible and stupid. Individualistic reasoning moves from the perpetrator being responsible for their actions to the victim being responsible for their lack of safety. Waterman further defined that normative individualism is the focus on personal responsibility for actions and decisions which minimises the social and wider contexts (Oyserman et al., 2002). These underlying concepts of individualism provide support for victim blaming comments such as 'she should have kept herself safe' or 'she should have made better choices'.

Rather than supporting initiatives to prevent sexual offending, this results in others profiting from the fears of women who feel they must seek the skills to protect themselves from sex offenders by selling anti-rape knickers, anti-rape rings, anti-rape necklaces, rape alarms and anti-rape self-defence programmes. This form of victim blaming is indirect.

It is not overtly saying that women deserve to be raped, but it is putting the onus on the woman to be able to physically fight off an offender, which ignores evidence indicating that the large majority of all rapes and sexual assaults are not perpetrated by strangers in unfamiliar environments using physical force (Egan, 2017; Sleath & Woodhams, 2014), and that many instinctive trauma responses include freezing and becoming unresponsive in an effort to minimise further physical harm (Moller et al., 2017).

Products sold to women using victim blaming

- Anti-rape wear (knickers, bras, skirts, trousers)
- Anti-rape jewellery (rings, bracelets, necklaces)
- Anti-rape nail polish
- Rape self defence classes
- Pepper spray
- Rape alarms
- Tracking apps

A concept linked with individualism is self-preservation, first set out by Freud in 1913 as an ego response to protect the self. In broader terms, self-preservation is defined as a 'behaviour based on the characteristics or feelings that warn people or animals to protect themselves from difficulties or dangers' (Merriam-Webster, 2019).

Self-preservation has led to humans developing personal safety rules and laws to avoid harm or death (Lyng, 1990). Specific to sexual violence and psychology, self-preservation and defence mechanisms are concepts from psychoanalytic theory, defined as being unconscious psychological mechanisms to protect the self from anxiety or something psychologically harmful (Schacter, 2011).

As an act of self-preservation, people are likely to assess the differences between the characteristics and behaviours of the victim and themselves, use those differences to explain why the rape or sexual assault happened to that particular victim and reinforce their sense of self-preservation and safety (Furnham, 2003; Shaver, 1970). They may also assess the actions of the victim and then conclude that they would never perform the same actions, would never 'allow themselves' to be found in those situations and therefore indirectly blame the victim for not being able to protect themselves (Shaver, 1970; Lerner, 1980). This provides comfort that if a person takes care of themselves and stays safe (like they have been told to do throughout their lives), they will remain safe because they will not have done anything to lead them to becoming a victim (Sleath, 2011; Furnham, 2003).

This bears resemblance to the logic of the BJW (Lerner, 1980); that if you are a good person and don't do anything wrong, you will not be harmed. In self-preservation or defence mechanisms, the observer may convince themselves that they would never make the same mistakes as the victim and therefore they are invulnerable to sexual violence.

The notion of self-preservation is important when considering victim blaming because there are several official responses to sexual violence that are about teaching young girls to change their behaviours, characteristics, physical appearance, knowledge levels and emotional states in order to protect her from future sexual violence (Jago & Christenfield, 2018; Women & Equalities Committee, 2016).

It is important to note that women in individualistic cultures and collectivist cultures both suffer from victim blaming, RMA and sexism (Kalra & Bhugra, 2013). Individualism is not a singular explanation of victim blaming, however, it does seem to support victim blaming messages, sexism, BJW and rape myths about women being able to predict, manage and protect themselves against sexual violence rather than sex offenders having to control their desire to offend against the woman. This raises the question of why the same burden of personal responsibility is not applied to the sex offender in the same way it is applied to the woman who has been subjected to their violence. This question may then raise a weakness in the theory of individualism, especially if it is only being applied to the woman. However, this might be another example of how standalone theories are unlikely to explain victim blaming.

Kalra & Bhugra (2013) make a parallel argument about ego-centric versus socio-centric cultures and how women (and their close support network) who are members of those different cultures respond to sexual violence against women.

In ego-centric cultures, as with individualism, the priority is given to the 'self' and achieving 'independence' which means that the consequences and responses of sexual violence remain with the woman, inducing feelings of private guilt. It is still common for women to be blamed for sexual violence but it is rare for the rest of her family members and support network to be tainted by these negative judgements.

By contrast, in socio-centric cultures, as with collectivism, the priority is given to the relations with others and maintaining interdependence. This means that the consequences of and responses to sexual violence are spread wider than the woman who was subjected to the violence, and therefore induces wider feelings of shame and embarrassment for the whole family and close support network (Kalra & Bhugra, 2013).

More research is required to understand the victim blaming of women in individualistic and collectivist cultures, especially as the research suggests that whilst victim blaming impacts women differently depending on whether their culture is individualist or collectivist, it remains prevalent regardless of the role of the individual in each culture.

Attribution theories

These theories are concerned with the way people explain the causes of events or behaviours. Heider (1958) argued that all people were naïve psychologists trying to make sense of the world and look for causal relationships for the things they observe and experience – even when there is not a cause. Heider (1958) proposed that humans had a cognitive bias towards attribution in which they would explain the behaviour or experiences of others using internal explanations but explain their own behaviour or experiences using external explanations.

Later on, Ross (1977) termed this phenomenon 'fundamental attribution error' and is also known as the 'actor-observer bias'. The error in attribution relates to victim blaming as it prioritises the characteristics or behaviours of the woman for rape and sexual violence, rather than prioritising the external forces such as the behaviours and motivations of the sex offender.

However, this has more recently been contested when a meta-analysis of 173 studies exploring the actor-observer bias showed that there were differing effect sizes for the asymmetry in attribution between the actor and observer in different situations (Malle, 2006). Whilst this is important, it must be noted that the studies were not specific to sexual violence, and due to the other interlinking societal factors and stereotypes surrounding sexual violence, the actor-observer bias may be different to general events.

Additionally, if the actor-observer bias was applied to women who were subjected to sexual violence, it should mean that women would not blame themselves using characterological or behavioural reasoning. It should instead mean that women would always attribute the sexual violence to external forces (as in the actor-observer bias) – but this runs counter to all of the evidence in the self-blame literature, which finds that women often blame themselves, their behaviours, their character or their choices (Ullman, 1996; 1998; 2001; 2010).

Clearly, there is a partially inverted effect in fundamental attribution error in sexual violence in which the external observer does attribute internal reasons for the event, but so does the actor. In sexual violence, this means that the observer is likely to blame the woman's behaviour, character or appearance – but so is the woman who was subjected to the sexual violence. This is an important finding as it raises questions about why this bias changes in sexual violence.

Also relevant to victim blaming, is the defensive attribution hypothesis (Shaver, 1970). The hypothesis stated that the level of blame put on the victim depends on observers' perceived similarity and identification with the victim: when victim and observer are increasingly similar, (the same sex or ethnicity, for example) the victim will be blamed less (Grubb & Harrower, 2008). Research by Fulero & DeLara (1976) showed that female students blamed the victim least when they were perceived to be similar and blamed the victim most when they were perceived to be dissimilar to the victim.

Increased victim blaming

No perceived similarity to the victim

Decreased empathy for victim

No identification with characteristics/demographics

Likely to attribute cause to the victim

The Defensive Attribution Hypothesis
(Shaver, 1970)

Reduced victim blaming

Perceived similarity to the victim of sexual violence

Increased empathy for victim

Identify with the victim characteristic/demographics

Unlikely to attribute cause to the victim

This finding could be applied to the family and friends of a woman subjected to sexual violence as they would arguably perceive a high level of identification to the woman (Perilloux et al., 2014).

However, in some studies, similarity and identification with the victim did not reduce victim blaming and instead found that women who had been subjected to sexual violence blamed the victim in scenarios twice as much as women who had no personal experience of sexual violence (Carmody & Washington, 2001; Perilloux et al., 2014).

This is an important finding, as the defensive attribution hypothesis would suggest that other women subjected to sexual violence would have high identification and should have blamed victims less.

These mixed findings may represent evidence of competing cognitive bias as when White & Rollins (1981) examined a community response to rape, they found that participant's responses were influenced less by the perceived similarity and identification to the woman in their family who was subjected to sexual violence – but more by the belief most participants had in a 'just world' (White & Rollins, 1981).

The defensive attribution hypothesis was tested by Mason et al. (2004) with participants who reported being a victim of sexual violence and participants with no identified history of sexual violence. Mason et al. (2004) found no difference in empathy or victim blaming between the two groups of participants.

Further studies found no difference in RMA or victim blaming when history of sexual violence was examined (Adams-Curtis & Forbes, 2001; Carmody & Washington, 2001). Therefore, findings did not support the theory that people who were perceived as similar due to experiencing sexual assault or rape would have higher empathy and have lower levels of victim blaming.

Indeed, evidence suggests that it is common for women to experience victim blaming from the members of their closest support networks, from people who they identify with and from other victims (Ullman & Vasquez, 2015; White & Rollins, 1981).

Counterfactual thinking and perceived control

Counterfactual thinking is the theory that suggests people naturally examine and critique their behaviour, experiences and possible reasons for their trauma which can often lead to women engaging in 'if only' thought processes that convince them that their experience may not have happened or would have ended differently had they done something different (Gavanski et al., 1993; Kahneman & Miller, 1986; Miller et al., 2010; Roese, 1997).

It has been proposed that the function of this thinking is to identify what behaviours, errors or actions supposedly led to the sexual violence to avoid making the same mistakes again in the future (Miller et al., 2010), which therefore contains high levels of self-blame. Examples given include a mixture of counterfactual thinking and gender roles stereotypes which led to thoughts such as questioning whether she was too trusting, whether she looked too provocative, whether she caused the rape due to her decisions or behaviours (Miller et al, 2010). Branscombe et al. (2003) reported that counterfactual thoughts following their sexual assault directly predicted self-blame and poor psychological well-being in women.

Their study found that when participants were asked closed questions about what they could have done differently to avoid being sexually assaulted, 90% of participants gave answers based in counterfactual thoughts. However, this was criticised by Miller et al. (2010) who chose to use open ended questions that did not direct the women to think about what they could have done differently. Despite this, both studies found that counterfactual thinking predicted lower self-esteem, poorer psychological wellbeing and higher self-blame (Miller et al., 2007).

Miller et al. (2010) concluded that these thought processes lead to future vulnerability, a perceived lack of control and a perception of inevitability of sexual violence. Self-blame may have a relationship with feelings of control, as Janoff-Bulman (1979) originally theorised that self-blame may be an adaptive coping mechanism to blame behaviours and actions. Blaming behaviours and actions were argued to decrease the belief of bad things happening by chance, and to increase wellbeing by blaming the event on controllable personal behaviours that could be changed in the future.

However, more recent studies conducted on domestic and sexual abuse have not supported this assertion, with one study finding that there was no relationship between characterological and behavioural blame and perceived control over the event (O'Neill & Kerig, 2000) and another finding that behavioural self-blame had a negative impact on the person, including making changes to their lives, withdrawing from social interactions and avoidance (Frazier et al., 2005). Overall, more contemporary research has argued that counterfactual thinking and self-blame to try to regain perceived control over the sexual violence has resulted in reduced wellbeing (Branscombe et al., 2003; Balzarotti et al., 2016).

In summary, theories of victim blaming and self-blame have been examined for decades, but researchers have not yet achieved an integrated approach to all of the theories and factors that cause, influence, increase or maintain victim blaming. Often, authors have attempted a singular explanation of victim blaming and where multiple explanations have been explored, it has been with measures of RMA, hostile sexism and BJW. The research findings have been shown to be inconsistent and nuanced, suggesting there is more to victim blaming than singular explanations. Many theories would benefit from wider social and feminist explanations of victim blaming of women as a specific class of people who exist within a broad system of oppression, stereotyping and objectification. Each of the current theories explain a small part of the process of victim blaming, but if viewed together, they may offer a broader, more holistic framework to understand why women are blamed for sexual violence. In the literature, there are many other factors that appear to influence whether and how much a woman is blamed or blames herself for sexual violence.

I will however, come back to all of these theories throughout this book, and again in my final chapters where I suggest a more integrated way of utilising theories of victim blaming.

7.

How does our criminal justice system blame women?

When it comes to victim blaming and self-blame after sexual assault or rape, one of the most influential factors in the exosystem is the police and criminal justice system. In society in which reporting crime is expected and encouraged, sexual offences are still the least reported crime and research frequently presents the experiences of women who were blamed for their sexual assault or rape either directly by the individuals in the roles of police and the wider criminal justice system; or more indirectly by the structures, laws, techniques and procedures used in the investigation and prosecution of sexual offences (Eaton, 2019)

Women are so aware of the views and attitudes held by the police and criminal justice system agencies that they have been shown to pre-empt victim blaming and therefore make a choice not to report their experiences at all. Women who have been blamed by the police or criminal justice system have been shown to blame themselves (Campbell et al., 2009; Fisher et al., 2003).

There is a large body of research that focusses on the experience of the victim in an adversarial criminal justice system following their rape or sexual assault. The research covers most parts of the process from the decision to report to police right the way through to the techniques used in the courtroom.

Due to nature of the system and processes of questioning, evidence gathering, trial and sentencing it has been frequently shown to blame the victim and to contribute to significant self-blame. In the literature surrounding this topic, women have reported feeling like they must fit the stereotypical rapes script or else their rape either didn't really happen or is too ambiguous for the criminal justice system to take forward. Many women in the research also talk about the feelings of shame, guilt, blame, fear and being very aware that they might not be believed or taken seriously if they do report (Fisher et al., 2003).

The 'classic rape' and the 'perfect' victim

Arguably, one of the biggest factors in this section is 'the classic rape' (Williams, 1984). The classic rape is essentially the stereotypical rape that includes common rape myths such as abduction, the perpetrator as a stranger, severe force, and serious injury. Williams (1984) suggested that victims of this specific type of rape are more likely to report to police because they see themselves as real crime victims. This very important suggestion, which has been evidenced by a considerable amount of research, is a powerful example of women that have absorbed rape myths into their own understanding of rape and sexual assault but also remain aware that others have done the same. They are predicting that when they report, their experience is not going to fit the rape stereotype and are therefore expecting to be disbelieved or discredited.

To support this mental process, Fisher et al. (2003) found that over 42% of rape victims who did not report to the police cited that their primary reason for not reporting was that they were not sure a crime had been committed because it did not contain the stereotypical factors. Finally, victims who were raped by a known person such as a partner or acquaintance were found to be less likely to be believed by police and are more reluctant to involve the police in the first place (McGregor et al., 2000; Sudderth, 1998).

This pattern is clearly problematic, given that 83.3% of sexual assault and rape victims indicated that they knew their perpetrator (Tjaden & Thoennes, 1998) and provides ample evidence for why the reporting rate is so low with between 89%-95% of all rapes and sexual assaults going unreported (CSEW, 2017).

There are clearly many barriers to reporting to police, many of which are coming from the internalisation of common rape myths and stereotypes. Krahe (1991) demonstrated how these rape stereotypes are also in the forefront of police officer's minds in a study in which German police officers were asked to apply features and characteristics to descriptions of female rape scenarios.

In the officers' definition of a credible rape, the victim was aged between 20-40 years old, wore non-distinctive dress, attempted physical resistance and incurred psychological consequences. There was no alcohol involved and the victim suffered injuries as a result of trying to escape.

The perpetrator was defined as psychologically disturbed and threatened the victim with physical violence with the use of a weapon.

The circumstances of the rape were outdoors, with no witnesses, where the victim and perpetrator did not know each other, and at night where the victim thinks they could recognise the perpetrator in a line up.

In 1991, German police officers were asked to describe a credible, real victim of rape. Their answers were clear:

- The woman was aged between 20-40 years old
- She wore non-distinctive dress, nothing sexual or revealing
- She attempted physical resistance and suffered injuries trying to escape
- She shows clear psychological distress
- There was no alcohol involved
- The perpetrator was defined as psychologically disturbed
- The perpetrator threatened the victim with physical violence with the use of a weapon.
- The rape was at night, outdoors, with no witnesses, where the victim and perpetrator did not know each other

This feature list bears significant similarities to William's (1984) classic rape, to the items on most RMA scales and to the stereotypical rape that women have spoken about in research. This common script is discussed by Campbell (1998) who found that rape cases that did not fit this rigid rape stereotype are highly likely to drop out of the legal system and the victim will probably not consider themselves to be a victim of rape (Williams, 1984). It was found that cases of female rape and sexual assault where the victim knew the perpetrator and the perpetrator did not use a weapon or physical violence were rarely taken forward for prosecution.

Attitudes of police officers

There has been significant effort and resources invested in the training of police officers and the development of specialist teams and staff to support disclosures and reports of sexual assault and rape since many of these studies were published, however, there are still important findings that show that police officers are just as prone to victim blaming and stereotyping as anyone else, even if they are classed as specialist officers in the field of sexual violence. In older research, Edward and MacLeod (1999) suggested that a police officer's belief in a female rape victim's allegation is based in their own individual beliefs about rape. It may be expected that officers with extra knowledge and experience would be less likely to be influenced by their own internal beliefs and acceptance of rape myths, however, research showed that police officers belonging to highly specialist sexual violence teams did not blame the victim any less than officers without the specialist training and experience (Sleath, 2012; Sleath and Bull, 2012)

This finding could mean several things. The first is that societal rape myths and victim blaming are more powerful than any programme that attempts to deconstruct them. The second possibility is the potential for confirmation bias within police in specialist teams.

If the data and research is correct, and the majority of cases of rape that do not fit the stereotypical rape criteria are never reported, then that would mean that police officers working in specialist sexual violence teams are more likely to work on cases that do fit the stereotypical rape criteria. Over time, this could lead to existing beliefs of police officers about the stereotypical rape being reinforced due to constantly working on and talking about cases that fit this stereotype.

Sleath (2012) argued that police officers are just as likely to be affected by rape myths such as the stereotypical rape as anyone else. As an additional possibility, Sleath (2012) found that police officers who had completed specialist sexual violence police training actually blame the victim for their rape and sexual assault more than ones that didn't have training. Sleath (2014) put forward that this increase in victim blaming was due to the training content focusing on the collection of accurate forensic evidence and striving for the strongest case possible to increase the chances of the CPS taking the case forward for a successful prosecution.

When police officers are specifically trained to look for solid forensic, physical and video evidence in order to secure a conviction, it is then easier to understand why so many cases that do not fulfil these criteria never progress to criminal prosecution. To link these points together, it is highly likely that stereotypical rape cases in which women suffer serious physical injuries, are attacked by a stranger, report straight away and are therefore able to supply DNA evidence are more likely to be taken forward for prosecution.

Women who report to the police

It has been established that many women never report their experience to police and those that do, face judgement and disbelief from police officers that are influenced by the same societal myths and stereotypes as everybody else. For those women who do report and have their case investigated, unfortunately, the victim blaming is shown to continue and causes women to feel like they are being revictimised by the process of investigation and prosecution.

One of the major criticisms that feature in the research is the amount of times women are asked to retell their story to numerous different professionals. During interviews and questioning which are designed to 'achieve best evidence' (ABE, 2013) they are often asked victim-blaming questions about what they were wearing, their prior sexual history, their prior relationship with the perpetrator, how they behaved during and after the assault, their reasons for not reporting sooner and the nature of their previous sexual encounters or relationships with men (Campbell, 2005, 2006; Campbell & Raja, 2005).

In Campbell (2005) and Campbell and Raja (2005) women were asked to self-report their psychological health resulting from their contact with the criminal justice system and the findings showed the impact of the process on the person. 87% of women said that they felt bad about themselves and 73% reported feeling guilty and reported that they blamed themselves. 89% of women felt violated and 80% were reluctant to seek further help due to the experience of the criminal justice system (Campbell et al., 2009).

A standard technique of defence solicitors in the UK is to attack the credibility of the victim by suggesting that in some way the victim asked for what happened to them and were responsible for getting themselves raped (Jordan, 2008). Comments about their sexuality, their personality, their behaviour before, during and after the rape or sexual assault, their history of mental illness and self-harm, any previous reports of rape or sexual assault, retracted statements and so on are used by the defence to harm the credibility of the victim so that the jury are influenced to disbelieve the account told by the woman.

The credibility of the rape victim can become the focus of the trial. Any stereotypical beliefs presented may be utilised to the advantage of the defendant to undermine the position and credibility of the victim as well as influencing perceptions of the victim's culpability (Sleath, 2014).

Arguably, one of the most pervasive factors to influence the perceptions of police officers and other professionals in the criminal justice system, underpinning and resulting in the blaming of women who have been subjected to rape or sexual assault is the notion of the unequivocal or credible victim (Christie, 1986). For example, research shows that jury members' attitudes toward rape were found to be the single best predictor of their decisions in rape case verdicts (I and Bienen, 1980).

If this is the case, it can be argued that the outcomes of sexual and domestic violence trials are heavily based on the woman or girl. The crime and the offender become less relevant and instead, what the woman was wearing, doing and saying become the central features of the trial.

This will not come as a surprise to anyone working in this field – many of us will have had cases fold or end in an incorrect 'not guilty' verdict because the woman or girl was not perceived as 'credible' or 'innocent' enough.

In the last ten years, I have dealt with or discussed cases in which women and girls have been raped, trafficked, abused and seriously injured but have been treated like the offender because unbeknownst to them, their character and behaviour is suddenly on trial.

Those of you who work in these services will know what I mean:

- Women who report to the police only to be questioned for hours about what they were wearing, why they were drinking and whether they were telling the truth

- Women who report to the police to be asked why they didn't report sooner

- Women who report to the police, initially believing they were not to blame, leaving the station convinced it was her own fault

- Women who try to report to the police but are told their evidence was not good enough or that their complaint would go nowhere

- Women who reported to the police but had their case NFA'd (no further action) because she was not 'credible' enough

- Women who reported to the police but were told they were not reliable enough because they have autism, mental health issues or addictions

Below is the real story of Lisa* who I interviewed a few years ago.

Lisa*

Lisa was raped on her way home from drinks with work colleagues. It was around 7:45pm and she was in familiar streets walking home. She says that a man came out of nowhere and attacked her, dragging her up the street before pushing her over.

She says there must have been witnesses because the street was full of people walking home in the light summer evening. After she was raped and the man ran away, she rang 999 and waited for the officers.

She was feeling hopeful, because she had been raped before when she was a teenager and because that happened in a relationship with no witnesses and no evidence, the case was closed. She thought, this time, she would be taken seriously, and she knew it was not her fault.

The police arrived and took her to the station and to the SARC for examination. It was when she was giving her interview that the officers asked her questions that made her question herself.

They asked her if she had been drinking because she smelled of wine. They asked her why she was walking home alone after drinking. They told her they knew she had reported rape before and 'it had come to nothing last time'.

They asked her why she couldn't remember what he was wearing. They asked her why she didn't fight him off or scream for help. Lisa explained she had mental health issues she was currently seeking help for and then realised that was making her sound even less credible.

Lisa started to cry and realised, she was not the 'credible' victim she thought she was. The case was NFA'd three weeks later and nothing was done to apprehend the offender.

As much as this might read like a 'worst case scenario' for women reporting rape, it really isn't. It's common. It's happening everywhere. Women are scrutinised from the moment they report.

Everything is considered: their behaviour, their character, their mental health, their background, their criminal history, their sexual activity, their story, their intoxication, their appearance and their body language. We know this to be true.

We know the research has been telling us consistently for the past 40 years that women who report rape to the police blame themselves more and wish they hadn't reported at all (Campbell et al, 2009; Ullman, 2004; Eaton, 2019). We also know that only around 13% of people (men and women) who are raped ever report to police (CSEW, 2017).

We know that the research explains this trend clearly: victims are measuring themselves against rape myths and stereotypes to consider whether they will be believed or not (Campbell et al., 2009; Sleath, 2011).

Even research from University of Bedfordshire (2015) showed that girls who had been sexually exploited in childhood who were encouraged to report and then go through a criminal prosecution process in court had worse outcomes, worse mental health and much higher rates of trauma.

So, the question must be asked: Why do we keep telling women and girls to report to police?

When the CSEW is reporting that 510,000 women were sexually assaulted or raped in 2017 but only 2991 offenders were convicted – that gives women a 0.5% prospect of conviction of the person who sexually assaulted or raped them.

So why do we keep putting women and girls through the process of questioning, interviews, evidence collection, trial, waiting and worrying for sometimes 12-18 months? Is this in their best interests? Is reporting to the police really the best thing for them as a victim?

No. It isn't.

Is it good for society?

Supposedly, but if the conviction rate is anything to go by, then no.

Will it protect others from being raped, as commentators such as Carlson Tucker claim?

Probably not.

8.

How do our cultures and beliefs blame women?

Belief in all of the major world religions has been explored as a contributory factor to victim blaming through the acceptance of rape myths, BJW and sexism (Franiuk and Shain, 2011; Muganyizi et al., 2010) – and religious belief has been shown to induce feelings of self-blame in women who have been subjected to rape and sexual assault (Bryant-Davis et al., 2011; Lonsway & Fitzgerald, 1995).

Almost all the religious influences can be reduced to two consistent factors that support victim blaming: the way women are portrayed as inferior to men or sexually manipulative towards men (Brownmiller, 1975; Turrell & Thomas, 2008; Weaver, 2007) and the way that religious teachings provide understanding of suffering in the lives of their followers, which lead to beliefs that rape only happens to bad women or women who are being taught a life lesson they must endure to become a better person (Heggen, 1996; Turrell & Thomas, 2008).

In the work by Turrell & Thomas (2008) there was also consideration for the way professionals should work with women who are religious, when the victim blaming and self-blame they experience are coherent with religious messages that encourage them to self-blame, endure suffering as a rite of passage or punishment and/or forgive the rapist (Franiuk & Shain, 2011; Gross, 1994; Khuankaew, 2007).

Religion has been explored as a contributory factor to victim blaming through the acceptance of rape myths and has been shown to induce feelings of self-blame, depression and PTSD in women who have been subjected to rape and sexual assault (Lonsway & Fitzgerald, 1994; Bryant-Davis et al., 2011). Religion has also been shown to influence the way that the event of a rape or sexual assault and the woman who experienced it, is perceived. It is not possible to give a full overview of the way in which all religions influence or contribute to victim blaming or self-blame in this literature review, but an attempt has been made to discuss academic research which discusses Christianity, Islam, Hinduism and Buddhism in this context.

Almost all of the religious influences discussed here can be reduced to two consistent factors that support victim blaming: the way women are portrayed as inferior to men and the way that religious teachings provide understanding of suffering in the lives of their followers. There are plenty of ancient writings about female chastity, family honour, rape, and marriage that may have influenced the way in which the religions discussed here developed and wrote about rape and sexual assault of women (Brownmiller, 1975). Therefore, as researchers have said before me, this chapter does not argue that inferior status of women originated with religion; but argues that religions have reinforced sexism for thousands of years.

Victim blaming in Christianity

To begin with Christianity, Heggen (1997) argued that there were four main messages that influenced the blaming of rape and sexual assault victims.

The first two fit closely with the issue of perpetuating sexism: that God intended that men dominate, and women submit; and that women are morally inferior to men. These messages reinforce the numerous sexist assumptions, expectations and prescribed ideologies of the way women 'must' behave in their relationships, in their sex lives and in the general public. The consequence of a woman violating these sexist norms is for her to be blamed for whatever happened to her and ultimately, the use of the supposed violation for the characterological or behavioural blame.

The third message is that suffering is an important Christian virtue and that women are to hold a role as 'suffering servants'. Whilst this message doesn't directly blame the woman for being raped or sexually assaulted, it does advocate and encourage her suffering during and after the offence and positions her experience as a necessary rite of passage if she is to be a good Christian woman.

Arguably, this could serve to reduce the empathy towards her from others and reduce her own feelings of empathy and self-love if she is under the impression that she is meant to suffer.

The final message has been shown to be especially problematic for women after rape and sexual assault: the expectation to forgive those who commit sin against them. In this context, a woman who is coming to terms with being raped or sexually assaulted is also expected to truly forgive their perpetrator as begrudging them or not being able to forgive them may affect their own virtue and sense of self-worth as a Christian. If the woman is not ready to forgive or feels as though she can never forgive the perpetrator of the rape or sexual assault, this may add to her distress and trauma through feeling as though she is not being a 'good Christian' who is expected to forgive.

Christians are regularly reminded that they can only be forgiven for sins they have committed if they can forgive those who commit sin against them. This could lead to the woman and/or others blaming the woman for her suffering because she cannot show forgiveness. In general terms, it has been argued that a significant amount of Christian teachings about women, suffering, abuse and rape place blame and focus on the victim of the suffering rather than condemning the perpetrator of the actions (Fortune, 2001) which is central to victim blaming but also holds parallel with other theories, such as the just world belief.

When just world belief is reported to have been supported in Protestant Christian teachings (Turrell and Thomas, 2008), it is not surprising that many of the Christian beliefs overlap with reasoning about blame, responsibility and belief in a just world when it comes to sexual assault and rape.

In the same way that the belief in a just world theory proposes that people believe in a world where if you are a good person, you should be rewarded and if you are a bad person, you will be punished with bad things happening to you in a cosmic balancing of justice, Turrell and Thomas (2008) discussed the way that people tend to believe that because they are Christian, nothing bad should happen to them.

When bad things do happen to someone, they can be taught to assume that the person must not be a good Christian, or they haven't been 'saved'. They do however point out a contradiction in the teachings of Jesus: that many Christians are also taught to believe that suffering is an important part of being faithful. Bad things are supposed to happen to them as a way to test them (James 1:1) or to metaphorically take up Jesus' cross (Turrell and Thomas, 2008).

To explain how this could affect a victim of sexual violence, it is useful to break the teaching down. In Christianity, suffering and painful events are attributed to Satan: Satan is said to rule this world and can do whatever he wants to people to cause them suffering. As rape and sexual assault is perceived as an evil in the world and as causing great suffering, it is attributed to the work of

Satan in the lives of religious people. However, instead of wallowing in their suffering, The Bible (James 1:1) says that individuals should 'count it all as joy' and as a useful teaching in the journey of their life.

Turrell and Thomas (2008) also questioned the confusion caused by the belief that a woman is supposed to suffer after sexual assault or rape and whether this would influence whether they would seek help for their trauma if they felt that they should suffer and use their experience as a lesson to change their behaviour or character in the future to prevent it from happening again. After sexual assault and rape, Christian women suffering from trauma may also believe that since they are really struggling with the experience and their mental health, it must mean that they are not good Christians and not really saved. Not only may the women themselves believe this, but other Christians around them may agree with these thoughts and blame them for what happened.

This is very similar to Just World Belief in that people can use reasoning about 'just' consequences to actions in life to explain the bad things that have happened to someone. Much like 'they must have done something in a past life' or 'they must have done something to deserve it' – Christian teachings can support the argument that 'it must have happened to them because they are not a good Christian – God wouldn't let this happen to a good person'.

Ultimately, women can internalise these beliefs about themselves which results in them doubting their purpose, their self-worth, doubting their instincts and decisions and therefore staying in sexually violent relationships or not seeking help for their experiences (Turrell & Thomas, 2008).

Sexism appears to play a major part in Turrell & Thomas (2008) findings and provides evidence for reasoning that mirrors some of the most common rape stereotypes and victim blaming messages.

They draw attention to Smith (1995), who writes that some Christians may view sexual assault and rape as an act of sex rather than an act of abuse or sexual violence. Reframing the event as an act of sex rather than an act of abuse or violence, places focus on the woman and moves the responsibility away from the perpetrator. By reframing it as an act of sex, the dress, actions and behaviour of the woman can then be called into question, leading her and others around her to believe that she must have done something to draw attention to herself (Smith (1995) as cited in Gioanovelli and Jackson, 2011).

An example of the way that teachings in Christianity can reinforce rape myths and victim blaming is provided by Turrell and Thomas (2008) who describe the story of Joseph and Potipher in which the wife of Potipher repeatedly makes sexual advances towards Joseph (a slave they had recently purchased) and when Joseph continues to decline her advances and harassment she rips her clothing and tells people that Joseph tried to rape her. Joseph is punished by life imprisonment.

This story is commonly used to teach women the consequences of 'crying rape' and is talked about in the context of the false accusations of rape made by angry women against men as revenge or punishment, which is very similar to the rape myths that women often lie about rape and that women accuse men of rape as a way to punish them. There are less teachings in the Bible about the consequences of raping a woman and where they do exist, the consequences almost always result in the abuse or death of the woman as well as the perpetrator.

Brownmiller (1975) discussed the consequences of rape that occurs within and outside of the city walls in the Bible. If a woman is raped outside of the city walls, she will either be forced to marry the perpetrator, or he will be killed. However, if the rape occurred within the city walls then both the woman and the perpetrator are killed. Brownmiller (1975) suggested that this was because the assumption was made that if the rape truly did happen, the woman would have been able to get help, scream for attention or fight him off and so he is killed for raping her and she is killed for not raising the alarm and stopping the assault from happening to her.

As is shown by Brownmiller's observations of the punishment of a woman who has been raped, a lot of the underlying reasoning is still present today in common victim blaming discourses, especially the familiar assumption that if a rape really did happen to a woman, she 'should' have been able to fight them off, scream for help, escape and report the rape immediately, probably with serious injuries from the fighting. These stereotypical and erroneous assumptions about the way a rape occurs are still being used to blame women and discredit their accounts in general discussion but also in the criminal justice process.

In the work by Turrell and Thomas (2008) the focus of the writing was to consider how best to support a Christian woman following rape or sexual assault amongst all of these biased, harmful and contradictory teachings that place blame on her. Many of their solutions involve the delicate and often difficult reframing of the stories and teachings from the Bible to ensure that their Christian identity and faith is not questioned or compromised, but that further harm is not done by the counsellor by perpetuating the harmful myths and sexist views portrayed in the teachings. Whilst the examples above are specifically taken from the Bible, it is interesting quite how many of these themes (sexism, blaming and punishment of women who have been raped, forgiveness) are repeated and perpetuated in other religions.

Victim blaming in Islam

The theme of sexism continues into Islam and the lower status of women in this religion is well-documented (e.g., King 2009). There are similarities to Christianity in the teachings about women who cause their own rape by the way they look or act with more of a focus on purity and chastity. In a study of over 1500 people, Muganyizi et al. (2010) found that identifying as a Muslim was associated with more victim blaming than any other religion.

Whilst it has been asserted that the Qu'ran sets out equal rights for men and women, many scholars argue that the interpretation of the Qu'ran has exclusively been carried out by men and therefore many of the messages about women have been distorted and manipulated over time to suit the ideologies and beliefs of the male senior figures and therefore need to be reinterpreted regularly in the context of a quickly-changing modern culture and society (Franuik & Shain, 2011).

Interestingly, there are very similar consequences to rape written in the Qu'ran as in the Bible, this is especially important considering the current climate of islamophobia in which the writings of the Qu'ran are heavily scrutinized and demonized, but other major religious texts are ignored or celebrated, despite containing similar rules and messages about women and sexual violence.

A woman's sexual purity and faithfulness to her husband and family are very important qualities in Islam and can therefore be used to blame her for her rape. Following this theme of violation of sexist norms and gender roles; characteristics and sexual behaviours of the woman can contravene the moral code a woman must adhere to in order to remain pure and honourable. Women and girls are killed for experiencing rape due to the dishonour and shame it brings upon the family or the potential of the rape actually being perceived as zina (sexual relations outside of marriage).

Even if it is accepted that a woman was targeted and raped by another man, if that man is not her husband, she is still guilty of zina (Weaver, 2007). In striking similarity to the consequences outside of the city walls in the Bible, the Qu'ran teaches followers to 'flog the adulterer and the adulteress, each one of them, with one hundred stripes' (Franuik & Shain, 2011). Whilst this is described as adultery, rape often happens outside of marriage and when this is then reframed as zina or adultery, it often results in women being punished or killed for being raped. To evidence this issue, Franuik & Shain (2011) discuss the following examples of women being punished or killed for their rape and sexual assault.

- In 2001, a woman in Pakistan reported her rape and was sentenced to death for violating zina

- In Saudi Arabia in 2007, a woman who experienced a violent gang-rape was sentenced to 200 lashes and six months in prison for being with an unrelated male at the time she was raped

- In 2011, a 14-year-old girl in Bangladesh died whilst receiving 80 lashes for committing 'adultery', after reporting being raped by her forty-year-old cousin

---

Much of the victim blaming and honour-based violence is committed when a woman breaches strict gender norms and is seen to be violating her sexual purity or facilitating rape and sexual assault. There is a large emphasis on the woman restraining her sexuality and her desirability by covering her body and face with cloaks or scarves so that she is not molested (Qu'ran 33:59).

The message of these passages is that if a woman does not follow the guidance to cover herself at all times and restrain her beauty and desirability, she is asking to be raped (Franuik & Shain, 2011).

In 2006, a senior Muslim cleric in Australia was speaking about the rape of women who do not wear hijab:

> "If you take out uncovered meat and place it outside on the street, or in the garden or in the park, or in the backyard

without a cover, and the cats come and eat it ... whose
fault is it, the cats' or the uncovered meat?"

(Franuik & Shain, 2011)

Victim blaming in Hinduism

This very closely relates to a concept in Hinduism in which a woman is described as being so sexual and so desirable (her Shakti) that a man should not be expected to restrain his desire to have sex with her and therefore the blame is placed upon the woman for inciting or asking to be raped, should he rape or sexually assault her.

In the Ramayana it states: "So soon as a woman sees a handsome man, her vulva becomes moist," (as cited in Starr 1991, pp. 64–65). This has been taken to mean that the woman becomes sexually aroused and wanting sex as soon as she sees an attractive man and underpins the rape myths that she both wanted to be raped and enjoyed being raped.

These messages about overt sexual desirability of women mean that a man would not be expected to restrain himself, which again bears similarities to Islam. Whilst it would be easy to assume that these theories about a woman's irresistible beauty seem to be contained to Islam and Hinduism, there are numerous non-religious examples of this exact line of reasoning and victim blaming all over the world.

In the IRMAS scale, there has always been a 'she was asking for it' scale of items that measures the prevalence of acceptance of beliefs such as the ones discussed here that have been shown to be accepted by very large proportions of people (Payne et al., 1999; McMahon and Farmer, 2011; Eaton, 2019).

In relation to these messages about men not being able to, and not being expected to restrain their sexual desires for women, the AMMSA and IRMAS scales have used items under the heading of 'men don't mean to rape' which encompass beliefs such as those discussed here – that men cannot help themselves, that men accidentally rape women when they get too carried away, that men sexually harass women because they are so sexy, that men rape women because they are wearing a short skirt and a low cut top.

It would therefore be incorrect to attribute these beliefs solely to Islam and Hinduism when the actual root of these beliefs lies in the sexism and gender role norms that the religions perpetuate. Due to the religious texts of these religions clearly stating these beliefs, it could be argued that Muslim and Hindu people are more likely to subscribe to victim blaming notions on this basis, but the religions themselves are not the only source of these beliefs.

Victim blaming using the concept of Karma

However, one concept that is central to Hinduism and Buddhism is that those that commit sins or become victims of their desires are destined to repeat their suffering or the suffering of others through karma and rebirth (Gross, 1994). Whilst Buddhism possibly holds the least examples of direct victim blaming in contrast to other religions discussed here, there are still prominent examples of sexism and hierarchy of gender, such as that rebirth as a woman is caused by negative karma and punishment for sinful behaviour in a previous life (Gross 1994), essentially positioning womanhood as an undesirable experience caused by previous sins. Khuankaew (2007) reported that Buddhist women who are suffering in violent relationships often believe that they have brought this suffering upon themselves through negative karma and Franuik & Shain (2011) confirmed that monks also believe women's abuse is brought on themselves through karma, meaning that Budddhist women may be receiving these victim blaming messages from numerous system levels in the ecological model at once.

If they already believe that they have brought their abuse or rape upon themselves by behaviours that they may have committed in a previous life that they cannot remember and then seek counsel from a Monk who reiterates this message, it is plain to see how Buddhist women may experience victim blaming and self-blame rooted in the teachings of their faith.

The concept of karma is comparable to the concept of redemption in Christianity and Islam as a consequence of behaviours and characters during one life affecting the next life or afterlife. It also draws similarities with just-world belief in that it creates reasoning as to why bad things may happen to someone and can result in a woman being blamed for being raped or sexually assaulted, rather than the perpetrator of the attack.

Where just world belief is described as an internal, cognitive bias, Karma offers an external, cosmic, eternal force of reasoning and balance that can be used to explain why a woman was raped or sexually assaulted rather than condemning the strategic targeting of the woman by the perpetrator. Karma ultimately moves the agency away from the perpetrator and forces Buddhists to consider current or past life behaviours as reasons for their experience of assault or rape.

This is possibly one of the more obscure or abstract versions of victim blaming because it rests neither on characterological blame or behavioural blame – but on hypothetical assumptions that in a potential previous life, the person may have done something that was judged as immoral and is being punished for their actions by (1) being born a woman and (2) being raped or sexually assaulted. This would prove very difficult for a woman to defend due to being taught that her gender is a punishment and that her suffering is of her own doing and could easily induce and reinforce feelings of self-blame.

Interpretation and White perspectives

Whilst discussing religions of the world in a piece of writing that is heavily centred on a western and even UK-focussed context, it is imperative to remain critically aware that all cultures and religions are historically and culturally specific and therefore interpreted differently by different people at different points in time.

Where some religious passages may be interpreted by a Western commenter (like me) as promoting inferiority of women or rape myths, leaders and followers of the religion may not interpret the passages in the same way.

Issues of interpretation and the power imbalance caused by who controls interpretation need to be at the centre of any discussion about religion and the perception of women's purpose and treatment. This argument of perception and interpretation has been central in the discussion surrounding the use of the hijab in which many western feminist writers have challenged the oppression of women by ordering them to cover their bodies and even most of their head so that they are not molested (as stated in the Qu'ran).

However, a number of Muslim and Arab feminist writers have replied to the criticism by saying that the only thing oppressive about the issue is that western people feel they can impose their views upon women and tell them that they are being oppressed when instead, they report feeling empowered by their choice to cover their bodies.

Whilst there are strong arguments on both sides, the purpose of this recent example is to show that when discussing the interpretation of religious or cultural texts, teachings and beliefs in relation to the oppression of women it is crucial to remain aware of the context, culture and position of the person doing the interpreting.

From the review I have presented here, conducted to explore the factors from each religion that may influence victim blaming and self-blame of women who have been subjected to rape or sexual assault; it is clear that religion has a large role to play not only in the direct victim blaming and perpetuation of rape myths but also in the influence to blame the self for rape and sexual assault. Turrell and Thomas (2008) provide a much-needed insight into the skills and consideration needed to support a person using teachings from their religion without the teachings themselves conveying messages of blame and sexism.

As discussed, all religions appear to reinforce sexism, one of the most common factors underpinning the victim blaming and self-blame of women following rape or sexual abuse but they also provide individual lines of reasoning and explanation for why a woman should be blamed, held responsible or even punished for being raped or sexually assaulted by another person. There is very little written in any of the religions about the motives, actions and punishment of perpetrators and this narrow focus on the behaviour, character and sexuality of the woman in society is reinforcing the victim blaming culture that impacts on women who have been subjected to sexual violence every day.

Cross-cultural responses to rape and sexual assault

In 2002, the WHO reported that sexual violence occurs in all cultures across the world. Any review on victim blaming and self-blame of women who have been subjected to sexual violence would be woefully inadequate if it did not consider the cross-cultural responses to women who disclose rape or sexual assault.

Whilst it happens to women all over the world, the definition and perception of sexual violence differs from country to country, language to language, generation to generation and community to community (Kalra & Bhugra, 2013). This section will explore literature that has focussed on the cross-cultural responses to sexual violence, specifically written on victim blaming, self-blame and consequent revictimisation.

Literature in this field has considered many different factors that may have a relationship with prevalence or experience of sexual violence, however, the common denominator seems to be the way these factors are directly related to the culture of that particular group of people (Robinson, 2016).

In a brief overview of the literature, Robinson (2016) states that ethnic minority men and women are more likely to victim blame than White men and women and that Latino, Black and Asian Americans are more likely to accept rape myths than White Americans. However, this must be understood in context with the finding from Jimenez and Abreu (2003) who argued that White Americans were more likely to victim blame if the woman was from an ethnic minority group. So, in a country in which racism is rife and over 64% of the population is White, it is reasonable to suggest that the powerful, overarching stereotypes held by White Americans (which were found to include the assertion that ethnic minority women from particular cultures are highly promiscuous (Jimenez and Abreu (2003)) could have been absorbed by women and men from those cultures and communities in the same way that women in general absorb sexist messages about their gender roles from the patriarchal society.

Where there are differences between cultures in general and more specifically, cultural responses to sexual violence, one factor that may enable the cross-cultural acceptance of rape myths and victim blaming attitudes despite the differences, could be the underpinning patriarchy that is present in many modern and historical cultures (Carmody & Washington, 2001).

One important difference between cultures is the way sexual violence is defined. Even when a woman lives in a country where the law has set out the criteria for a sexual assault or rape, her cultural norms may have an effect on whether the legal definition is accepted or adhered to. Kalof (2000) and Sigurvinsdottir and Ullman (2014) found that women from ethnic minorities who had experienced a legally defined rape still asserted that they were not victims of rape and in any case, they blame themselves for the incident. This finding that is further supported by Littleton et al. (2007) who argued that Latina women are less likely to disclose a rape to anyone and are less likely to have ever heard another woman disclose a rape to them. In their paper in which they compared the responses of European American women and Latina women, they found that Latina women are more likely to internalise misogynistic gender role stereotypes and sexual scripts which focus on the purity and virginity of the woman as a major contributor to her dignity and respect of her family.

Most researchers when attempting to write about the differences of victim blaming in culture and ethnicity tend to caveat their work with the complaint that there is a severe lack of research in this area from which to draw.

Littleton et al. (2007) are no exception to this but do provide an overview of the small research area, beginning with citations from qualitative studies in the 1990s.

They report on the work of a handful of others on page 510:

> 'Latina rape victims engaged in more self-blame and perceived their community as more victim blaming than did African or European Americans. Finally, there is some evidence that Latinos/as are more likely than European Americans or African Americans to adhere to traditional, patriarchal gender roles (Kane, 2000). Adherence to patriarchal gender roles could be associated with greater belief in the notion of sexual precedence (Caron & Carter, 1997; Livingston, Buddie, Testa, & VanZile-Tamsen, 2004), that is the idea that if a woman has had previous consensual activity with a man or is in a committed relationship with him, then he has a legitimate claim to her future sexuality (Shotland & Goodstein, 1992). Thus, greater belief in sexual precedence would be associated with less belief that rape can occur within the context of an established romantic relationship.'

They go on to justify their own study rationale by stating that a literature search found that there had never been any other studies which explored the rape scripts of women from different ethnic groups, or from different social class groups.

A little more than a year later, Shana Maier wrote in 2008 about the perceptions and responses of women from different ethnicities. She wrote specifically about the influence race and ethnicity would have on the victim's own responses to being raped.

In her work, she argued that African American women were likely to stay silent about being subjected to sexual violence due to their awareness of racial bias. Maier (2008) wrote that African American women were scared of turning African American men into the police in a system that was inherently racist, were fearful of being seen to be being disloyal to the race – and being suspicious and fearful of a White-dominated rape crisis movement.

Maier suggests four key issues which affect African American women subjected to rape:

1. The stereotype of Black women as a 'jezebel' who is hypersexual, promiscuous and deserving of male violence

2. The stereotype of Black women are strong, powerful matriarchs who are responsible for controlling and holding the family together. They are therefore seen as capable of, or unmoved by, dealing with sexual victimization.

3. The 'sapphire' stereotype of Black women that they are aggressive, overbearing and seek to emasculate Black men. Because Black women are seen as strong and powerful, the actions of Black men are seen as less impactful or serious.

4. Linking to the stereotype above, is the belief that Black men only rape and abuse White women and girls. This stereotype harms Black women because it reduces belief and credibility of women when they are raped, abused or assaulted by Black men. Arguably, the rape and abuse of Black women by Black men is seen as less serious and less harmful than the rape of White women by Black men

Together, these stereotypes have a profound impact on the way African American women are perceived when they are subjected to male violence – and the way they perceive themselves. I strongly recommend reading her paper and have included it in the reference list.

I also agree with her criticism of our academic and activist work, when she states on page 305:

> *This research addresses issues of racial and ethnic diversity by examining if and how rape victim advocates understand victims' experiences and responses to rape within a cultural context. A multicultural component is critical to current research on rape crisis centers in light of criticism that rape crisis centers have been dominated by White women who ignore the complex situations experienced by women of color (Matthews, 1989; Riger et al., 2002; Washington, 2001; White, 2001).*

Individualism and collectivism

Another interesting difference relates to the section earlier in this review about individualism versus collectivism. Kalra and Bhugra (2013) make a parallel argument about ego-centric versus socio-centric cultures and how women (and their close support network) who are members of those different cultures respond to their experiences of sexual assault and rape.

In ego-centric cultures, as with individualism, the priority is given to the 'self' and achieving 'independence' which means that the consequences and responses of a sexual assault or rape remain with the woman, inducing feelings of private guilt. It is still common for women to be blamed for experiencing a rape or sexual assault, but it is rare for the rest of her family members and support network to be tainted by these negative judgements.

By contrast, in socio-centric cultures, as with collectivism, the priority is given to the relations with others and maintaining interdependence. This means that the consequences of and responses to a sexual assault or rape are spread wider than the woman who actually experienced the violence but induces wider feelings of shame and embarrassment for the family and close support network (Kalra & Bhugra, 2013). Women in socio-centric cultures are not only blamed for experiencing the sexual assault or rape but are also under secondary pressure due to the dignity and status of her family being called into question by the rest of their community. Many of these issues stem from the dichotomy afforded to the sexuality of women in many cultures in which their sexuality is simultaneously viewed as a dangerous temptation to men, but it also given the status of holding the honour of the woman. Therefore, any actions or incidents that include her sexuality will induce judgement about either her culpability or her purity and whether this has affected her honour. One of the most harmful effects of honour being related to women's sexual behaviours and experiences is that women can experience a non-consensual experience such as rape or sexual assault, and still be judged for bringing shame on herself and her family for having sex outside of marriage (known as zina).

So not only may a woman be subjected to a traumatic violent sexual experience, but she may then suffer from victim blaming from her support network and the added judgement due to 'committing zina' (Weaver, 2007). The concept of rape or sexual assault being categorised as extra-marital relations that bring shame on the family of the woman rather than the act of interpersonal violence demonstrates the way that the culture of the woman has rated the rights of the male perpetrator to commit acts of violence against women above the rights of the woman to be protected from violence.

The experiences of Latina and Hispanic women are also influenced by racial and ethnic issues. When women and girls are sexually victimized, they bring shame to their family because they are 'tainted' and no longer chaste (Lefley, Scott, Llabre & Hicks, 1993; Low & Organista, 2000). A woman's sexual purity, conceptualized by the notion of marianismo, is essential in Latino and Hispanic cultures, and the lack of 'sexual purity' after being subjected to male violence dishonours her family.

Due to many of these issues being underpinned by patriarchal belief systems and gender inequality, it is no wonder that a number of studies into culture and ethnicity in sexual violence have shown a relationship between victim blaming and high levels of gender role stereotyping (Kalra & Bhugra, 2013). In cultures where sexism and gender inequality are deeply embedded and even encouraged, victim blaming is a reflection of the woman being seen as less worthy and having been prescribed rigid gender roles which include her permitted roles in sex and relationships. For example, stigma and negative response to disclosure of rape or sexual assault is particularly noticeable in Asian cultures due to the taboo surrounding anything sexual in general (Kalra & Bhugra, 2013).

It can begin to sound as though there are a number of specific cultures in which rape and sexual assault of women happens much more frequently than other cultures, and in those specific cultures, those women are much more likely to be blamed for their experiences.

However, Sanday (2003) argued that following this logic would mean that there would be cultures that were rape-free and cultures that were rape-prone, and the key would be to look at whether the rape-free cultures were in fact feminist cultures that challenged patriarchy. Unfortunately, Sanday (2003) could not identify any rape-free cultures in the world but did report that other researchers such as Otterbein (1979) had examined 17 different cultures and had concluded that the cultures with the most patriarchal belief systems had the highest prevalence of sexual violence against women.

Unfortunately, this is a poorly researched topic area (Kalra & Bhugra, 2013) and so further studies have been very difficult to find.

Both male violence and victim blaming of women and girls (underpinned by a patriarchal belief system) is evident all over the world but there are differences in the way these feelings of guilt, shame and self-blame are owned and responded to depending on whether the culture is ego-centric or socio-centric.

Much further research is warranted here, especially as the victim blaming of women and girls from particular cultures in which cultural norms are entwined with religious beliefs will be even more difficult to challenge and change.

In my personal experience of working and supporting women from these communities, there is a distinct difference in the self-blame between religious and non-religious women. The same can be said for women from egocentric and sociocentric cultures and communities. It is not that any of our cultures or communities are any better or worse at victim blaming or encouraging self-blame, but they are different, and we must recognise those differences.

9.

How do family and friends blame women?

Whilst it is statistically rare for a woman to report her rape or sexual assault to the police, it is more common for a woman to disclose her experience to a member of her closest support network, defined in the ecological model as friends and family members.

In an exceptionally diverse and large sample of women who had been subjected to sexual assault or rape and told someone about it, 82.5% had told their friends and 62.9% had told their romantic partner (Mason et al., 2008) and of the support network, friends were rated as the most supportive and parents were rated as the least supportive after a rape of sexual assault disclosure.

Research has shown that the decision to disclose her rape or sexual assault to the support network is based on the reaction they predict they may receive from them (Browne, 1991), meaning that if a woman believes that the response will be supportive, she will disclose but if she has reason to believe that the response will be negative, she will not disclose.

Deitz et al. (2015) said that if a woman's support network responds by blaming her, self-blame is much greater than if she is not blamed by her support network. This section will examine research that sought to explore the responses from the close support network after the rape or sexual assault of a woman they know and the response to disclosure from the support network on subsequent self-blame.

Victim blaming within the family

In 1949, Reuben Hill theorised that a family crisis was defined as 'any sharp or decisive change for which old patterns are inadequate' (p.51). Hill put forward three components of the crisis: (a) the event itself, (b) the family's crisis-meeting resources and (c) the definition the family makes of the event.

This was contextualised to consider rape by White (1984) in which the factors that affect the response of the family and friends were examined using the Hill's adapted model with additional factors by Burr (1973). Of most relevance to victim blaming and self-blame are the definition of the event and how the family has been influenced by cultural views and stereotypes of rape. Consistent with earlier sections, the absorption and acceptance of rape myths and stereotypes can seriously affect the response the woman receives from the support network (White, 1984).

One such rape myth that has been discussed in the literature is whether the woman invited or caused the rape and the ability of the support network to place the blame on the perpetrator rather than the woman. As rape stereotypes and perceptions tend to define rape and sexual assault as an act of unwanted sex, it is unsurprising that White (1984) and Holstrom & Burgess (1979) also talk about the tendency of support networks to see the woman as a recipient of a sexual act rather than a victim of violence who was targeted due to a personal vulnerability.

In the sudden event of a female family member being raped or sexually assaulted, the views on gender roles, rape myths, victim blaming and sexism are brought into unexpectedly sharp focus; focus that rarely occurs in other family discussions or crises (Burgess & Holstrom, 1979). The families who perceive the event as sex and blame the woman for her assault or rape were more likely to experience significant family crisis and struggled to provide support for the woman (White, 1984).

More recently, Campbell et al. (2001) carried out research from the perspective of the women who had been raped or sexually assaulted to explore their perception of the responses they had received from their support network and (whilst finding that women have mixed perceptions of what a healing or harmful response is) they could conclude that negative social reactions included family members and friends telling the woman that she was to blame for her rape or assault, being told she was irresponsible and being told to get on with her life which were again consistent with much of the common rape stereotypes that currently fuel victim blaming.

In addition, Campbell et al. (2001) observed a cumulative effect in that the more negative responses from the support network, the more severe the psychological harm was to the woman. In addition, their research provided support for Ullman's 1996 and 1999 studies which found that only the negative reactions from the support network were strongly and consistently related to increased psychological harm and delayed recovery whereas positive reactions had a negligible effect (Ullman, 1999).

Findings from Campbell et al. (2001) suggested that women usually experience both positive and negative responses to their disclosure in fairly equal quantities but that negative responses had the biggest impact on their psychological wellbeing and their propensity to develop depression, post-traumatic stress disorder and other health issues. Whilst the negative responses have been shown to be more impactful than positive responses, the participants in the study reported that having the members of their family and friends believe what they said and were allowed to talk about the assault when needed reduced feelings of post-traumatic stress, depression and health issues (Campbell, 2001).

Familiarity and friendship do not reduce victim blaming

The Defensive Attribution Hypothesis (Shaver, 1970) is relevant to this microsystem factor. The hypothesis states that the level of blame levied on the victim depends on observers' perceived similarity and identification with the victim: when victim and observer are increasingly similar, (the same gender, for example) the victim will be blamed less (Grubb & Harrower, 2008).

Traditional research by Fulero and DeLara (1976) showed that female students blamed the victim least when they were perceived to be similar and blamed the victim most when they were perceived to be dissimilar to the victim. This finding could be applied to the family and friends of a woman who has been subjected to sexual assault or rape as they would arguably perceive that they had a number of similarities and a high level of identification to the woman as someone they know and love, and would be expected to be even more prominent in female family members.

However, to critique this hypothesis, I presented findings that similarity and identification did not reduce victim blaming and instead found that women were just as likely to blame female victims of rape and sexual assault as men and that observers that were perceived as similar to the victim did not blame the woman any less (Mason et al., 2004).

These mixed findings may represent evidence of competing cognitive bias, as when White (1984) examined a community response to rape, they found that their participant's responses were influenced less by the perceived similarity and identification to the woman who was raped or sexually assaulted in their community but more by the belief most participants had in a 'just world'. (White, 1984).

Another potential variable in the way that families and friends respond to the woman who has been subjected to rape or sexual assault could be their own experience of rape or sexual assault. When it is considered accurate that 20% of women and 3% of men (Office for National Statistics, 2015) will experience rape or sexual assault during their life time, it is probable that at least one of the woman's family members or friends have also experienced the same thing. Along this line of thought, being a victim of rape or sexual assault would provide an extra level of similarity and identification and it was assumed that those people would victim blame less than people who had not experienced any rape or sexual assault (Shaver, 1970).

The defensive attribution hypothesis was tested by Mason et al. (2004) using participants that reported experiencing rape or sexual assault and participants with no identified history of rape or sexual assault. Mason et al. (2004) found no difference in empathy or victim blaming between the two groups of participants. This finding was also replicated by Carmody & Washington (2001) and Forbes & Adams-Curtis (2001) as both of their studies found no difference in rape myth acceptance when history of sexual assault was examined and therefore the findings did not support the theory that women who had been subjected to sexual assault or rape would have higher empathy and have lower levels of rape myth acceptance. It is therefore common for women to experience victim blaming from the members of their closest support networks (Ullman, 2014).

Relyea & Ullman (2015) state that the negative responses are particularly hurtful because they are usually experienced when a woman has disclosed very sensitive information and is expecting to receive support from her friend or family member. They borrowed a term from couple counselling to explain this reaction: 'turning against'; to represent the feeling of a loved one turning against their family member or friend by blaming them, disbelieving them or reframing them as the cause of the rape or sexual assault.

Reyea & Ullman (2015) go on to provide evidence from their own research that showed that 78% of participants had experienced the 'turning against' reaction from their loved ones and then discussed previous research that has shown that when loved ones do 'turn against' the woman who has been sexually assaulted or raped, it is more likely that the woman will blame herself and importantly, in the context of revictimisation, will be less likely to show assertiveness in sexual refusal in future instances of attempted rape or sexual assault.

These potential negative reactions make it very difficult for victims to heal from the rape and rebuild their lives (Ullman, 1996). Ullman recommended that the support networks of women need to be educated about the reactions that will help or hinder the recovery of their loved one. Campbell et al. (2001) has more recently described this idea in more detail and said that rape prevention programmes should include information or training on how to support women who have been raped or sexually assaulted so that if a friend or family member was ever to disclose to them, they would not continue the negative responses of victim blaming and disbelieving women in distress.

Like all topics in this field, a lot of the previous research has been based on White, western populations of women. Researchers have long been calling for more culturally diverse and relevant pieces of research that presented the experiences of women from different ethnicities and cultures who may have different coping mechanisms following rape and sexual assault.

Bryant-Davis et al. (2011) conducted a much-needed study into the role of social network support and religion in the recovery of African American women. A number of studies have found that African American women utilise social support networks as their primary resource when they have been subjected to rape, sexual assault or intimate partner violence (Coker et al. 2002).

The findings from Bryant et al. (2011) support previous work and showed that strong social support from family and friends reduced PTSD and depression following sexual assault or rape. Both of these findings warrant further exploration into whether the families, friends and closer support networks of Black women are either less likely to blame her for the rape or sexual assault or are more approachable and equipped to support a woman in crisis than the support networks of White women.

The family and the immediate support network play a pivotal role in both the external response the woman will experience and also in the way she will perceive herself during and after being subjected to rape or sexual assault.

This area of research has provided evidence that suggests that negative responses from family and friends are common but that women are still likely to look to those family members and friends for support and advice. There is an interesting parallel between the role and response of the family – and the role and response of the police.

Women's choices to report to the police and to disclose to their close support network are dependent upon their predictions of the reaction they will receive from those two groups of people. It has been shown that the general public will have a fairly high level of rape myth acceptance and it has been shown that the response that women get from the police and larger criminal justice system can be negative and blaming.

Therefore, there is a pattern emerging that seems to suggest that women are so very aware of the victim blaming culture that they make an assessment of whether they think they will be blamed and responded to negatively before they disclose to an informal network such as family or friends and also before the decision to report to a formal network such as police.

Despite women being acutely aware of victim blaming culture, the way their family members and friends (and police) subsequently respond to them has been shown to increase the likelihood that they will blame themselves for what happened.

A limitation of this area of research appears to be the diversity of participants. This is becoming quite the pattern, a pattern that Black colleagues, activists and readers will be all too familiar with.

Whilst a lot of research is focussed upon White, western support networks, more complex and varied findings are coming from research that has talked to Black and Asian women about their relationship with their support network and the way they were responded to when they sought support after rape and sexual assault. As argued earlier in the previous chapter, further research would benefit from seeking the experiences of women from different communities and cultures to broaden the narrative and the understanding of close support networks' responses to women who have been subjected to rape and sexual assault. This is especially important considering that there appears to be significant differences in the ways in which Black and Asian families respond to women being subjected to male violence.

10.

How does the media blame women?

The mass media now includes television, radio, internet, and printed communications and is intended to reach the majority of the general public. Every day, an individual now spends more time engaging with mass media outlets through technology than sleeping. Ofcom (2014) reported that people in Britain spend an average of 8 hours and 40 minutes per day accessing media in comparison to only sleeping for an average of 8 hours and 20 minutes per day. With individuals relying heavily on media for information about social and political issues, pop culture, product information and general news, it is easy to see the power that these outlets have when it comes to presenting messages about sexual violence (Shaw et al., 2009).

Even studies from the early 80s and 90s found that large proportions of children's prime time television dramas contained sexual imagery, kissing, flirting and discussion of sex and intimacy (Cope-Farrar & Kunkel, 2011).

Despite feminist groups fighting the objectification and sexualisation of women and girls in the mass media for decades (Long, 2012) media outlets can be selective when it comes to the portrayal of women and girls. Further, media portrayals of sexual assault and rape have been shown to increase victim blaming and influence the way women, the general public, the police, the criminal justice system and in some cases, the way juries have perceived a female victim (Shaw et al., 2009; Eaton, 2019). In a review examining depictions of young women in a range of media, (APA, 2007) findings showed that women and girls are frequently depicted in sexualized and objectified manners. The same report argued that this was causing girls as young as seven years old to view themselves through the 'male gaze' and judging themselves based on their own sex appeal (APA, 2007).

This chapter will discuss the ways in which mass media and pornography influence the way we all perceive sexual violence – and the ways we seek to prevent sexual violence by encouraging women and girls to protect themselves.

As suggested by Sandra Walklate (2020), preventing sexual violence requires a good understanding of the causes of sexual violence against (predominantly) women and girls. However, as this report will demonstrate, the harmful messages being communicated by different forms of media may be playing a role in misguided and poor prevention strategies taken by local authorities, government, and police.

Dominant messages: The sexualisation, pornification and objectification of women and girls

The media communicates influential messages about the gender role stereotypes of women, girls, men, and boys. Whether it is the consistent depiction of women in the kitchen, boys playing construction games whilst girls apply make-up to a plastic doll head and men doing DIY in their garage – the media has considerable power to influence gender role norms. Sexualisation and objectification of women and girls in the media is commonplace. The media play a key role in communicating information, cultural norms, attitudes, and approaches not only to sexual violence as a topic, but also to the prevention of sexual violence. Therefore, it is relevant to consider the way the media portray women, sex, and sexual violence.

Sexualisation of women and girls is defined as occurring when the value of the person is derived from their sex appeal, excluding their other characteristics; when a person is defined by their physical attractiveness, and when a person is sexually objectified (APA Task Force, 2007). Objectification is defined as perceiving and treating a person as a sexual object (Loughnan, 2013). Sexualisation and objectification in mainstream media has been shown to affect the perceptions of the general public. Sexualised and objectified women and girls are dehumanised, dementalised and therefore perceived as less worthy of moral concern. Consequently, when women and girls are sexualised and objectified either directly or indirectly, they are more likely to be blamed for rape and sexual assault and less likely to be perceived as suffering from the experience of being subjected to sexual violence (Loughnan et al., 2013).

Cope-Farrar and Kunkel (2011) report that sexual imagery or sex-related talk occurred 8-10 times per hour and 1 in 4 conversations between lead characters were about sex on prime-time television shows in the nineties. Less than two decades later, Eyal and Finnerty (2009) found that 16% of all sexual intercourse depicted on TV involved teenagers or young adults.

Attractive female characters were more likely to be victims of sexual crimes in television shows than male characters. The authors found that whilst HBO included the most shows with sexual intercourse, few differences across channels were observed in the presentation of sexual intercourse (Eval and Finnerty, 2009). Television shows and advertisements were largely presenting sex and relationships in the same way: women and girls are frequent victims of sexual assault, whereas men are rarely victims of sexual assaults or rapes; sex is framed as positive and casual, but negative depictions of sex are presented as having very serious and long lasting consequences for the female victims (Eyal and Finnerty, 2009).

In recent television, internationally popular 'Game of Thrones' was criticised for the staggering number of rapes of women and girls in the episodes across all series, with 50 rapes in the TV series and over 200 rapes in the original book series. When questioned about this by The New York Times in 2014, author George R.R. Martin argued that sexual violence was a common part of history and war – and that he was reflecting an everyday occurrence. However, critics called the significant amount of sexual violence against women and girls gratuitous, unacceptable and disgusting (The New York Times, 2014).

However, this is not the only globally viewed production that has been criticised for the sexualisation and sensationalism of the rape and abuse of women. Other films include Gone Girl (2014) and Red Sparrow (2018), which were criticised for sexualising the rape of women and for perpetuating the rape myth that women lie about rape and domestic violence for revenge or attention. In May 2019, newspapers reported that audiences had walked out of screenings of The Nightingale (2019) due to the inclusion of three violent rape scenes of the female character within 20 minutes. Reviews described the film as 'vacuum-packed with a non-stop supply of rapes, deaths and beatings' (The Independent, 2019).

Mass media play a large role in depicting and reframing issues of gender role stereotypes, sexualisation and objectification of women (APA, 2007; Eaton, 2019). Authors have also argued that the media depiction of gender roles of women and girls often intersect with the depiction of race, which causes further problems for women of colour who are not only subject to the misogyny of sexualisation and objectification, but also the racism related to their ethnicity or cultures.

Fredrickson & Roberts (1997) found that the sexual exploitation of African American women and girls in slavery has led to media stereotypes of Black women as sexual aggressors and sexual savages (Thomas et al., 2004). They also reported that Asian women and girls were generally portrayed in the media as sexually submissive, childlike, and exotic (Root, 1995). Finally, women and girls of all ethnicities and cultures that belonged to lower social classes were portrayed as gross, overly sexed, untamed, crude, and deserving of sexual exploitation and aggression (Pharr, 1988; Smith, 2008). Whilst this may result in seemingly benign popular adverts containing, for example, African women dressed like carnal, sexual animals in a jungle or chained naked in a metal cage, the reality is that women of colour are depicted as non-human animals, savages or submissive slaves.

Film Director and Photographer, Jean Paul Goude is behind many famous images of Black women. His book, questionably entitled 'Jungle Fever' (1982) and much of his most influential work depicts Black women as sexual savages, usually naked in cages, in jungles and animalistic poses. In the book, he speaks candidly about Black women he dated and married, comparing their body parts and characters to animals and savages.

In 2009, famous Black actress and model Amber Rose was depicted as an animal in a cage for a photoshoot for Complex Magazine. Naomi Campbell and Grace Jones are among other famous Black women who have been repeatedly depicted as savages or animals in fashion and advertisement. The media reinforces the powerful historic White, misogynistic power over 'exotic' women and girls of colour who are hyper-sexualised objects of sex to be used or tamed by the dominant class: White, privileged men.

Long (2012) argues that all these media representations of women and girls reduce women to an object for sex, holes to be filled or a body to be used. This has direct links to the victim blaming of women and girls who have been subjected to rape or sexual assault because it reinforces the notion that they are insatiable sex objects for men and boys to conquer and use. This systemic representation of the sexual purpose of women means that rape is often seen as an act of sex, not as an act of violence. It perpetuates rape myths such as 'women who are forced to have sex, enjoy it really' (Payne, Lonsway and Fitzgerald, 1999) which features as an item in the Illinois Rape Myth Acceptance Scale.

Sexualisation and objectification is important when considering prevention of sexual violence because this positioning of women as objects has been shown to reduce concern for women who are subjected to sexual offences. If the concern is reduced, the prevention strategies may be misguided or even blame women and girls for being subjected to sexual violence.

This was demonstrated by Loughnan et al. (2013), who found that participants presented with a case study of an objectified, sexualized woman who had been raped were less likely to feel moral concern for her, and she was more likely to be held responsible than women who were not objectified or over-sexualised. Not only this, but the hyper-sexualisation of groups of women can be absorbed and accepted by the women themselves (Loughnan et al., 2013), meaning that they can buy into the popular misrepresentation of their own gender roles and self-worth; thereby increasing self-blame (Eaton, 2019).

Arguably, one of the most devastating effects of buying into the representation by the mass media of women as sexual objects is that women can learn that their self-worth lies within sex and remaining constantly sexually available to men and boys (Garcia, 1999; APA, 2007b). This can lead to women and girls judging and blaming themselves using common rape myths for why they were raped – or not even realise that their sexual encounter was non-consensual, forced or exploitative (Ullman, 2011; Eaton, 2019). Indeed, Fairchild and Rudman (2008) have shown that young women who were subjected to sexual harassment and objectification in the street by unknown men had a variety of coping mechanisms but those young women who responded to sexual harassment passively or by blaming themselves were much more likely to self-objectify.

The effect of pornography and porn culture

Pornography is now one of the most consumed forms of media in the world. Each year, PornHub.com releases statistics on usage and trends. They reported that:

- In 2017, PornHub.com received 28.5 billion visits. That's 78.1 million per day.

- In 2017, people watched 92 billion porn videos on PornHub.com

- In 2017, 4.6 billion hours of porn were watched on PornHub.com

This immense consumption of pornography is not confined to adults. A report by online security company BitDefender, showed that children under 10 years old accounted for 22% of under 18s consuming porn and that out of all people using porn, 1 in 10 visitors to porn websites every day are under 10 years old (BitDefender, 2016). Porn culture or 'pornification' is defined as 'the prevalence or normalisation of sexual themes and explicit sexual imagery in popular or mainstream culture'. Examples of this can be seen in advertisements, music videos, drama, fashion and even fast food.

As pornography and porn culture is often based upon both sexualisation and objectification of women, there is evidence to show links between all three and victim blaming. Pornography is linked to victim blaming because it provides validation of the hyper-sexualisation and objectification of women and girls (Katyachild et al., 1985) and the minimisation, trivialization, and glorification of rape and sexual assault (Layden, 2010).

Pornography and porn culture in the media convey compelling messages about what sex is, how it should be performed, how a woman or girl should respond to sex or sexual advances and what men and boys should expect and want from sex. In a study conducted by NSPCC in 2013, young people of 15 years old were found to be imitating or requesting sex acts that they had seen in porn. Indeed, many pornographic materials watched by adults and children exploited the 'rape loophole'. The 'rape loophole' was a method in which film makers were legally allowed to depict rape and sexual assault in their films up until 2013 when Rape Crisis England and Wales put pressure on the government to make it illegal.

In a study carried out by Rape Crisis (2013) as part of their campaign, it was found that of the top ten Google search results for the search term 'free porn', half of the websites hosted free 'rape pornography'. Their study also found that on the top 50 UK porn websites, 78% advertise content simulating rape of girls under 18 years old under keywords such as 'schoolgirl rape' and 'young teen rape'. Further to this, PornHub.com reported that one of their most common search terms in 2017 was 'stepdaughter porn' and 'stepsister porn'. This not only sent messages to established and potential perpetrators that incest, child abuse, rape and forced sex is acceptable, exciting and enjoyed by women but also sent strong messages to women and girls, who may feel obliged or pressured to perform a sexual act that they have seen in pornography.

This is especially concerning when added to the research findings from Corne et al. (1992) who found that women and girls who were exposed to pornography from an early age were more likely to accept common rape myths and even experience sexual fantasies where they were raped. Researchers argued that this was due to the way that exposure to porn had socialised these women and girls to believe that sexual aggression and sexual submission was a part of a romantic or intimate event/relationship. Further still, Layden (2010) found that young women who watched pornography depicting rape and sexual violence would recommend a prison sentence half the length of young women who had not watched the material. It is arguable that exposure to porn of any kind that repeatedly presents women and girls as subordinate, insatiable and 'enjoying' forced sex acts will distort a person's perception of healthy consensual sex.

In a study conducted in Japan in 1994, Ohbuchi and colleagues found that young men who watched porn depicting rape and forced sexual acts where the actresses are directed to show pleasure are significantly more likely to believe that high percentages of rape cases are invented by women and girls in society. The same study also reported that the young men who had watched this type of pornography were significantly more likely to believe that women and girls enjoy being raped. More recently in Britain, reports of rapes of girls being perpetrated by boys on school grounds is increasing, with recent statistics showing 5500 rapes of girls happened in their schools in 2016. Bates (2018) reported that when interviewed, schoolboys had said that they thought it was normal for girls to cry during sex and foreplay, which Bates attributed to the prevalence of porn now containing women and girls crying in pain (Long, 2012).

To explore these comments, a keyword search was conducted on the 30th August 2018 of PornHub.com.

Keywords searched included 'crying', 'hurt' and 'pain', to explore how accessible free porn videos were that contained women who were in clear physical pain and might normalise sex with women who are crying in pain.

The results from the brief keyword search resulted in 1129 videos of women 'crying' in pain during sex acts, 983 videos of women being described as 'hurt' during sex acts and 2364 videos of women described as 'in pain' and 'in extreme pain' during sex acts. All words featured in the titles of the videos.

It is important to note that this was a brief search of only one free porn website conducted at one moment in time, but that there was clearly a very large collection of videos depicting women who were crying from physical pain during sex, therefore sexualising and normalising painful and abusive sex.

This effect was found years before the internet made porn so readily available. In a piece of research with male undergraduates, Garcia (1984) found that the more sexually violent and coercive materials consumed by the participants, the more likely they were to believe that women and girls are responsible for their own rape, that rapists should not be severely punished and that women and girls should not resist non-consensual sex. However, this study was based on male undergraduates accessing hard copy pornography such as books, magazines and occasionally, video tapes in the eighties.

The participants reported that around 50-60% of the pornography they had seen showed physical violence towards the woman. With the expansion of the internet, social media and mobile technology, the modern figure of violence in pornography is now reported to be around 90-97% (Long, 2012; Dines, 2011).

A meta-analysis was conducted by Paolucci et al. (2000) to explore the impact that watching pornography has on committing sexual violence and accepting rape myths that blame women for their rape and sexual assaults. The meta-analysis of 46 studies between 1962-1995 with over 12,000 participants showed that there was a 22% increase in men committing sexual violence and a 31% increase in the acceptance of rape myths by men (Paolucci et al., 2000) and that rape myth acceptance has been repeatedly positively correlated to all forms of porn (violent or non-violent) due to the degradation and sexualisation of women contained within the materials (Van Maren, 2014; Long, 2012; Dines, 2011).

These issues could be central to prevention strategies. For example, if women and girls are consistently framed as sexual objects in widely consumed media and pornographic materials, then abuse, sexual assaults, rapes and harassment may be perceived as 'the norm' for the way women and girls will be treated in society, in their relationships and in sexual intercourse.

Before we move on, it is imperative that pornography is not discussed passively, as if there is no harm or sexual violence occurring to the actresses themselves. It is argued that the population of porn actresses and sex workers who appear in pornography has been very difficult to access for research purposes and therefore many of the reports about experiences in this line of work are anecdotal or from small sample size qualitative interview studies.

Despite this, there is justified concern for the women in porn ranging from the way they are targeted, recruited, deceived, exploited, abused and threatened by their pimps, directors, co-stars and agents (Long, 2012).

A number of world-famous porn actresses have quit the industry to speak out about the exploitation and abuse they have experienced. Their personal experiences provide an insight into the way pornography and objectification relates to victim blaming and self-blame with many of the actresses now working for the Antipornography.com campaign.

Across interviews with a variety of actresses (and actors) the alarmingly well-hidden examples of rape, sexual assault and increasingly dangerous, painful and degrading sex acts are discussed as factors that cause normalisation and escalation of the derogatory attitudes towards women in the industry.

These anecdotal experiences support past arguments from Garcia (1984) that the more sexually violent the material, the more likely the observer is to accept pro-rape attitudes and to perceive that women do not suffer significant trauma from rape (Malamuth & Donnerstein, 1982).

Actresses that reported feeling objectified and victimised are now campaigning against the hyper-sexualisation of women and the strategic recruitment of naïve, young amateurs into porn where they are quickly abused, exploited and addicted to drugs to cope with the pain and treatment from Directors and other actors (Antipornography.com, 2016).

They give detailed accounts of being coerced or forced into scenes that were non-consensual or unexpected and then being threatened with their pay cheque to continue performing. After submitting to the Director's demands, the women blame themselves for being stupid, naïve and not being worth anything more than the body that is being used.

Victim blaming, rape myths and misogyny

If sexual violence against women is presented as the norm, prevention strategies may focus on what women could have done differently to protect themselves from inevitable sexual violence, rather than stopping perpetrators of sexual violence. Clearly, the victim blaming of women and girls may play a role in which prevention strategy is developed and adopted. If women and girls are sexualised and objectified as a social norm, rather than telling perpetrators not to rape, we may issue advice to women about covering their bodies and ensuring that they do not lead men on.

When I conducted interviews with women (discussed in Chapter 15) who had been blamed for not preventing rapes and sexual assaults against them, I found that women were being encouraged, advised or forced to change something about themselves as a 'preventative' measure.

Among the things women had changed about themselves to prevent sexual violence, women had cut their hair off, wore baggier clothes, hid their body shape, quit their jobs, moved areas, stopped walking home from work, stopped dancing and singing, stopped hugging friends and family and stopped drinking alcohol or socialising in bars and clubs. One of the key findings from my interviews was a theme that suggested that women who were blamed for sexual violence were given 'prevention' and 'protection' advice that involved changing herself, despite most women understanding that it would not really protect them from an abusive partner or rapist.

Whilst rape myths and victim blaming from the 1960s through to the 1990s often cited the clothing of the woman and her modesty (Burt, 1980; Brownmiller, 1970; Eaton, 2019); other rape myths communicated by the mass media have focussed on extreme, rare and unusual sexual violence against women – which has played a role in the prevention advice being given to women and girls.

The mass media tend to report on the rarest cases of rape and sexual violence (stranger rapes, sudden abductions, imprisonments). Whilst this makes sense from a 'news' perspective (to sensationalise rape as the 'stranger waiting in the dark alley', to gather more clicks and shares or to attract more readers to the website), it can reinforce stereotypes about rape and sexual assault and can increase the misconception that most rapes and sexual assaults happen to women and girls when they are walking home alone and are violently attacked by a stranger (Brownmiller, 1975; Ward, 1995; Payne et al., 1999; Eaton, 2019). Over half of media reports of rape describe a rape that has occurred in a deserted public place and committed by a stranger (Maier, 2008), despite this being one of the rarest forms of sexual violence (Sleath and Woodhams, 2012; Eaton, 2019).

Victim blaming is also prevalent in the media and directly affects attitudes towards sexual violence. For example, results from a content analysis of television dramas found that 42% of storylines depicted a female "wanting" to be raped, 38% depicted a female victim lying about rape, and 46% featured females "asking" to be raped (APA, 2007). In an experimental study examining whether newspaper headlines influence readers, Franuik et al. (2008b) exposed participants to an article with either a rape myth-endorsing or non-rape myth endorsing headline. Results showed that participants exposed to the rape myth endorsing headline were less likely to believe that the perpetrator was guilty of rape and more likely to hold rape-supportive attitudes about women and girls.

An international report that reviewed studies and law enforcement estimates reported that approximately 2–8% of reported sexual assaults are believed to be false (Lonsway et al. 2007). However, the general perception of false rape allegations is much higher. In 1980, Burt found that half of men and women from a community sample believed that women lie about being raped and almost thirty years later, Kahlor and Morrison (2007) found that participants believed that an average of 19% of sexual assault and rape accusations were false.

Culkanz (2000) outlined the most common messages on prime-time TV:

- Women often lie about rape
- Rapists are always a stranger
- Women are responsible for their attack due to how they behaved or what they wore
- Rapists are mentally ill or psychologically abnormal
- Women who are raped must prove their prior sexual purity to be taken seriously
- Black men are more likely to rape women than White men

As so many people watch television (such as soap operas, dramas and documentaries) on a daily or weekly basis, it is important to explore how the stories of the rape and sexual assault of women and girls are told in fiction, too. Culkanz (2000) outlined the most common messages on prime time TV as being that women and girls often lie about rape, that rapists are always a stranger, that women are responsible for their attack due to how they behaved or what they wore, that rapists are mentally ill or psychologically abnormal, that women and girls who are raped must prove their prior sexual purity to be taken seriously and that Black men are more likely to rape women than White men.

TV shows increasingly focus on policing and law; therefore, it is important to examine how this potentially contributes to victim blaming in prevention campaigns and responses to sexual violence.

Whilst it could be argued that this extra media exposure to sexual violence could increase awareness of the general viewing population, the success of this would depend on the nature and the style in which the drama productions represented rape and sexual assault. For example, when hit TV show 'Glee' ran a storyline about sexual abuse of a boy, RAINN (2014) reported that their online chat service usage increased by 60% and calls to their National Sexual Assault Hotline increased by 80%. Not only this, but because the storyline was based on a male experiencing sexual abuse, RAINN (2014) also reported a large increase in men and boys calling for support about their own sexual abuse.

However, if storylines are stereotypical and contain victim blaming responses from authority figures in crime and law contexts, this could have a detrimental impact on the public and professional attitude towards women subjected to sexual violence. Examples of such shows are the multiple CSI series', Law and Order: Special Victims Unit and Criminal Minds, all of which contained examples of victim blaming and rape stereotypes. This was explored by Magestro (2015) who suggested that over one quarter of all aired episodes of Law and Order: SVU and CSI are based on the rape of women.

Magestro provides the examples of victim-blaming language use in NCIS such as a police officer saying 'she got herself raped and killed' (Magestro, 2015, p.8) and the repeated use of the word 'relationship' instead of the word 'abuse' or 'rape'. Also discussed are the general storylines and possible effects on the viewer. All ten of the rape storylines featuring in the first ten seasons of NCIS (100% of episodes) were found to blame the woman or girl for her rape (Magestro, 2015).

Further examples include a storyline in which a woman is seen as undeserving of empathy and justice because she had an online dating profile whilst her husband was away serving in the military and another involving a girl being raped which concluded with suggesting she had made up the accusation. Magestro (2015) also found several jokes and threats of rape including a police officer mocking a man about being raped 'like prom queen on prom night' in prison (Magestro, 2015, p.13).

Crime and law dramas are not the only shows to discuss or depict rape and sexual assault. As previously discussed, British national chat shows, such as ITV 'This Morning', have found themselves at the centre of justified criticism due to the way their presenters and journalists have discussed rape to an audience which averages 1 million people per day in the UK.

Television, film, advertisements and pornography have been shown to have considerable impact on the perception of sexual violence and of women subjected to such violence. But as technology has advanced, media is more than just television and film – and the messages about sexual violence have spread to gaming. Violent and sexist video games, such as Grand Theft Auto (GTA) that had sold over 220 million copies in February 2016 (IGN, 2016) have been shown to reduce empathy for female victims of sexual violence (Gabbiadini et al. 2016).

Gabbiadini et al (2016) argue that male characters tend to be hyper-masculine and aggressive and all the female characters in the game are prostitutes, pole dancers and victims of the male characters; females in this game are therefore sex objects. For example, players of GTA can have sex with a prostitute but then make the decision in game play to kill her after the sex and steal their money back (Gabbiadini et al., 2016). The researchers concluded that playing video games in first-person that endorsed violent, abusive and sexist behaviours towards women increased the masculine beliefs of adolescent male players and therefore reduced the empathy towards victims of sexual violence and increased their levels of acceptance towards violence against women.

In a more extreme example, a popular immersive computer game called 'Rapelay' was released in 2006 which was available worldwide through Amazon.com and Microsoft. The game was a first-person story-mode from the perspective of a man who stalks and rapes a mother and her two child daughters. Whilst tracking them down, the person playing the game can sexually assault, rape, gang rape or kill other women. The gameplay includes incredibly graphic scenes and even has 'forced fellatio' option and an 'internal ejaculation' counter. It took three years for government officials to launch campaigns against the game and its creators in Japan. Despite clearly encouraging and glorifying the rape and sexual assault of women and girls, the large scale action to ban the game was met with confusion from the creators, fans of the game and even academics who argued that there are thousands of games that depict worse crimes than rape, including murder and war crimes. The game is no longer available to purchase from the creators and Amazon agreed to delete any listings of new or used versions of the game in 2009.

It appears that mass media in all its forms, is the vehicle in which sexual violence is embedded as normal, trivial, exciting and fun – and women and girls are framed as sexual objects to be used and abused. However, there may also be a problem with the media being used to raise awareness about sexual violence.

An interesting criticism by Kitzinger (1999) considers wider media influences such as posters, adverts, articles, case studies and even sexual violence support organisations and campaigns that are often forced to use the most extreme examples of rape and sexual assault to push governments, authorities and public to take the issue seriously or to campaign for change. This results in frequent representations of rape and sexual assault that include severe physical injuries, stranger rapes, unfamiliar places, night-time scenarios and 'vulnerable' girls and women. The distorted 'real rape' scenario is therefore upheld and reinforced not only for general public and for those working in the criminal justice system, but for women and girls who have been subjected to sexual assault or rape and may be questioning whether what happened to them was really a sexual offence (Campbell, 2009; Eaton, 2019).

This frequent misrepresentation of sexual violence as occurring outside, in dark unfamiliar places, perpetrated by violent strangers has been recognised in the forensic psychology literature for decades, with Williams (1984) naming it 'The Classic Rape'. This is central to discussions of prevention, as the classic rape stereotype teamed with the previously discussed victim blaming, sexualisation and objectification of women and girls has arguably led to some questionable prevention strategies in the UK.

11.

How does the education system teach us to blame women?

Schooling provides a mixture of organisational and social structure and close peer relationships with lots of children around the same age as the individual. A review of the literature has revealed that schooling and RSE has an important links to victim blaming and self-blame in sexual violence. The links to victim blaming vary from the way traditional notions of education are seen to perpetuate gender roles right the way through to the sexual harassment and assault of girls in schools where they feel their complaints are not taken seriously and that sexual violence is a normal everyday occurrence.

The school as a victim blaming environment

Researchers have shown considerable curiosity about whether schools promote gender role stereotypes and the oppression of females for decades.

In 1992, Bailey wrote about the way teachers socialise girls from a very early age to be quiet, neat, calm and to recognise popularity and likeability as important characteristics whereas boys were socialised to speak out, be independent and active. Not only that, but when boys were surveyed, they ranked competence and independence higher than the girls, who ranked popularity and being well-liked as their most important characteristics at school. Bailey (1992) argues that this is coming from the school as an environment and as a social structure.

Reay (2001) found that teachers were more accepting of boys showing disruptive behaviour but labelled girls who showed assertive, disruptive behaviour in contradiction to traditionally accepted femininity as, 'real bitches'.

Chapman (2015) gives examples in which masculinity is prized in schools and femininity is posed as a weakness, providing fertile ground for sexism and misogyny in schools – where doing anything 'like a girl' is an age-old insult and the boys bully the girls and weaker, 'less masculine' boys.

Teachers have also been found to hold strong gender biases about students such as stating that boys are naturally better at math and science subjects and girls are more emotional and defined by their relationships with the boys. Studies have shown that teachers give significantly more supportive time to male students in secondary schools; which has shown to result in girls being behind their male peers by the end of secondary schools despite being ahead of them at the end of primary school (Chapman, 2015).

So why does this environment relate to victim blaming and self-blame in sexual violence?

As this book has already established, victim blaming and self-blame seems to be strongly linked with gender role stereotypes, insidious sexism, rape myths and the objectification of women and girls.

A recent example of how schools are perpetuating these issues is the argument raging in the press for the last three years about the way girls' school uniforms are 'distracting male teachers and students.'

This message directly blames sexual harassment, male comments and male behaviours on the clothing worn by female children. There have been nationally published examples of schools banning skirts due to male teachers feeling distracted and due to male students touching and making comments about the girls. Instead of responding to the fact that the school potentially had male teachers who viewed their female children sexually and male students who were sexually harassing their female students based on what they were wearing – the school decided to ban skirts and to make the school uniform more conservative for girls.

The school may have been held up as an example of victim blaming and overt sexism but soon, many other schools were exposed for measuring skirt lengths, advising girls to wear shorts under their skirts, banning skirts, not allowing female students to show their collar bones, backs and shoulders, not allowing female students to wear shorts for PE and so on. It soon became apparent that schools were changing the behaviours and appearances of the girls as a solution to sexual harassment, comments and assaults in their school environment.

Clearly, the link can be made to the 'she was raped because she was wearing revealing clothing' rape myth and victim blaming rhetoric. One school was found to have implemented these rules and then written a letter to female students which stated that the new rules were to ensure that 'boys don't intimidate or target you'. This complete disregard for the sexually harmful behaviours of the male student population and the focus on the clothing of the female children is a current and relevant example of victim blaming in modern day schools in the UK and in the US.

In 2016, the Women and Equalities Committee published a parliamentary report entitled 'Sexual Harassment and Sexual Violence in Schools', describing the issue as 'widespread' and recommending that OFSTED include the reduction of sexual harassment and sexual violence against girls as part of their inspection schedule. The report found that 5500 sexual offences were committed by school children against other school children within the school between 2012-2015 which included 600 rapes. The report also published key findings I have included below:

In 2016, the Women and Equalities Committee published a parliamentary report entitled 'Sexual Harassment and Sexual Violence in Schools'.

- 5500 sexual offences were committed by school children against other school children within the school between 2012-2015 which included 600 rapes.
- 71% of school children reported hearing sexual name calling such as 'slut', 'slag', 'whore' and 'bitch' every single day
- 59% of girls had been sexually harassed in their school or environment
- 29% of 16-18-year-old girls had experienced unwanted sexual touching in the school environment
- 22% of girls aged 7-12 years old reported experienced 'sexual jokes' or 'sexual banter' from boys at school.
- Boys pulling down girl's trousers or lifting their skirts up was commonplace by the age of 10 years old

---

The national report consulted with schools, third sector organisations, councils and young people to understand the experiences and prevalence of sexual harassment and sexual violence in schools around the UK and found that boys pulling down girl's trousers or lifting their skirts up was commonplace by the age of 10 years old and that sexual bullying, sexism and sexual violence (including harassment) are normal, everyday occurrences by the age of 13 years old.

Within the report, academics and practitioners offered theories as to why this culture may flourish in UK schools, with many of the explanations focus on the insidious nature of sexism, the 'lad culture' in which boys and adults normalise and justify sexual harassment and sexual violence against the girls due to it being viewed as inevitable, normal or just 'boys being boys'.

Some pedagogical arguments were made that the curriculum and school environment is inherently sexist and that education in sex and relationships for children was not being prioritised which was evidenced by a fall in SRE teaching hours across the UK which have been decreased by 21% in the last three years with schools registered as academies not having to provide sex and relationships education at all (Women and Equalities Committee, 2016).

Victim blaming in sex and relationships education

Current sex and relationships education (SRE) was criticised for being inadequate and for employing 'shock tactics' and 'victim blaming' with the report giving examples of teachers who excused the sexual assault of girls in the school if she was not behaving 'appropriately' (Women and Equalities Committee, 2016). The survey of young people revealed that over 50% of children would not tell their teachers if they were being sexually harassed or assaulted at school because it would not be taken seriously.

Over 40% of schools were found to have inadequate teaching around sex and relationships education with only 3% of teachers saying that they felt confident teaching and supporting students in this area. Comments from Ringrose also criticise current sex and relationship education as being based on preventing pregnancy, preventing disease and about girls managing the sexual urges of the boys.

In addition, the report criticised the use of 'awareness raising films' which were based on fear, shame and risk taking of girls. Focus groups undertaken as part of this report found that these types of films in which a girl is depicted being sexually harassed, assaulted or becoming the victim of shared sexual images actually lead the children to victim blame the girl in the film despite the fact that the perpetrator in the films were clearly shown to have committed or forced sexual acts without consent. Schools were reported as currently developing programmes in which all of the girls in the school year must attend on topics such as 'combatting and preventing sexual violence and harassment' and then doing absolutely nothing with the boys in the year group, with some schools reporting that they just ask the boys to watch a short film, explaining that the boys are emotionally illiterate and uninterested in the topic (Haste, 2013).

Women and Equalities Committee Report (2016) found:

- Current SRE was criticised for being inadequate and for employing 'shock tactics' and 'victim blaming'

- Teachers excused the sexual assault of girls in the school if she was not behaving 'appropriately'

- 50% of children would not tell their teachers if they were being sexually harassed or assaulted at school 'because it would not be taken seriously'

- 40% of schools were found to have inadequate teaching around sex and relationships education

- Only 3% of teachers reported that they felt confident teaching and supporting students in this topic

In 2012, NSPCC published a qualitative report about the impact of 'sexting' on boys and girls in schools in the UK. The researchers conducted focus groups and interviews with children between 11 and 16 years old and found that the foundations of 'girls are sluts but boys are congratulated' if they are sexually active underpinned many of the experiences of girls and boys who had taken part in the interviews.

Behaviours such as asking for, collecting and taking 'bare' photos on smartphones and then sharing them without permission to 'expose' girls was commonplace. Whilst the action of taking and sharing sexually explicit images (even when self-generated) is the topic of current national debate around youth behaviours, this report went on to talk to the young people about their thoughts on sexual images and sexual behaviours which revealed ample evidence of victim blaming of the girls in the schools.

Examples include a 14 year old girl, Kylie, who told an interviewer that that she was asked to write 'JASON OWNS ME' across her breasts by her boyfriend who had recently told her to wear shorts under her school skirt at all times to prevent other boys touching or seeing her legs.

Shorts under her skirt

She told the interviewer that her boyfriend had advised her that if she wore the shorts under her skirt, no one could say she was asking for it. The reports states that Kylie understood his 'advice' in terms of him being protective of her. This is a clear example of victim blaming and absorption of self-blame between two children at school, employing the common rape myth that girls and women who are seen to be wearing revealing clothes (in this case, school uniform) then they are seen as asking for sexual attention. This led to a teen boy advising a teen girl to cover her body so other boys did not sexually touch her.

Kylie admitted that her boyfriend, Jason, lifted her skirt up every day to 'check' that she was wearing the shorts and would question her about her motives if she was not wearing shorts under her skirt, even in summer weather. Whilst this clearly shows that Jason felt that Kylie should have to cover her body and protect herself from sexual touching and sexual attention from other boys, it also gives an example of control of her sexuality and her appearance which was another common theme in the report (NSPCC, 2012).

When boys as young as 12 years old were interviewed, they told interviewers that they often touched or grabbed girls as they walked past them in the school because the girls provoked them and wanted it, whilst then explaining that 'it wasn't like they were raping them, it was only touching them up'.

This example came from a focus group of young boys who had adopted victim blaming to excuse why they would touch, grab, 'dagger' (which meant to force a girl to the ground and to dry hump them from behind) and pinch girls that walked past. The excuses given were multi-faceted – that the girls provoked them to act in this way, that the girls wanted this to happen to them and then a minimising explanation at the end, that it was not as bad as actual rape. This second example and many others in this report provided evidence that young children used common rape myths and victim blaming responses when questioned about their behaviours towards girls.

Sexy but not a slut… again

Finally, a 14-year-old boy, Raja, explained to interviewers that girls who had self-respect would not send sexual images in the first place so they deserve to have them shared because any girl who shares pictures of herself is a 'slag'.

When the researcher asked him whether that was the same for boys who shared topless pictures of their six-pack, he laughed and said that its different with girls because they should 'act appropriately and dress appropriately if they want to be respected' by him.

This final example from the report displays evidence of victim blaming based on the common explanation that victims of sexual violence have no class, self-respect or were seen to contravene the accepted feminine gender role and therefore deserve whatever happens to her. What is interesting about his comment on 'self-respect' was that boys in these interviews were found to say that the girls who refused to send them pictures had self-respect but were simultaneously described as frigid and no fun. The girls were also reported to be very aware of this assigned dichotomy and were fighting a constant battle to be seen as fun and sexually mature but not to be seen as a slut and lacking self-respect because then they would be harassed, used and sexually assaulted and then blamed for it.

It is apparent just from this small collection of evidence that the school environment as an influential social structure harbors and perpetuates sexist and victim blaming cultures through the teaching styles, support, responses to sexual bullying and the ignorance of sexual harassment in schools every day.

This is teamed with a population of school children who are already employing victim blaming to excuse and to explain sexual behaviours of boys and of girls in their peer groups. This toxic pairing of a long term environment in which an authority perpetuates or ignores misogyny and victim blaming whilst the children employ victim blaming to navigate conversations about sex and sexual relationships means that the school environment is a prominent meso/exosystem factor contributing to victim blaming of women and girls who have been subjected to sexual violence.

12.

How do mental health services blame women?

It was of vital importance to include a chapter on the way our current approaches to mental health and trauma seek to blame women and girls for the responses they have to male violence.

As discussed in the introductory chapter, women have been pathologised for centuries. Even the most respected and cited philosophers and scientists described women as defective, deformed versions of men who had mental and physical health issues that no one could decipher (or cared to decipher).

As the systems of mental health moved from burning and drowning women to exorcising and torturing women, to isolating and sectioning women and then towards diagnosing and medicalising women – we have continued to blame women and girls for responding to trauma and abuse.

It is no secret that many of the mental health issues and symptoms that psychiatrists use to tell women and girls that they are disordered or mentally ill are related to abuse, trauma and oppression. Mental health sequalae are normal and common after women and girls have been subjected to male violence.

And yet, as I write this book in 2020, we are still commonly telling women and girls that their responses are unnatural, disordered, irrational and over-emotional.

This response has its roots in misogyny and sexism. To understand it, we must critically analyse the gender role stereotypes women and girls are forced to perform – and what happens when they do not conform.

Women and girls are expected to conform to the feminine stereotype. The feminine stereotype includes everything from what we wear, how we look, who we are attracted to, what body type we have, how we speak, our lifestyle, our ambitions, our role within the family and community to our likes and dislikes, hobbies, talents, knowledge and opinions.

When a woman or girl falls outside of these expected norms, she is likely to be criticised, humiliated or oppressed. This is no different within the realms of mental health and wellbeing.

A brief overview of history

From the 18th century, 'hysteria' was classed as a women's disease, linked to femininity and the female form. Laycock (1840) wrote that, 'Hysteria is the woman's natural state' and some decades later, Mitchell (1885, p.266) wrote, 'The hysterical girl is a vampire who sucks the blood of the healthy people around her.'

The word 'hysteria' comes from Ancient Greek which was used to describe the female uterus, and the belief from 4th and 5th centuries BC that the female uterus can move around the body, causing health issues and mental health issues. This mythical health issue was named 'wandering womb syndrome' and hysteria was listed as a medical disease until 1952.

Interestingly, theorists and philosophers believed that hysteria mostly affected childless women, women without husbands, women who did not have enough sex and women who had different sexual attractions and needs. Here, we can see that these are two examples of women who do not conform to the gender role stereotypes of the feminine woman.

Not surprisingly, the original cure for hysteria was for women to have more sex with men. It was believed that women's menstrual blood and the 'retention of the female seed' was causing hysteria.

Later on, in the 17th century, women and girls showing signs of trauma and mental health issues were accused of being possessed by demons. Whilst sex with men and getting married were still seen as the most effective cures for hysteria, masturbation for single women was seen as sinful or taboo.

By the 19th century, the concept of hysteria was being discussed in more and more 'scientific' ways. Rather than believing the uterus was wandering around the body, doctors started to argue that hysteria was caused by disorders of the brain in women.

However, in the wider context of women's trauma and mental health, the attack on gender non-conforming women continued.

Women were being sectioned, medicated and tortured for decades in asylums and hospitals for so many different reasons that any woman or girl could find herself in there, with no way to get out.

It is clear from the list of reasons for admittance to the asylum that women could be sectioned and treated for anything from reading books to not having enough sex with their husbands (again).

When looking carefully at the list, it is important we consider how women in the 19th century would have been perceived if they studied, were interested in politics, used their intellect and refused to marry or date men. Depressingly, not much has changed.

Reasons women were admitted to asylum

West Virginia Hospital for the Insane (1899)

- Novel reading
- Ill treatment by husband
- Imaginary female troubles
- Immoral life
- Over taxing mental powers
- Menstrually deranged
- Political excitement
- Religious enthusiasm
- Dropsy
- Masturbation
- Grief
- Not fulfilling wifely duties
- Studying

Whilst we might not section and medicate women for 'over taxing mental powers' or 'not fulfilling wifely duties' anymore – there are still psychiatric diagnoses that rely on gender role stereotypes and denying male violence towards women and girls.

Borderline Personality Disorder (BPD) and Emotionally Unstable Personality Disorder (EUPD)

In 2019, women and girls are 7 times more likely to be diagnosed with BPD or EUPD than boys and men showing the same symptoms. This is despite clear guidance from NICE (2020) which states that children under the age of 18 years old should never be diagnosed with personality disorders. This advice is routinely ignored and thousands of girls in the UK are told that they have borderline personality disorder or emotionally unstable personality disorder. It is common in girls in looked after care services and girls who have disclosed abuse, violence and exploitation. Again, the origins of this oppression hark back to hundreds of years ago.

Emotionally Unstable Personality Disorder (EUPD) is the latest rebranding of Borderline Personality Disorder, which was an updated way of diagnosing people (mainly women) whom doctors felt 'bordered' on psychotic.

According to current NHS (2020) definitions, BPD is:

> *'A disorder of mood and how a person interacts with others. It's the most commonly recognised personality disorder. In general, someone with a personality disorder will differ significantly from an average person in terms of how he or she thinks, perceives, feels or relates to others.'*

Research shows that most of the BPD or EUPD diagnosis is based on gender role stereotypes and sexism. Women and girls are ideally polite, nice, happy, content, quiet, have no opinions or ambitions and live to serve others. 'Difficult women' are frequently diagnosed with borderline personality disorder (Ussher, 2013).

There are also diagnostic criteria around the sexuality of women and girls, including some vague indicators around 'being confused about their sexual preference' or 'changing their sexual preference', which most would agree, is inherently homophobic.

The typical 'borderline patient' has been described as a 'demanding, angry, aggressive woman', who is labelled as 'mentally disordered' (Jimenez, 1997: 162, 163) for behaving in a way that is perfectly acceptable in a man. Research found that men's sadness and anger was considered to be related to situational factors – such as 'having a bad day' – whereas sad or angry women were judged as 'too emotional' (Barrett and Bliss-Moreau, 2009).

Indeed, I always make the point of telling frontline practitioners that the diagnostic criteria from DSM II for 'hysteria' and the diagnostic criteria from DSM V for 'borderline personality disorder' are very similar. Hysteria has been described as the 'wastebasket of mental health' and BPD has been described as a 'catch-all diagnosis'.

They are essentially the same diagnosis. They are both targeting women and girls. They are both built around gender role stereotypes. They both oppress traumatised and abused women. Where hysteria (or 'wandering womb syndrome') was said to be caused by women's hormones and biology – BPD is said to be a disordered personality. Both innate, internal causes which need to be medicated, treated and dealt with.

The 'symptoms' or 'diagnostic criteria' of BPD are:

- Fear of abandonment
- Unstable or short relationships
- Unclear or shifting/changing self-image
- Impulsive, self-destructive behaviours
- Self-harm
- Mood swings lasting minutes or hours
- Feelings of emptiness
- Intense anger
- Feeling suspicious, paranoid or disassociating

Most people would agree with me when I say the following three things:

1. Anyone who is traumatised by abuse or exploitation would hit enough of these criteria to be diagnosed with a personality disorder

2. Most people at pretty much any point of major stress, would exhibit these behaviours as a normal response to distress and change

3. These feelings are completely justified in traumatised and abused women – and therefore do not constitute a disorder or abnormality. These responses are normal.

We need to think much more critically about how many of the girls and women on our caseloads are being told that their responses are abnormal and are caused by personality disorders, rather than caused by the people who abused, oppressed, scared and harmed them. Why would we want to collude with the victim blaming and encouragement of self-blame of women and girls like this?

Timoclea (2020) found that professionals discussed women with a diagnosis of personality disorder in derogatory and harmful ways – with one professional calling the women they worked with 'demonic, little mini-skirted Machiavelli's'. By interviewing professionals working with women in the criminal justice system, Timoclea (p.9) argued that, 'clinicians often diagnose BPD in women based on judgments regarding her perceived social desirability.'

Similar arguments can be made for women and girls who display anger. Angry women were often characterised as problematic, disordered, mentally ill or dangerous. It is not socially desirable for women and girls to be angry, challenging or articulate.

This is especially true when considering that anger can be used to diagnose personality disorders in women and girls – even when their anger is justified. This is a clear example of secondary victim blaming – the woman is pathologised and 'treated' because she is angry that she was raped, abused, oppressed or harmed by male violence. In this approach, women are not allowed to express their anger, because their anger breaches the gender role stereotype of femininity and is therefore abnormal, or unhealthy.

There are many examples of natural responses to trauma and abuse being used to pathologise women and girls after they have been subjected to male violence. In 'The Little Orange Book: Learning about abuse from the voice of the child', Dr Claire Paterson-Young and I wrote about the way girls who have been abused can be pathologised and diagnosed with 'attachment disorder'.

Attachment 'disorder'?

A further example of the pathologisation of common trauma responses to sexual violence comes from attachment theory. Research in attachment has often been nuanced, but the same cannot be said for practice. Frontline workers are often taught that there are four main styles of attachment in children – and that attachment styles are static and affect/direct the child for the rest of their lives.

More recent research has rejected the notion of fixed attachment styles that are static over the lifetime, arguing that children (and adults) can have many different attachment 'patterns' with many different people in their lives. A child can have a very unhealthy attachment to an abuser, but a very secure attachment to their grandparents, for example.

Meins (2017) started an important debate in the British Psychological Society magazine, in which she argued that attachment was being overrated and overused to 'predict' outcomes of children or to pathologise them as disordered. Meins (2017) also argued that a large proportion of the population would be categorized as having 'insecure attachments' and that the most recent research clearly showed that attachment was fluid, changeable, and individual to each person in the life of the child.

Deana*

Deana was 11 when a group of her family members started to sexually abuse her at family gatherings. They took videos and photographs of the abuse and shared the imagery online with paedophile networks. As she got older, the family members took Deana to hotels on motorways where people from the online networks paid her family to rape and abuse her.

At 15 years old, Deana was taken into care by the local authority and legal action started against her parents and wider family.

In care, Deana trusted no one. When professionals showed her care, attention, and respect, she rejected them and became defensive. She refused to be left alone with any staff members and she was unable to form a healthy relationship with any of them. At school and in the home, Deana struggled to maintain friendships or relationships with anyone. If anyone got too close to her, she would push them away or make allegations about them so she could be alone again.

After a few months, staff asked for a referral for Deana to CAMHS who diagnosed her with a borderline personality disorder and attachment disorder.

The issue with examples such as the one above is that Deana's trauma responses were perceived as abnormal and problematic. Her coping mechanism was to defend herself against any further harm from people who profess to care for her.

Throughout her abuse and trafficking, her parents and family had always told her that they loved her and cared about her, and that she was special. She knew that when they started talking like that, they were going to do something bad to her.

In the example, Deana was taken into care where she trusted no one. She rejected any adults who showed her care, attention, and respect, likely because she had learned that this was a precursor to violence and abuse. Deana's coping mechanism after the abuse was to use what she had learned about humans (that they trick you into thinking you are cared for and loved in order to harm you further) to keep herself physically and psychologically safe from the new people, professionals, carers, and even other children.

Rather than viewing Deana's behaviours as adaptive coping mechanisms that were both useful and rational, they were viewed as symptoms of both a psychiatric disorder of the personality and a disorder of attachment.

For a girl to experience repeated rapes and abuse by people who professed their love and affection for her to then conclude that other people who treat her in that way are likely to be dangerous is not disordered – it is rational reasoning from a girl who is trying to keep herself safe.

The implication of these diagnoses is that interventions will begin to 'correct' or 'improve' these 'disorders', rather than accepting that the behaviours are coping strategies for cumulative and complex trauma. There will also be assumptions made about Deana's ability to form healthy relationships in the future, not only with new partners but possibly even with her own children.

This is something Meins (2017) raises as a central issue in the misunderstanding and overreliance on attachment as a predictive factor. She argues that attachment patterns are fluid and changeable across the life span and across the support network, and that other factors were more likely to an impact on the child and their outcomes, such as the presence of other vulnerabilities, trauma experiences, positive coping mechanisms, and resilience.

Recent experiences of women

All of these issues led me to invest in a large study in 2019 with 395 women who had been subjected to male violence. I wanted to explore their experiences of seeking help for their mental health after trauma caused by male violence. In particular, I was interested to hear from women about their own feelings about being diagnosed or treated for different mental health issues and whether they felt this helped or harmed them.

Of the 395 women who responded to the study, 87% of them reported that they felt the mental health professionals had a poor understanding of trauma arising from sexual and domestic violence.

One woman wrote:

> 'NHS CMHT's have been the least trauma informed in my experience. Have been quick to diagnose conditions rather than trauma. In many interactions, I was expected to talk about trauma in meetings, in depth, which could and did trigger flashbacks. When I explained it was emotionally harmful to continue to do that, unless in a therapeutic environment, I was told I was not willing to engage, hostile, dismissive, difficult, passive aggressive, rude among the more polite labels. 'Traumatised' I do not remember being mentioned or understood well at all.'

79% of the women said that they were diagnosed with at least one mental health issue after they disclosed sexual violence and abuse. Of these women, only 40% were told they had post-traumatic stress responses. The rest were diagnosed with psychiatric disorders ranging from personality disorders, psychoses and neuroses.

Of all women, 67% were given medication after they disclosed male violence – but only 17% were offered any trauma therapies. What was common however, was cognitive behavioural therapy (CBT). 42% of women were given CBT after they disclosed being subjected to male violence. This is concerning because the aim of CBT is to change the way the woman thinks and responds to those thoughts. It does not provide space to process or explore the sexual traumas.

In the study, women discussed the ways they felt about being diagnosed with disorders. The responses were varied, but most women wrote about the complex feelings of being diagnosed:

> *'I felt there was something wrong with me. My brain didn't work properly. Told to take tablets. I know what was wrong. I was shattered into fragments I could never find again after years of sexual violence, not being believed by social services and police, the CPS dropping my court case, domestic abuse in the family and my beloved precious younger siblings, being abandoned to a similar or worse fate. THAT was the issue.'*

Another woman wrote:

> *'Two months after it happened, I was diagnosed with type 2 bipolar. I wasn't 100% sure why because I'd never had anything that I agreed was a manic or hypomanic episode. I was definitely depressed but lots of the symptoms didn't match. At the time I just wanted to feel better, so I accepted the diagnosis, took medication and went to counselling but nothing really helped. So, at the time I probably would have said it was helpful but in hindsight it wasn't.'*

Reading the hundreds of accounts of women, in addition to working with women and girls for over a decade has definitely changed the way I feel about the psychiatric diagnosis of adults and children who have been subjected to violence, abuse and oppression.

Specifically, there is so much misogyny within psychiatry that I have become increasingly concerned with the way women and girls are told that their responses to male violence are abnormal, disordered and broken. The impact on women is evident – they believe they are ill and that there is something fundamentally wrong with them

Isn't this the ultimate form of victim blaming of women subjected to violence and trauma?

As Ussher (2013) sums up well:

> *'As the outspoken, difficult woman of the 16th century was castigated as a witch, and the same woman in the 19th century a hysteric, in the late 20th and 21st century, she is described as 'borderline' or as having premenstrual dysphoria disorder.'*

13.

An attack on the woman: All the other ways we blame her

This chapter contains factors which pertain only to the individual such as sexual experiences history, socio-demographics, biological/genetic factors and the experience of the assault itself. The factors at the individual level of the ecological model tend to be the factors that are most commonly cited in victim blaming and self-blame but are framed as arising from the individual, as if they exist in a vacuum.

However, it is understood that there are also factors at the individual level (such as their values, beliefs and perceptions of rape, sexual assault and gender) that are influenced by macrosystem level factors like rape culture, sexism, porn culture, rape myths and so on. This chapter provides evidence for considerable interaction between higher-level factors and individual factors. I will therefore acknowledge that the individual factors in victim blaming and self-blame may appear to sit with the individual but rarely arise in a vacuum within that individual and are likely to have originated from society or other external pressures and social norms.

This section is split into some of the most common individual level factors that were found to be discussed in the literature on victim blaming and self-blame. However, it would be impossible to cover them all in the depth they deserve and there are certain factors that lack the level of interest that other individual factors have received, resulting in little empirical research findings and conclusions.

As a brief overview, White (1984) identified just some of the variables that have been shown to impact on the way the woman and the rape is perceived and the way that the woman also perceives the rape experience. These variables included the types of behaviours of the woman during the sexual assault or rape, the personal details of the woman such as her age, her class, her life, her marital status, her personality, whether she knew the perpetrator of the rape or sexual assault before it occurred, when and how (or whether) she reported the rape to the police and how they then responded to her. White (1984) therefore argued that one of these, some of these and/or all of these factors can influence the way the woman and the rape is perceived by external people and can also have an effect on the way the woman understands what happened to her. Depending on the values, beliefs and messages she has absorbed throughout her life, this could lead to her blaming herself.

Acceptance of rape myths and sexual stereotypes

This section will focus on the impact that personal acceptance of rape myths and stereotypes have on the woman who has been subjected to rape or sexual assault herself. Studies have shown that when women absorb and accept rape myths and stereotypes, they are more likely to victim blame and more likely to self-blame, often citing common rape myths and stereotypes as their reasons for blaming themselves or not reporting their experience to the police (Woodhams and Sleath, 2012).

However, Payne (1999) has also argued that the acceptance of rape myths by women who may not have been subjected to rape or sexual assault actually serves to reduce feelings of vulnerability to future sexual violence by reinforcing stereotypical messages of how, why and who rape happens to so women can make decisions or take action to attempt to 'avoid' rape and sexual assault by not behaving or acting in the way of previous stereotypical and largely mythical victims.

For example, the large amount of mass media stories of women being attacked in dark places alone could have led to the common and frequent message given to women about never walking home alone – a message that is less likely to be given to men.

There is also evidence that rape myths affect the disclosure and reporting decisions of the individual. When women are subjected to rapes that conform to the widely accepted rape stereotype that includes injuries and physical violence, they are much more likely to identify as a victim of rape and are seven times more likely to report their experience to the police (Du Mont, Miller & Myhr, 2003; Clay-Warner & Burt, 2005).

Along the same lines, when women are raped by a stranger, they are much more likely to identify that event as rape and report it to the police (Campbell et al., 2001). This can be taken as evidence that the acceptance of rape myths appears to affect the identification of the event as a sexual offence and will be covered in more detail in the section below entitled 'Understanding of the word 'rape''.

Whether the woman identifies as having been raped or not appears to be closely related to how high their levels of rape myth acceptance are, meaning that the higher their acceptance of rape myths and rape stereotypes, the less likely they are to identify the event as a rape (Peterson & Muehlenhard, 2004). They are also more likely to blame themselves for the assault whilst taking away the responsibility from the perpetrator and refocusing on their own actions, behaviours and personal qualities (Harned, 2005).

This could be presented as a lifelong process of being exposed to rape myths, rape stereotypes and victim blaming messages that, in the first instance, give women erroneous beliefs and actions to take in order to convince themselves that they can stay safe if only they do not act, dress, speak or live in particular ways.

In addition, they have learned throughout this same lifelong process of exposure to only very specific types of stereotypical rapes, that there are a number of criteria that must be fulfilled for their experience to be a 'real rape', and only when they are certain that they have been fulfilled, will they identify as having been raped and then report that rape to the police.

The increase in self-blame when levels of rape myth acceptance are high is likely to be related to the confusion that would be caused when a woman is subjected to abuse or rape but not all of those criteria are fulfilled or when a woman is subjected to what she thinks might have been rape but perceives that her character or behaviours led to her own assault based on the rape stereotypes she has learned her whole life.

That argument is based on rape myths being fairly subtle and women transforming rape myths into victim blaming of their own volition but actually, there is no need for them to have done this themselves. As it has been shown in the section on mass media, women have been presented with overt victim blaming statements and explanations for rape and sexual assault from many different outlets during her life.

The relationship between rapes that do not conform to the 'perfect victim/violent rape' template and the blaming of the female victim is well documented and can commonly follow most reports of a rape or sexual assault of a woman in the mass media. Therefore, it is sensible to argue that women have been taught to criticise and dissect the behaviour, actions, character, history and intentions of the woman – even when that woman is themselves. This leads to thoughts of self-blame and moves the focus away from the perpetrator and back to the woman who has been subjected to the rape or sexual assault.

As other sections of this literature review have shown, even women who have been subjected to rape or sexual assault themselves can still retain high levels of rape myth acceptance and can still go on to victim blame other women despite having real lived experience. The fact that the real experience of being raped does not affect their own levels of rape myth acceptance or victim blaming is a testament to how influential these societal messages really are.

Previously subjected to child sexual abuse

A factor that appears to be thoroughly considered in the literature is whether the woman has previously been subjected to child sexual abuse and whether this has a relationship with self-blame and revictimisation after being subjected to more male violence in adulthood. Revictimisation is defined as the experience of sexual victimisation in childhood and then again in adulthood (Messman-Moore & Long, 2003).

Quantitative studies have shown a wide range of statistics that indicate that from 15-72% of children who were subjected to sexual abuse go on to be subjected to adult sexual assault or rape (Mason et al., 2008) with studies also showing that women who have been subjected to child sexual abuse are twice as likely to be subjected to adult sexual assault or rape than women who were never subjected to child sexual abuse (Ullman & Vasquez, 2015).

Studies that have sought to explore why this likelihood of subsequent revictimisation is so high have focussed on the individual behaviours, characters and circumstances of the person. Ullman and Vasquez (2015) found that an array of studies had reported that people who had been subjected to child sexual abuse had a greater number of partners, had more unprotected sex, were more likely to use alcohol and drugs prior to sex and were more likely to 'exchange sex for money'.

It could be argued that some of these are stretching tenuous links and are even employing rape myths if linking these behaviours with revictimisation and victim blaming, especially the higher number of sexual partners and the use of alcohol before sex, both of which are very common in modern sexual relationships.

In fact, Ullman & Vasquez (2015) found that most of those behaviours are common amongst adults and all but one of them has no relationship to prior abuse or subsequent abuse. The only behaviour that increased risk of revictimisation was the act of 'exchanging sex for money', which depending on the circumstances, could be another act of abuse and sexual exploitation in itself – and not an indicator of behavioural risk at all.

There is a relationship between being abused in childhood and women who blame themselves for being subjected to male violence later in life.

Results from Filipas & Ullman (2006) presented that over 42% of women who reported childhood sexual abuse also reported a further sexual assault or rape in adulthood and of those 42% of women, more than half of them blamed themselves at the time of the sexual abuse and over 40% of them still blamed themselves to the present day (the time of the study).

A number of explanations for these results have been offered including the social learning that occurs during childhood sexual abuse, the adaptation of maladaptive coping mechanisms such as characterological and behavioural self-blame and finally, the assertion that many perpetrators of sexual offences deliberately target women who appear to be vulnerable (Filipas & Ullman, 2006).

In terms of social learning, Seligman (1975) suggested that children who are sexually abused in a private, systematic manner learn about adult-child relationships, about interpersonal physical intimacy and about their self-worth from their perpetrator; eventually feeling helplessness and powerlessness as the abuse continues without any intervention from others. Over a period of time, the children either normalise the abusive experiences or they learn that they must accept the sexual abuse as a part of life.

This normalisation or acceptance of sexual abuse is said to put adult women who have been subjected to child sexual abuse at greater risk of sexual revictimisation and increase their propensity to self-blame.

Hazzard et al. (1995) did conduct a study related to this issue and to extend their work, it would be of value to explore whether the increased propensity to self-blame comes from the woman's adult understanding of 'real rapes' as they contrast those stereotypical rapes against their own experiences. It could be that women who self-blame as adults feel as though they 'should' have responded differently to the child sexual abuse and also to their adult experiences of sexual violence – which is something that will be discussed in greater detail in the section entitled 'behaviour during or after the assault'.

Due to the messages from the perpetrator to the child during the abuse (that it was their fault, that they deserved it, that they were special or that they wanted it to happen) and due to the wider societal messages and stigma about sexual abuse, women who are raped or sexually assaulted again in adulthood are more likely to believe that they brought the sexual violence upon themselves and that they deserve the abuse, or at the least, do not deserve to be truly loved (Filipas & Ullman, 2006).

To further this point about the absorption of societal messages about sexual abuse, even children appeared to employ rape stereotypes in their attributions of blame that are similar to the way adult women attribute blame. Hazzard et al. (1995) reported that girls and women were more likely to attribute blame to the perpetrator if greater levels of violence and physical force were used against them.

This is very close to the commonly held rape stereotype that for a rape to be a 'real rape' and the for victim to be considered the 'infallible victim' with lesser blame for what happened, there needs to be clear evidence of physical violence, force and injury to the victim. If this belief is perpetuated by rape culture and then other people that they disclose to throughout their lives, it makes sense that when they are adults they may not even realise they are being subjected to sexual assaults or rapes if the perpetrator does not employ violence or force.

This is one of the most damaging and successful outcomes of rape myths and misogynistic views of women – that women and girls are sufficiently socialised not to know what sexual violence really is, so men can continue to abuse, rape and harm them without women and girls ever knowing they are being violated.

Finally, women who have been sexually abused as children and then again as adults are likely to blame themselves, causing them to question their judgement, their own self-worth and their value in future relationships. The findings from Finkelhor & Browne (1986) showed that children who are sexually abused experience a myriad of mental health issues. There have also been findings that show that women who self-blame are much more likely to attempt suicide and much more likely to develop PTSD (Campbell et al., 2001).

Repeat revictimisation in adulthood

In 2005, a literature review conducted by Classen et al. (2005) found that two out of every three women who have been subjected to rape or sexual assault were revictimised more than once.

In a study by Mason et al., (2008), 271 of the 625 women in their sample reported a sexual assault or rape in the previous 12 months. When researchers went back to participants 12 months later, almost 60% of those women reported that they had been subjected to male violence again.

Despite a large number of studies confirming that there are some factors that appear to influence revictimisation, there is still no consensus or widely accepted theory to explain sexual revictimisation risk over the lifetime (Miller et al., 2011). However, blame and self-blame have been found to play an important role (Miller et al., 2007) in the adult literature surrounding sexual revictimisation with Mason et al. (2008) finding that women who have been subjected to repeated sexual assaults or rapes are significantly more likely to receive blaming reactions from others and that revictimisation is more likely when women blame themselves for a prior rape or sexual assault. Researchers also found that when women self-blame, they are less likely to show 'assertive refusals to sexual advances' in the future, with the lowest levels of assertiveness in sexual refusal predicting sexual revictimisation in a longitudinal study of women at college (Greene & Navarro, 1998).

The concept of sexual refusal assertiveness is a concerning one.

On the one hand, it appears that the topic is looking at the actions of women during unwanted sexual advances as they attempt to assert that they do not want the sex act to take place. However, the findings from many of these studies have crept into victim blaming fairly quickly. Authors argue that 'sexual refusal assertiveness' is protective against sexual revictimisation. Specifically, that women who show 'assertiveness' when refusing sex are less likely to be raped or sexually assaulted and that 'sexual refusal assertiveness' needs to be taught to all women and girls in schools and colleges to protect from completed rape or sexual assault.

When examining these findings in the context of victim blaming and self-blame and from a radical feminist perspective, it does sound very much like blaming women for not being 'assertive' enough. These studies pull the focus back to the behaviour of the woman during the assault and I would argue that it is not helpful or progressive for us to create programmes that will re-focus young women on how they 'should' assert that they do not want sexual intercourse and should be more assertive in sexual violence situations.

Whilst this shouldn't be about hanging the responsibility of the rape or sexual assault on the alleged lack of ability to refuse someone who is making unwanted sexual advances towards them, it could be that when women have been subjected to rape or sexual assault and have then gone on to blame themselves or have experienced victim blaming from their support network or people in authority, it may have left them with a feeling of helplessness, worthlessness and dehumanization.

This could have an impact on the way they respond to future situations of sexual violence if their last response was deemed inadequate by others or even by their own internal standards of how they expected to behave when faced with a forced sexual act. This finding of 'less assertiveness' should also take into account, the natural trauma responses of which three of them (friend, freeze and flop) would more than likely be perceived as 'less assertive' than the most traditional responses to trauma (fight and flight).

It is worth considering whether a woman who has a natural 'freeze' trauma response who therefore does not conform to the stereotypical standards of fighting the perpetrator off or screaming for help also reinforces her self-blame and feelings of guilt because she also expected herself to be able to fight off or get away from a rapist. Many women and girls I have worked with have been very confused as to why they were not able to move, speak or fight off the perpetrator. In their mind, they had always imagined that if a man ever attacked them, they would simply fight him off and scream for help. The majority of women and girls do not do this, because they are so traumatised, they are not able to.

There is also ample research that suggests that once the brain has developed a response to sexual trauma, it will repeat that response in all sexual traumas in an effort to minimise harm and to do what worked last time. In that case, could it be that women who are perceived as 'less assertive' in sexual refusals are actually experiencing the 'freeze' response to trauma (common to between

69%-89% of all women subjected to rape according to Moor et al. 2013) from the last time they were raped or sexually assaulted and are therefore experiencing a natural, self-preservation response to their experience of subsequent sexual trauma rather than a lack of sexual refusal assertiveness? Moor et al. (2013) concluded the study by recommending that the 'freeze' trauma response is considered in the literature on sexual refusal assertiveness given that it is the most common way to respond to a sexual assault or rape, rather than 'assertive refusal'.

Self-blame was found to predict sexual revictimisation in a study that considered the different thought processes that can occur after being subjected to a rape or sexual assault (Miller et al., 2007). Some women were found to engage in counterfactual thinking to consider how preventable their rape or sexual assault was and what they could have done differently, some also reported negative self-talk and negative thought processes about the self. Miller et al. (2010) concluded that these thought processes lead to future vulnerability, a perceived lack of control and a perception of inevitability of sexual violence. These cognition-based arguments could also lend an explanation to the issue of 'low assertiveness' in sexual refusal.

However, and this point is important to remember, much of the research on 'revictimisation' is influenced by positivist victimology and vulnerability theory. Therefore, revictimization is seen as a problem within the woman or girl – we start to ask, 'Why does this keep happening to her?' or 'Why does she keep putting herself in these situations?'

Due to this, much of the literature suggests that revictimization is due to something wrong with the woman: her character, her behaviour, her cognitions, her assertiveness or her beliefs.

I intend to challenge this in my next large piece of exploratory work starting this year. I am interested in the link between victim blaming women and revictimisation theories – and how we can show that women are not the cause of their own revictimisation, as I discussed in the introduction chapter of this book.

Personal characteristics – ethnicity, age and body type

Not only do the mass media and general public pay a great deal of attention to the personal characteristics of women who are subjected to sexual violence, this is also the case for researchers in this field. All three groups of people have searched (formally or informally) for causal links and relationships between characteristics of women such as their age, ethnicity, body type, sexual history and social status and their experience of sexual violence.

Whilst academic researchers are attempting to explore links objectively, there are deeply embedded cultural messages and assumptions made about women with particular characteristics that have led to them being blamed for being sexual assaulted or raped by men. This section will explore the literature surrounding the individual level factor: personal characteristics of the woman.

A lot of victim blaming and self-blame focusses on the factors in the assault or circumstance that are perceived as being within the control of the woman, such as the clothing she was wearing, the places she went and how she behaved. The fact that those factors are seen to be within the control of the woman means that people who blame victims can use arguments that suggest that the woman should have made better decisions or behaved in a different way. However, there is now more research being conducted that looks into the way women are blamed using factors that are outside of her control, such as her ethnicity, her body shape and her perceived attractiveness to others (Coates & Wade, 2004; George & Martínez, 2002; Maurer & Robinson, 2008).

Other research suggests that the factor most strongly associated with whether people blame the woman for being raped is her prior sexual history (Coates & Wade, 2004). However, some would argue that this is a factor that the woman had control over (how many sexual partners she had, how often she had sex etc.). I would argue that this factor could not be changed or controlled at the time of the rape or sexual assault and is therefore irrelevant to the motivation and actions of the sex offender.

The research goes on to explain that whilst chastity and purity are no longer commonplace in everyday life, the connotations of these traditional concepts still influence the perceptions of victims now. For example, Bogle (2008) argues that the rape of a sexually active 'unchaste' woman is still perceived as less serious than the rape of a virgin or sexually inactive woman.

Gotovac & Towson (2015) put forward the suggestion that women who are perceived to be overweight, in theory, should be blamed less for their rapes or sexual assaults based on the assumption that women who are overweight are sexually inactive. However, this was not to be the case. Their findings showed that anti-fat attitudes correlated with victim-blaming attitudes, meaning that women who were perceived as overweight were actually blamed more for being raped or sexually assaulted than women who were not perceived to be overweight. This contradicts the argument surrounding sexual history and activity. Instead, it started a discussion about whether it was because their lack of sexual activity was not a choice or a virtue, but because they were perceived as undesirable.

In trying to unpick this, Gotovac & Towson (2015) suggested that this is also related to rape stereotypes in which people may assume that a woman who was physically attractive was more likely to be raped, so therefore assume that a woman who was overweight and then deemed unattractive, was less likely to have been raped so must have provoked the rape.

In contrast to this idea, the Clarke & Lawson (2009) study which reported that female jurors were more likely to blame thin, attractive women (stereotypically connecting thin with attractive) due to assuming that they were raped because the man could not control his sexual urges, which is yet another rape stereotype.

When Clarke & Stermac looked at this issue again in 2011, the findings were similar in that thin women were blamed more than overweight women. So, Gotovac & Towson (2015) found that overweight women were blamed more than thinner women and Clarke and colleagues (2009, 2011) found that thinner women were blamed more than overweight women.

Both sets of authors give valid explanations for why this could be, both explanations based in rape stereotypes about blame and desert. However, whilst it is unclear as to which group of women is more likely to be blamed, one clear conclusion about weight can be drawn: it doesn't seem to matter whether women are perceived as thin or overweight – they can still be blamed for what men did to them, whether that is because they were perceived as so attractive that the man couldn't possibly help himself, or because they were perceived as so unattractive that the man must have been provoked to rape them. Both issues demonstrate how strong but illogical the pathway to victim blaming is.

Victim blaming is the solution, and the route to that solution can be literally anything we want it to be, it would seem.

In a national study of over 3,000 women, Kilpatrick et al. (1997) found that the biggest 'risks' for being subjected to sexual violence were minority status within a community and historical victimisation which is covered in other sections of this book. The statistics on prevalence for different ethnicities has been inconsistent but there are definite differences between ethnic groups.

When it comes to cross-cultural and cross-ethnicity studies in sexual violence, there are significant gaps in the literature. Again.

There needs to be much more research that does not 'control' for cultural differences and actually embraces them as an important factor. If sexual violence is being seen as a cultural issue, then differences between cultures should be the most obvious field of study. However, there is not much research that looks at the difference in victim blaming and self-blame across different ethnicities or cultures.

One piece of research that does look at these factors however is Mason et al. (2008) who reports that they did not find any differences between post-rape effects and coping strategies but did find differences in the messages and thoughts the women had about their experience in the context of their culture which led to self-blame.

African American women were found to be more likely to believe the 'Jezebel' image to explain why they were raped. The explanation put forward for this difference was the experience of feeling undervalued or discriminated against in society. This related to findings from Wyatt (1992) who found that African American women who had been subjected to rape felt at more risk of it happening again, than White women. However, this topic has also been covered by Maier (2008) in which she explores the experiences and responses to sexual violence by African American women in much more detail.

The discussion begins with the issues that hail back to slavery and colonialism, in a time where White people used Black women for whatever purpose they wanted. Due to Black women being oppressed as 'property' for such a long period in history, Maier (2008) argues that the enduring racist myth that African American women are 'unrapeable' and are sexually promiscuous by nature has increased their own feelings of objectification, self-blame and experiences of victim blaming by others.

Maier (2008) also goes on to describe three main racist stereotypes that harm African American women who have been subjected to rape or sexual assault, including the 'jezebel' image. The image of the sexualised, animalistic, rape-deserving African American woman has been found to be internalised by African

American women themselves, leading them to conclude that they would not get support from the criminal justice system, that they are to blame for what happened to them and that they would be treated less seriously than White women (Maier, 2008). These internal conclusions are not incorrect, though. Studies have shown that White people do view African American women who had been subjected to rape or sexual assault as more promiscuous than White women (Donovan, 2007). Therefore, Black women's fears about not being taken seriously by police or justice systems are also justified when studies have shown that both African American and White males and females perceived the rape or sexual assault of an African American women as less serious than the rape of an Asian or White woman (Foley et al., 1995; George & Martinez, 2002).

The study by Maier (2008) looks at whether rape advocates felt that Black women responded differently or faced different issues than White women who were subjected to rape or sexual assault. Findings showed that 57% of advocates believed that Black women do respond to rape differently or face different issues than White women do.

According to advocates, the most commonly cited differences were that Black women receive less support by their support network and are more likely to be blamed for bringing shame on their family (which supports the ego-centric versus socio-centric argument about the difference between shame and guilt in different cultures after rape or assault).

Maier et al. (2008) also discussed the experiences of Latina and Hispanic women and, consistent with findings from Miller et al. (2008), Latina women experience an increased level of shame and victim blaming. It is suggested that this is due to the strong gender role stereotypes employed within Latino culture and the way a woman's sexual purity and virginity denotes the dignity and honour of herself and her family.

This adherence to patriarchal and stereotypical ideas of a woman's role and worth could be leading to higher levels of self-blame in Latina women. As a result of this, Latina women blamed themselves for their rape or sexual assault more and experienced more victim-blaming from their support network than African American or European women (Lefley et al. 1993). These findings are similar to those from Williams in 1985, who found that Mexican American women who had been subjected to rape and assaults themselves were still more likely to self-blame, victim blame other women and were less likely to attempt to take any legal action against the men who raped them.

There are clearly differences between the victim blaming and self-blaming responses and experiences of women of different ethnicities, even in the small sample of studies that explore this factor.

However, a factor with an even smaller sample of studies to draw from is the experiences of older women who have been raped or sexually assaulted. No studies were found that explored the victim blaming or self-blame of older women who had been raped or sexually assaulted, but one of the most comprehensive studies of this nature is considered here in contrast to the high levels of victim blaming and 'real rape' scripts that have been shown to be prevalent in younger women throughout this literature review.

Lea et al. (2011) begins by discussing these rape scripts and stereotypes, stating that the stereotypes do not identify or even consider older women as a potential victim of a sexual offence which leads to the disbelief in older women's accounts. So much so, that longitudinal prevalence data for older women does not exist in the UK. Walby & Allen (2004) pointed out that the British Crime Survey (now known as Crime Survey England and Wales) only collated responses from respondents aged 16 to 59 years old until 2017. Therefore, all domestic and sexual violence data we had in the UK ignored the experiences of women over the age of 60 for the past 40 years. We have never had accurate data about how many older women (aged 59 and over) are being subjected to male violence. In 2017, the government lifted the maximum age of participants to 74 years old, which is arguably an improvement, but still begs the question: Why cut the data collection off at 74 years old? Why have a cut-off age at all for crime data?

There have been a very small number of studies that have sought to explore the experiences of women over 60 years old.

Muram et al. (1992) had a sample with a mean age of 69 years old of which they asked questions about the type of rape or sexual assault they experienced. They found an interesting set of characteristics that were significantly more likely for older women than younger women and were qualitatively more similar to the 'real rape' and 'infallible victim' stereotypes.

For example, they found that 79% of older women were raped by a stranger despite the fact that 72% of the rapes happened in their own homes. This suggests that the majority of older women were subjected to rape or sexual assault where a man gained entry to their home – and this suggestion is confirmed by the finding from Lea et al. (2011) who found that 73% of women were subjected to a 'surprise' attack in which the woman was approached suddenly within her own home with no prior knowledge of the offender, no prior conversation with the offender and with ample use of physical force and violence used to control the woman during the assault.

Whilst it is impossible to speculate whether older women experience victim blaming or self-blame based on the characteristics of their experience (because we have no data or studies to draw from), especially when the available literature suggests that they have been largely silenced, it is worth exploring the highly stereotypical nature of their assault when compared with the 'real rape' scenario.

The findings describe a rape in which a vulnerable older woman with no way to defend herself, is attacked by a complete stranger using ample force or violence. This is much more stereotypical than the varied experiences of younger women who are more often abused and raped by men they know or men they are in relationships with.

It is therefore of great interest to explore whether older women hold the same stereotypical views about rape and sexual assault that they have absorbed from society over decades. Would this mean that they identify as 'real' rape victims easier? Would they therefore blame themselves less and experience victim blaming less? Who knows? We never asked them.

This section considers some personal characteristics that have been explored in relation to victim blaming of women. It is concerning but necessary to conclude that a significant amount of personal and even protected characteristics come under scrutiny when a woman discloses sexual violence. Her appearance, her weight, her attractiveness, her age, her ethnicity and her colour all become factors that appear to affect the level of blame she is attributed.

Whilst this is only a small sample of personal characteristics, it is clear that there is a very narrow stereotype of the 'perfect victim' who would not experience victim blaming: a young White woman of a socially acceptable weight, attractive enough to be raped but not overly attractive that she would be deemed to have provoked or seduced her attacker.

However, it is clear from the sections on rape myths and stereotypes that situational factors also affect the blame of the woman, so personal characteristics are only part of this story. It is difficult to conclude whether personal characteristics of the woman or the situational details of the rape are more influential when exploring the factors leading to victim blaming. This is especially relevant for older women who are stuck in a unique place in which their rape experiences tend to be violent stranger attacks that cause injury (which fit well with the 'perfect rape' stereotype') but have personal characteristics, such as their age, that exclude them from the 'perfect victim stereotype'.

In this case, just the personal characteristics alone are enough to cause the invisibility of older women in national data, despite their experience fitting the criteria for a rape that society would accept as legitimate. This complexity warrants further research. It would be useful to be able to test whether the situational factors surrounding the type of rape are more likely to cause blaming responses than the personal characteristics of the woman or vice versa. I think that now would be a good time to appreciate the current work of Dr Hannah Bows, Assistant Professor of Criminal Law who is committed to a four year project exploring the criminal justice experiences and outcomes of victims of serious crime aged 60 years and over. Her work continues to be vital in our understanding of this gap in literature.

Behaviour before, during or after the assault

The way in which the woman behaved before, during and immediately after the rape or sexual assault has strong ties to victim blaming and self-blame. It is likely that the consistent theme of the rape stereotype and the 'real rape' scenario runs through this individual level factor too. This section will discuss the evidence available on the topic of the behaviours and responses of the woman immediately before the assault, whilst she was being raped or sexually assaulted and her behaviour and responses immediately afterwards and how this may influence victim blaming and self-blame.

In 2014, Perrilloux et al. found that the most common types of self-blame could be split into five categories which all included behaviours before and during the sexual assault or rape. The five categories were putting themselves in the situation, being drunk or high, not resisting enough, sending mixed messages to the perpetrator and being too trusting of the perpetrator. Even from this small group of common types of self-blame, it is easy to see how influential the 'real rape' myth and the 'infallible victim' stereotype has affected the perception of how the woman 'should' have behaved. All five categories also show that the most common responses shift all of the responsibility of the rape or sexual assault away from the perpetrator and back to the victim. They imply that had the woman not put themselves in that situation, had been sober, had resisted the perpetrator, had sent clear messages of disinterest and had not trusted the perpetrator, rape should not have occurred.

Using the 'real rape' stereotype as a guide, it can be deducted that women are blamed less when they do not know their perpetrator, did not spend personal time with the perpetrator and therefore cannot be blamed for leading him on, flirting with him or bringing it upon herself due to some message she gave off to the perpetrator.

This directly leads to women who have been raped or sexually assaulted by a partner, friend or date to be more likely to be blamed along those lines. Miller et al. (2010) suggest that high levels of self-blame and victim blaming occur when the woman is perceived (or perceives herself) to have acted in a socially undesirable manner such as drinking too much, being sexually active, being too naïve or trusting or even wearing something that is then criticised for being too revealing. A central issue for victim blaming and self-blame is the way in which the behaviour of the woman is brought under close inspection in order to judge culpability.

The behaviour and response of the woman during the experience of being sexually assaulted or raped is also under scrutiny and this is shown to have direct links to victim blaming.

One of the most common lines of reasoning, is to blame the woman for not fighting the perpetrator off, not screaming for help and instead staying still or waiting for the assault to be over. There are five common responses to trauma which are regularly used in teaching, medical models and training of psychologists, therapists and professionals working in trauma informed environments: fight, flight, freeze, friend, and flop.

Whilst fight and flight are well-used in the general knowledge of responses to trauma and fear, they are erroneously held up as the 'correct way' to respond to a sexual trauma, with many rape myths implying that women should be able to fight off their attacker, escape their attacker or at the very least, experience injury due to struggling to get free and to shout for help.

The lesser known responses to trauma are freeze, friend and flop – with more research focus on the freeze response, which Moor et al. (2013) reports as a common form of paralysis and behavioural inhibition which prevents the person from any type of response to the sexual trauma – resulting in the person being silent and feeling 'frozen' to the spot, unable to move or respond. This response is so common in fact, that Bucher and Manasse (2011) found that 42% of all women who were raped experienced a complete freeze response during their rape which included being incapable of verbal or physical response. More recent research found that over 70% of women who are raped, freeze during the attack (Muller et al., 2017).

Despite this common response, which Moor et al. (2013) argue is an adaptive survival tactic to reduce further damage to the body – it is still viewed as an inadequate victim response and therefore contributes to the social blaming and personal self-blame of women who have been subjected to sexual assault or rape.

Moor et al. (2013) confirmed this by stating that victim blaming messages and rape myths are based on the misunderstanding or purposeful reconstruction of the freeze trauma response as a deliberate lack of resistance on the part of the woman or even a signal that the woman wanted to be raped or sexually assaulted, supporting the rape myths that some women 'want to be raped' and some women 'enjoy being raped'.

Due to these strong messages, it is no wonder that many studies have found that counterfactual thinking is common in women who have been subjected to sexual assault or rape. The theory suggests that women naturally examine and critique their behaviour, experiences and possible reasons for their trauma which often leads to women engaging in 'if only' thought processes that convince them that their experience may not have happened or would have ended differently had they done something different.

Examples given included a complex mixture of counterfactual thinking and perceptions of socially desirable behaviour of women which led to thoughts such as questioning whether she drank too much, whether she was too trusting, whether she looked too provocative, whether she caused the rape due to her decisions or behaviours (Miller et al, 2010). N'gbala (2003) reported that counterfactual thoughts following their sexual assault directly predicted self-blame and poor psychological well-being in women.

This criticism of women's behaviour during sexual assaults is a common feature of victim blaming and rape myths. Moor et al. (2013) suggests that deconstructing these rape myths and victim blaming messages by showing that a freeze response is not only common but is also a natural, self-preservation tactic when faced with extreme trauma. This deconstruction could not only break down myths and victim blaming in the general population but may also reduce the self-blame that women put on themselves when they are measuring their responses against the rape stereotypes and myths they have absorbed their whole lives.

Own understanding and recognition of the assault

As well as all of the factors contributing to social victim blaming women for their rape or sexual assault, a number of recent studies have started to explore whether the woman's own understanding of her assault, her perpetrator, her perception of and feelings towards the word 'rape' contribute to victim blaming and self-blame.

Many of these factors overlap with the ones already discussed in this book – suggesting that one of the impacts of the cumulative power of social victim blaming, objectification, rape myths is that women's understanding, acknowledgement and recognition of their experience is affected. This could appear to impact the woman in a cyclical pattern in which the woman absorbs the messages about sexual violence and her culpability. She is then subjected to sexual violence but does not acknowledge it or understand it, therefore does not report or respond to the experience in the way society expects a victim to respond to sexual violence which then leads to further victim blaming, self-blame and revictimisation. This line of reasoning could be applied to the low disclosure and reporting rates of sexual violence in the UK – not just because women are scared to speak out about what happened to them – but because women may not be sure they were really raped at all (Peterson and Muelenhard, 2004).

This confusion has led to a body of research that references the 'unacknowledged victim' as a woman who has had an experience which meets the criteria of a sexual offence but does not acknowledge it as such. The discovery of this type of victim led to the authors of the Sexual Experiences Survey adding a final question that directly asks the participant 'have you ever been raped?' to enable researchers to explore whether participants were responding positively to descriptions of sexual offences that would constitute rape but were responding negatively to the question in which the word 'rape' was used to label the experience.

There are a number of issues that arise from this including whether language is the key to acknowledgement – that the word 'rape' is loaded with so many myths, stereotypes and stigma that women do not identify with it. Another reason could be the word 'rape' (because it is generally used to mean a stranger attack) seems so extreme and causes such publicly accepted scrutiny of the victim that women prefer not to use it to apply it to themselves.

The literature appears to show that the difference between a woman who has recognised and understood their experience as rape or sexual assault and a woman who does not, seems to lie within their own acceptance of sexual scripts, gender roles and most importantly, rape myths (Miller et al. 2011).

If women have accepted powerful messages from the media, society, culture and their support network that rape is where they would be attacked, beaten, injured and forced to have sex with a stranger, women who are asked whether they have ever been 'raped' are not going to respond positively if their experience of a rape was being blackmailed into performing a sex act in bed for their husband of 25 years.

Women in Miller et al. (2011) reported significant confusion and uncertainty about whether they had been raped and whether rape was a common experience. Heath (2011) found that women who were raped or sexually assaulted would only feel confident that they were raped and then report their experience to the police if they had bruising or obvious injury. A further concern is highlighted by Littleton et al. (2009) who found that women who were being raped or sexually assaulted but did not acknowledge their experience as such, were more likely to have continued their relationship with the perpetrator and were more likely to be revictimized several times, whilst blaming themselves.

Self-blame and revictimisation were argued as direct costs to not acknowledging or labelling a rape or sexual assault. In Miller et al. (2011) self-blame and revictimisation were found to be linked by the acknowledgement of the event as a sexual assault or rape. Women who did not acknowledge the event as a sexual assault or rape were more likely to blame their behaviours or character for what happened and were then more likely to be subjected to sexual revictimsation in the future.

With the rate of revictimisation of women who have been subjected to rape and sexual assault already sitting at two out of three (Miller et al. 2010), this link between victim blaming, self-blame and revictimisation needs careful exploration, especially as revictimisation has consistently been found to be associated with self-blame (Classen et al. 2005).

However, this does beg the question: why would women who don't acknowledge that they are a victim of a sexual offence blame themselves for the non-consensual sexual experience? Some theories come from counterfactual theory, some from just world theory and some from research on sexual scripts but all posit that women employ types of self-blame that enable them to feel control over their sexual experiences whilst not having to acknowledge them as abuse, assault or rape. But if the woman does not acknowledge that the man has raped or abused them, why would they still experience such high levels of self-blame?

Crome and McCabe (2001) suggest that when women have no previous or direct experience of a sexual assault or rape, they are the most likely to use sexual scripts and stereotypes to fill in their missing knowledge. This argument would mean that women who were repeatedly victimised would be more likely to acknowledge the experience as a sexual assault or rape and would be less likely to employ sexual scripts and stereotypes – but this does not account for the fact that studies have shown that even women who are repeatedly raped and abused can still employ rape myths, stereotypes and sexual scripts that mean that even years of sexual abuse is sometimes not acknowledged as sexual abuse.

Miller et al. (2011) cite Faccenda & Pantaleon (2011) who said that belief in a just world provide a version of the world that is fair, just and predictable. They made the argument that it is common for women subjected to sexual violence to feel that if they do not take the blame or responsibility for the incident, then they must admit that they did not have any control of the decisions, actions and situations that led to them being sexually assaulted or raped.

Therefore, by engaging in self-blame, they are taking back some control of the of the event by making decisions not to allow those same precedents to occur again – thereby convincing themselves that they can avoid that particular sexual experience happening again.

Unfortunately, Heath (2011) discussed the self-blame women engage in in these situations is not so much related to other people blaming them – but are related to those original rape myths, scripts and stereotypes in which they have learned about wider society blaming women for sexual violence. This meant that many women chose to make decisions that correlated with common rape myths (telling themselves that they will fight back in future, not drink in future, not go to places alone and not provoke the perpetrator in future).

The final theory that may answer the question about why women who have not acknowledged their experience as a sexual assault or rape still blame themselves is closely related to the reasoning used in just world belief.

Counterfactual theory suggests that the negative feeling about the event triggers a cognitive response which focusses on the so-called behavioural errors that led to them being sexually assaulted or raped. Once these behaviours are identified, they are remembered for future reference.

Whilst this may work in non-personal situations ('in future, I will not touch a hot stove because it will burn my finger') this type of reasoning places undue emphasis on the behaviours or decisions of the woman subjected to sexual violence where the emphasis should be placed on the behaviours and decisions of the man.

Unfortunately, the reasoning tends to follow the same pattern, even when women report that they know that the perpetrator was to blame for their sexual assault or rape, they still engage in counterfactual thinking which causes significant levels of self-blame (Miller et al., 2010).

Even when there are no obvious behaviours or decisions that could be perceived as having led to their sexual assault or rape, women were still shown to consider numerous other behaviours and decisions that had no rational relationship with the sexual assault or rape (Alicke, 2000).

Branscombe et al. (2003) conducted a counterfactual thinking task in which they found that women who engaged in counterfactual thoughts were more like to self-blame and more likely to experience poor psychological health.

This section has provided significant evidence for the way factors at all levels of the ecological system influence the way the individual woman understands and processes her experience of sexual violence.

The research has shown that women employ common rape myths, gender role stereotypes, sexist values and misogynistic stereotypes to understand and identify the experience of male violence, to blame themselves for what happened or to attempt to regain a locus of control over their experience of being subjected to male violence and over their future sexual experiences.

From the research, it is not clear whether there is a difference in this self-blame behaviour depending on whether the women have been directly blamed for their rape or assault by someone or whether they have absorbed those messages over the lifespan, but there is likely to be an opportunity for useful research to be conducted which explores whether women who have absorbed the many complex messages about victim blaming and victim culpability blame themselves as a way to counteract the blame they think they will experience from external people and so that they can offer a solution or reason for why their experience happened and how they are going to ensure that it doesn't happen again by changing their behaviour or personal characteristics.

Whether it is the way she responded during the rape, the decisions she made in the time running up to the rape or the way she understands and labels her experience – the culture of victim blaming has been shown to have significant effects on the recognition, understanding and response to sexual violence at the intrapsychic level.

14.

Blaming the woman, blaming the girl

Child sexual exploitation (CSE) is a topic that has featured heavily in media, policy, procedure, research and practice for almost a decade. However, whilst much has been invested into the field, this chapter will argue that there are fundamental misunderstandings about victims of CSE that have led to ineffective and punitive preventative and intervention approaches. This chapter will critically discuss three underpinning assumptions in child sexual exploitation theory and practice related to prevention and practice:

(a) That children (mainly girls) take risks which lead to being sexually exploited

(b) That vulnerability of the girl leads to sexual exploitation; and

(c) That education of girls can prevent sexual exploitation.

Why is the definition of CSE important?

There have been several definitions of child sexual exploitation over the years, and whilst it has continued to evolve, the definition has still not reached a form that is accepted by everyone. Before 'child sexual exploitation' became a term in common usage, girls being sexually exploited by adults were generally called 'child prostitutes' (Hallett, 2017). The term was written into law, with the Sexual Offences Act (2003) containing offences pertaining to 'child prostitution' and 'child prostitutes' until it was amended in 2015.

Campaigners including individual professionals, politicians, feminist groups and child rights activists argued that girls could not be 'prostitutes', and if they were being sold for sex, or found 'selling sex', they were always being sexually abused and exploited by adults (usually adult men). They argued that the act of calling girls 'prostitutes' conveyed a level of choice, agency and knowledge that they did not and could not have as minors. Ann Coffey MP was particularly instrumental in the removal of the term 'child prostitution' from the Sexual Offences Act (2003).

Over time, the term was changed to 'abuse through prostitution' and then 'commercial exploitation'. Whilst these terms signalled a shift away from perceiving girls as choice-making individuals 'selling sex' within the context of prostitution; there was still a lack of focus on the fact that the girls were children being abused, assaulted, raped and harmed by adults.

Finally, the term 'child sexual exploitation' and commonly used acronym 'CSE' was adopted into common usage around 2009, positioning the victim firmly as a child, and the crime as the sexual exploitation of the person. However, whilst the improvement from 'child prostitute' to 'child sexual exploitation' was something to celebrate, the definition of child sexual exploitation continued to remain in flux for many years – and still contains remnants from the days of 'child prostitution'.

Figure 1 – The evolution of the term 'child sexual exploitation' versus the definition

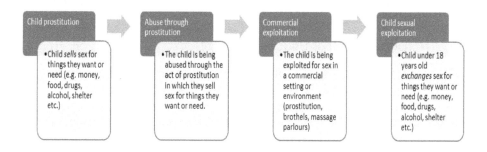

The diagram shows that whilst the terminology changes slightly, the most recent definition published in 2017 by the Department for Education (the fourth boxes) uses the concept of children 'exchanging' sex and sexual acts for things they want or need.

It can be seen in the diagram that the concept of child prostitution is not dissimilar from the concept of CSE, in which the definitions focus on children exchanging sexual acts for things they 'want or need'. This remains problematic, as it positions the child as having agency and choice.

Recently, women who were subjected to sexual exploitation in childhood from Rotherham have challenged the notion of 'exchange' by arguing that the concept is offensive to victims and survivors because it reframes the violence and abuse as reciprocal and 'it positions us as little business women making an exchange' (Woodhouse, 2017).

The definition of CSE has also been raised by Gladman and Heal (2017) who argued that the term 'child sexual exploitation' had become hygienic and abstract, whereby the current DfE (2017) definition does not represent the true harm, violence, injuries and death of children, but describes a vague process of exchange with no reference to harm or trauma to the child:

> Child sexual exploitation is a form of child sexual abuse. It occurs where an individual or group takes advantage of an imbalance of power to coerce, manipulate or deceive a child or young person under the age of 18 into sexual activity (a) in exchange for something the victim needs or wants, and/or (b) the financial advantage or increased status of the perpetrator or facilitator. The victim may have been sexually exploited even if the sexual activity appears consensual. Child sexual exploitation does not always involve physical contact; it can also occur through the use of technology.

(Department for Education, 2017)

Gladman and Heal (2017) raise an important point, and one that can be seen with ease when we contrast the definition of child sexual exploitation with the definition of child sexual abuse; one that is explicit, detailed and clear in its description of the harm and crimes committed against the child:

> Involves forcing or enticing a child or young person to take part in sexual activities, not necessarily involving a high level of violence, whether or not the child is aware of what is happening. The activities may involve physical contact, including assault by penetration (for example, rape or oral sex) or non-penetrative acts such as masturbation, kissing, rubbing and touching outside of clothing. They may also include non-contact activities, such as involving children in looking at, or in the production of, sexual images, watching sexual activities, encouraging children to behave in sexually inappropriate ways, or grooming a child in preparation for abuse (including via the internet). Sexual abuse is not solely perpetrated by adult males. Women can also commit acts of sexual abuse, as can other children.

(Working Together to Safeguard Children, HM Government, 2018)

The difference between the two definitions is clear: child sexual exploitation (whilst described as a form of child sexual abuse) is still being defined as a process of exchange in which children are getting something in return for performing sex acts – whilst the definition of child sexual abuse positions the child as a victim of violence, harm and sexual crimes. There is no mention of the words 'rape', 'assault', 'grooming', 'trafficking', 'violence' or 'harm' in the definition of child sexual exploitation.

The definition of child sexual exploitation is central to critical discussions of preventing sexual violence against children and protecting them from abusers. Whilst the definition still positions the child as having the agency to perform an exchange, prevention approaches will focus on changing the behaviours and decision making of the child, rather than protecting the child from adults who are raping, trafficking and abusing them. Arguably, this assertion can be seen in the approaches, prevention methods and responses to victims in recent years, including the higher level of victim blaming of girls who had been 'sexually exploited' when compared to victim blaming of children who had been 'sexually abused'. I first presented this argument in the diagram below in Eaton and Holmes (2017, p.12).

Figure 2 – Definitions of abuse change the perception of the victims

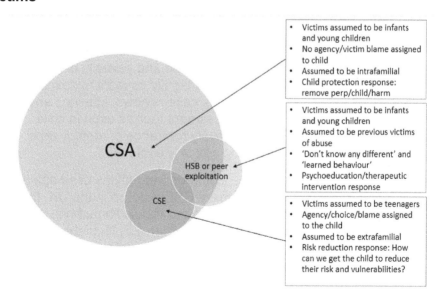

In the diagram and chapter for the national evidence review, I argued that children were assigned different victim stereotypes and victim agency depending on the terminology used to describe what was happening to them – which in turn influenced the intervention or preventative approach they were subject to. Children being subjected to child sexual abuse were likely to be perceived to be infants and small children without agency or choice in the abuse, but children being subjected to child sexual exploitation were likely to be perceived to be teenage girls with some level of choice and agency to 'take risks' (Eaton & Holmes, 2017).

Generally, child sexual abuse still fits within a traditional child protection response, but child sexual exploitation has developed an alternative 'risk reduction' response, in which children who are being raped and abused in exploitation are given educative 'awareness raising' sessions and support to change their behaviours to 'reduce their risk' of being sexually exploited. This could be considered a form of victim blaming that places responsibility on the child to change rather than the adult to stop harming the child.

Rape myths are used in CSE practice to blame girls

As many rape myth studies and victim blaming studies tend to focus on the actions and characters of adult women, it would be reasonable to expect that rape myths and victim blaming would not apply to children being raped, trafficked and sexually exploited, especially as many of them cannot legally consent to sexual activity. However, several serious case reviews, inquiries and even published policies and risk assessment toolkits used in child sexual exploitation practice actively reference or employ rape myths with girls who are being sexually exploited.

In the table on the next page, common rape myths used against women are compared with current CSE practice in the UK. In the left column are items from the Updated Illinois Rape Myth Acceptance Scale (McMahon and Farmer, 2011). In the right corresponding column are examples from current practice with children subjected to sexual violence, that support the rape myth.

Rape myth U-IRMAS (2011) McMahon & Farmer	Operationalisation of the rape myth in CSE practice
Subscale 1: She was asking for it If a girl is raped while she is drunk, she is at least somewhat responsible for letting things get out of hand	This rape myth is most often seen when girls are being given alcohol and/or drugs as part of grooming offences and sexual exploitation, but instead of the alcohol and drug use being recorded as part of the offence committed by the adult, girls are criticised and stigmatised for being intoxicated. Girls who are raped whilst under the influence of alcohol or drugs are perceived to be unreliable witnesses or problematic victims in a prosecution. Girls who are being actively sexually exploited using drugs and alcohol can be given 'alcohol and drug awareness sessions' instead of safeguarding them from sexual violence. The concept of exchange also compounds this rape myth, in which CSE is defined as children 'exchanging sex for items such as alcohol and drugs'. This positions the children as having more agency and responsibility than the offender, who is not mentioned.
Subscale 1: She was asking for it When girls go to parties wearing slutty clothes, they are asking for trouble	This rape myth appears on most of the risk assessment toolkits under the heading 'wears provocative dress' or 'oversexualised attire/makeup/clothing'. These items are used as 'risk indicators' that a child may be sexually exploited, but they only apply to girls which presents two problems. The first being the presence of sexism, that clothing causes rape and the second being that the tool is also used to assess boys, who would not be categorised as wearing 'provocative dress' as boys' bodies are not policed in the same way as

	girls' bodies.
	Therefore, girls are being assessed against sexist stereotypes and rape myths; and boys are being assessed against a harmful, female-centric tool with items not culturally or socially relevant to them.
Subscale 1: She was asking for it When girls get raped, it's often because the way they said "no" was unclear **Subscale 3: It wasn't really rape** If a girl doesn't say 'no', she can't claim rape	These rape myths are prevalent in CSE due to the way preventative measures focus on teaching children about consent and saying 'no' when they do not want sexual activity with others. Sessions with children who are already being raped and abused often include lessons on giving consent, healthy and unhealthy relationships and boundaries. This perpetuates the myth that the reason the children are being sexually exploited is because they didn't understand enough about consent and relationships to be able to say 'no' clearly.
Subscale 4: She lied A lot of times, girls who say they were raped agreed to have sex and then regret it A lot of times, girls who say they were raped often led the guy on and then had regrets A lot of times, girls who claim they were raped have emotional problems	This subscale contains three rape myths which feature heavily in CSE practice, especially when considering the failings of authorities and police forces who perceived girls to be lying, exaggerating or making malicious complaints. Whilst many children never disclose abuse, rape and exploitation, there were many cases of CSE in which girls repeatedly disclosed or were found in premises with the men who were harming them – but they were not believed. In serious case reviews from Rotherham, Telford and Oxford, girls were found to have been called liars and their disclosures were ignored as they were positioned as consenting, promiscuous teenagers who led men on.

	Girls who have been subjected to sexual violence are also very likely to be diagnosed with psychiatric disorders and mental health issues, rather than being acknowledged as victims of complex and multiple traumas, displaying natural and rational trauma responses rather than symptoms of a psychiatric disorder.

Three assumptions that affect CSE practice and theory

Child sexual exploitation practice and theory has developed based on three core assumptions. The first is that sexual exploitation happens to 'vulnerable' girls. The second is that girls who engage in 'risky behaviours' will be sexually exploited and that girls increase and decrease their own 'risk level' to sexual violence. The third is that prevention of this form of sexual violence is based on educating the girl about sexual exploitation and teaching them not to 'take risks' that would lead to being sexually exploited. This preventative method is assumed to protect them from child sexual exploitation and abuse, by raising their knowledge and awareness of sexual exploitation and therefore giving them the power to exit abuse or the knowledge to spot a perpetrator early on in a grooming process.

All three assumptions are problematic and have heavily influenced the preventative approaches taken by local authorities, police and national children's charities in the UK. Currently in child sexual exploitation practice, prevention involves changing something about the child for the abuser to stop abusing them, or not to target them in the first place. Generally, this is confined to two main preventative approaches: stopping girls from 'taking risks' and 'reducing vulnerabilities' of girls.

Stopping children from 'taking risks'

One of the most common methods of identifying and responding to children who are, or are suspected of, being sexually exploited is to measure factors known as 'risk indicators' and by changing or reducing the 'risk level' of the child by modifying their behaviour or character in some way. Professionals in multi-agency teams measure the risk of child sexual exploitation happening to the child using a matrix of 'CSE risk indicators' on a toolkit adopted by each local authority, police force or larger strategy area. Notice, that they do not measure the risk of the offender as standard, but the 'risk' of the child.

The items on the CSE toolkits have a central focus on the child, their behaviours, their backgrounds, upbringing, character and appearance. Professionals are required to tick or score the indicator on the toolkit to raise concerns or make referrals for children to safeguarding teams or specialist CSE teams (Brown et al., 2016;2017). CSE toolkits vary from authority to authority but are generally based on original or hybrid versions of the SERAF Tool from Barnardo's and the NWG CSE Toolkit. Both toolkits contained long lists of 'risk indicator' items, which when scored, give a calculated outcome of the 'risk' the child is at.

Brown et al. (2016) found over 110 individual indicators being used to assess children despite the items having never been validated or evaluated empirically or in practice. Further, the authors concluded that the CSE toolkits were perpetuating victim stereotypes in CSE and causing professionals to focus on the characters and behaviours of the child, rather than where the risk was really coming from: the perpetrator.

Brown et al. (2016;2017) published a second report about the use of CSE toolkits with children which explored the way social workers and other professionals understood and employed the CSE risk toolkits and indicator lists across the UK. The authors concluded that CSE risk toolkits were unreliable and should not be used to make decisions about children.

CSE risk toolkits are generally understood to be a preventative measure, in which professionals calculate the 'risk level' of children (usually 'low', 'medium' and 'high') and then act to protect the child. However, as Brown et al. (2016;2017) pointed out, many of the items that measure risk are evidence of sexual abuse or are current sexual offences, not risk indicators that the child may be sexually abused in the future.

In support of the argument by Brown et al. (2016;2017) the table on the next page demonstrates a gross misuse of the word 'risk' in preventative practice. Indicators that describe actual abuse and harm to children, are categorised as low, medium or high 'risk'.

Examples of 'risk indicators' that are evidence of abuse already occurring

Risk indicator	Risk level
'Superficial self-harm as a consequence of CSE'	Low risk
'Associating with young people who are also being sexually exploited'	Low risk
'Being groomed online or offline by perpetrators over 18 years old'	Medium risk
'Offering to have sex for money or other payment and then running before sex takes place'	Medium risk
'Being involved in CSE through being seen in hotspots i.e. known houses, recruiting grounds or parties'	Medium risk
'Child under 13 involved or coerced into sexual activity'	High risk
'Pattern of street homelessness and staying with an adult believed to be sexually exploiting them'	High risk
'Child under 16 meeting different adults and exchanging or selling sexual activity for goods or a roof overnight'	High risk
'Being bought/sold/trafficked'	High risk

(Risk indicators taken from current CSE toolkits in UK, based on NWG CSE Toolkit)

When used correctly, the word 'risk' means the probability or chance that something negative may happen. In CSE the word 'risk' is used to describe harm that has already occurred or is actively occurring *and* the risk that may occur. Current CSE risk toolkit outcomes lead to girls who are being trafficked, raped and sexually exploited being labelled as 'medium risk' or 'high risk' rather than being acknowledged as a victim of sexual offences and serious crime.

The focus on measuring risk also leads to girls being framed as 'risk takers' or 'displaying risky behaviours' rather than the perpetrators being framed as the risk. When it comes to prevention, this has influenced the way girls are supported and protected. Rather than the offender being risk assessed and changed, stopped or apprehended, CSE strategies focus on changing the 'risk level' of the girls.

At professional meetings, girls are assessed based on the CSE risk toolkit and given a 'risk level'. Based on the risk level they fall within; each girl will then be prescribed general interventions and support based on reducing their own risk level in an attempt to stop or prevent the sexual exploitation from occurring or continuing. This approach essentially erases the perpetrator from the crimes against the girl, leaving the girl as the cause and the solution to the sexual harm they are being subjected to. Interventions can include stopping the girl from going to certain places, seeing friends, walking to school alone, wearing certain clothing and makeup, using the internet, having a mobile phone, having a games console or even living in their hometown.

Case example

Fifteen-year-old Selina talks to unknown men when playing games online. They ask her to send photos of herself. She sends photos, mainly silly ones but a couple with her bra on. Workers and parents stop her from playing on the Xbox, disconnect her internet access, remove her phone and laptop and report that she is now at low risk of CSE because they have changed her behaviours. The accounts are not investigated, and Selina is left feeling like it was her own fault.

Examples like the one above are common in CSE practice across the UK. In an attempt to protect a girl or prevent CSE, the girl is assessed for 'risks' they are 'taking' which may lead to being sexually exploited or groomed – and then changes are made to reduce those risks.

In Selina's case, her parents were told to stop her from playing on the Xbox and disconnect her access to the Wi-Fi internet in the house. Despite many older teens playing online and talking to strangers, this was perceived as a 'risk-taking behaviour'. It was reported that because she was no longer able to game online, her risk level decreased. A girl like Selina may well have also received education on 'risk taking online', to change her online behaviours to 'reduce his risk' of being sexually exploited.

However, an approach focussing only on changing the girl and placing responsibility on her actions and behaviours, is not truly preventative and is often perceived as punitive by girls who were targeted by a potential perpetrator, disclosed to an adult and then had their belongings or freedom limited or reduced as a consequence.

In serious case reviews, it has been reported that approaches such as these leave a new gap for a perpetrator to fill: a girl who suddenly has no access to the internet, games console or mobile phone will seek one out – and a perpetrator can be the person who supplies that access.

Unwittingly, professionals can create an opportunity for a perpetrator that did not exist before the intervention to 'reduce the risk'; meaning that the intervention increases the risk of the offender targeting or controlling the girl.

Another argument is that changing the behaviour of one child does not prevent sexual violence but means it will happen to another child instead – because the perpetrator was never confronted or stopped and was free to continue abusing other children.

Risk levels originating from the CSE risk toolkits also cause preventative work to be conducted, even when the girl is already being sexually abused or exploited. Girls at 'medium' or 'high' risk of CSE, which as we have seen, often means the girl is already being harmed – still results in direct case work in which girls are educated on topics of consent, healthy and unhealthy relationships, reducing risk taking behaviours, risks of alcohol and drugs and sexual health.

Whilst girls have a human right to access education and information on the topics that concern them and affect them, and all children should have comprehensive relationships and sex education – it is arguably not appropriate to deliver this education whilst the girl is being actively sexually abused, trafficked or exploited, as a preventative method or intervention; especially where the education is being used to attempt to reduce 'risk levels' of the girl instead of stopping the offender (Eaton, 2019a).

The concept of risk is currently misused in CSE practice. Risk is perceived as belonging to and originating from the behaviours, background and characteristics of the child. This leads to ineffective or punitive preventative approaches to CSE as a form of sexual violence, that focus on changing the child and reducing their 'risk level', rather than assessing the risk of the offender committing crimes against children.

'Reducing vulnerabilities' to CSE

The second core assumption in CSE practice is that girls with specific vulnerabilities are more likely to be sexually abused than other girls with little or no vulnerabilities. This assumption is not specific to CSE, however, and I have discussed in other chapters the way in which psychological research seeks to discover the vulnerabilities of the woman that make rape, sexual abuse and domestic abuse more likely. Despite the ongoing search for 'vulnerabilities' that lead to sexual violence, findings are highly contested and variable (Eaton & Holmes, 2017; Brown et al., 2016). When it comes to child sexual exploitation, for example, there is very little evidence that any 'vulnerabilities' are linked to a higher chance of being sexually exploited (Brown et al., 2016).

To begin, it is important to define what is meant by 'vulnerabilities to CSE'. Society tends to perceive children as inherently vulnerable, due to being children (James & Prout, 1997), however, if we did truly see all children as vulnerable to sexual abuse and exploitation, there would not be specific lists of vulnerabilities that children are scored and measured against.

Lists of vulnerabilities to CSE are widely used in practice, with many lists of vulnerabilities attached to the previously discussed CSE risk toolkit. The lists of vulnerabilities vary widely from toolkit to toolkit and have not been validated or evaluated to show causation or correlation yet (Brown et al., 2016;2017). Vulnerabilities include having a learning disability, being a looked after child and witnessing domestic abuse at home. Generally, the lists of vulnerabilities include adverse experiences from throughout the lifespan of the child, however, some are vaguer and include items such as moving to secondary school, illness of a family member, a change in appearance or fashion and having low self-esteem.

It is thought that the more vulnerabilities the child has, the more likely they are to be sexually exploited. This approach to working with children represents a deficit model of children, rather than a strengths-based model of understanding their lives and potential. In a deficit model of prevention and support in sexual violence, negative and adverse childhood experiences increase the likelihood of sexual abuse and exploitation.

The problem with this approach is two-fold. The first is that it positions girls with trauma histories or adverse experiences as 'predisposed' to be continually abused and exploited, with little hope of positive outcomes and safety. Rather than focussing on the many strengths the girl has, the risk assessment and interventions become focussed on the vulnerabilities and experiences of the girl, ignoring her strengths, desires, skills and talents. In this approach, girls become 'CSE cases' and all interventions become focussed on the CSE and not the whole person (Eaton & Holmes, 2017).

The second problem with the vulnerabilities approach to CSE, is that measuring the risk of being abused or exploited by how many vulnerabilities the girl has, erases the actions, decisions and motivations of the sex offenders that choose to target children of all ages, sexes, ethnicities, backgrounds and life experiences. This leads to a narrow, stereotypical view of which children would be sexually exploited (girls with existing vulnerabilities) and which children would not (girls without existing vulnerabilities, and boys). Sex offenders are therefore erased from the narrative, from assessments, practice and prevention.

One example of the way vulnerability approaches to CSE perpetuate stereotypes is the way younger children are seen as more vulnerable; but become less and less vulnerable to sexual violence as they get older. Once over the age of 16 years old, there is a markedly different response to girls who are being sexually abused and exploited. This was first reported in a publication by The Children's Society in 2015 which explored the way 16 and 17-year-old girls in the UK who were being sexually exploited were being failed by organisations and professionals. It was argued by the authors that this failure was due to older teenage girls being perceived as less vulnerable, less susceptible to harm and 'old enough to know better' (which became the title of the report).

If children did become less and less vulnerable as they aged, the prevalence of abuse would dramatically reduce as the child reached adulthood, but this is not the case. A meta-analysis of over 9000 cases by Cockbain et al. (2015) showed that the sexual abuse and exploitation of girls appears to increase significantly as she ages and peaks between 13 and 16 years old. The decrease after 16 years old may be related more to the issues raised by Pona and Baillie (2015) in The Children Society report rather than being a true decrease in prevalence.

Another argument would be that if vulnerability to sexual abuse and violence did reduce with age, the prevalence of female adult rape, abuse and exploitation would be much lower than that of female children, which is also incorrect.

In Eaton & Holmes (2017), I created another diagram which separates vulnerabilities from the act of sexual violence against children, placing the offender in the centre of the process.

Diagram from Eaton & Holmes (2017, p38) arguing that the experiences of a child are separate from the abuse, with the central factor being the offender's motivations and opportunities to abuse

Girls' experiences may or may not be relevant or known to a sex offender, but research has only identified three that have any correlation with experiencing CSE – previously being subjected to sexual abuse (Ullman and Vasquez, 2015; Gagne et al, 2005), having a disability and being in looked after care (Brown et al, 2016). These are included in section 1 of the diagram. It is currently taught that vulnerabilities of children are detected by intelligent sex offenders who only target children with multiple

210

vulnerabilities and then utilise those vulnerabilities as opportunities or leverage. However, there is little to no evidence of this in sex offender theory and research.

Whilst girls who are sexually abused may have experienced other issues in their lives before the sex offender targeted them, it would be inappropriate to link these as causal, or in some cases even correlational. Studies such as the Adverse Childhood Experiences (ACE) Study frequently find that over 70% of adults report at least one adverse childhood experience and over 12% report more than four. However, only around 5% of adults report being sexually abused or exploited in childhood (NSPCC, 2017). This means that, statistically, a large majority of children in the population have experienced harm or trauma (which would be perceived as vulnerabilities in CSE practice) but have not gone on to be targeted by an offender.

In the diagram, I suggest that the previous or current experiences of the child stand independently from the abuse process unless the child is being targeted by a sex offender. A child might experience multiple harms or vulnerabilities but will not be sexually exploited unless a sex offender targets them. If there is no sex offender, there will be no sexual offence against the child.

Vulnerabilities, therefore, do not lead to CSE – sex offenders lead to CSE.

The sex offender operates independently on their own motivations coupled with the utilisation or creation of an opportunity to abuse, which may or may not include the girl's existing experiences. This means sex offenders may know and choose to use the girl's adverse experiences to groom or control them – or they may not know (or not need to know) about any previous or current experiences, because they aim to create a new experience, such as offering drugs or alcohol, that was not already a feature of the girl's life.

This more nuanced view of vulnerabilities has implications for current CSE practice, which not only employs the vulnerabilities of the girl as a predictive measure of CSE, but also views those vulnerabilities as changeable or able to be reduced with education and support. Much direct preventative work in CSE involves efforts to 'reduce vulnerabilities' of girls in order to protect them from a sex offender, who is assumed to only target vulnerable girls.

'Education is preventative'

Both risk reduction and vulnerability reduction are argued to be achieved via education – and in CSE practice, education is viewed as a preventative measure to being sexually abused or exploited.

Much work has been conducted in the UK to develop educational films, resources and session plans with the aim of increasing the awareness of CSE with children and the claim of being able to reduce risks, reduce vulnerabilities and even enable children to identify and leave sexual violence. Whilst education is welcomed – and all children should have access to education which informs and empowers them, education is not preventative and cannot protect a child from an adult sex offender who wields power and control over them in a myriad of ways (Eaton, 2018).

Despite education being used as a preventative method for several years, there is very little evidence of impact or success. In a meta-analysis by Bovarnick and Scott (2016), the authors concluded that education did not influence experiences of sex, abuse or relationships later on – and new information was rarely retained longer than a few months by the children.

Much preventative education has no evidence base and longitudinal studies exploring the impact of education on prevention of sexual violence are rare. Studies of longitudinal impact of education are also methodologically complex due to the high level of variables that would affect the interpretation of findings. High quality education covering topics such as sex, abuse, relationships and health are vital for children, but it is not the solution to CSE and cannot be considered preventative in nature.

In 2018, I published the first report documenting the harm caused by preventative CSE films in which children (mainly girls) watch scenes of other girls being raped and abused. Whilst the method has been used with hundreds of thousands of children in recent years, there is no evidence that showing traumatic imagery of child rape and abuse would prevent children from being sexually exploited by powerful and controlling offenders.

For practitioners, education is a well-established intervention to use with children who are being subjected to sexual exploitation. The showing of films and educational resources is often built into care plans, action plans and strategies for individual girls and even entire schools or local authority areas.

This real example was provided by a woman who was shown educational resources when she was being sexually exploited.

Case Example: Faye*

As a child I worked with an organisation in (area name) and was shown the film 'Sick Party.' I remember the worker coming to my home, she brought her laptop and set it up on the dining room table. We began to watch the DVD. I remember it being approximately half an hour long, during this time I became very upset and panicky. She paused the film several times so I could 'compose myself until we could continue.' At the end of the film I was extremely upset, and the worker seemed shocked how upset I was. She ended my visit earlier to 'leave me to calm down' and said she'd come see me next week, then she left.

I vividly remember feeling so confused, embarrassed and ashamed. At that time what I had just seen made me feel so angry at myself that I'd not kept myself 'safe.' I felt stupid that I hadn't 'seen the signs.' I know I self-harmed that night, the shame felt unbearable.

I specifically remember being told I would see a worker for 6 weeks and each week we would have a specific 'topic' to work on. This was set in stone with no negotiation. It was a set plan they worked from with children they supported. One week, she brought some cards. Each card had a 'scenario' on it, I then had to match up whether I thought this was 'okay' 'maybe okay' or 'not okay'.

One scenario that I remember was along the lines of 'I'm going to take and send a nude photograph' another was 'I am going to meet an older man after school.' The point of the exercise was to look at ways of 'keeping myself safe in the future' – like it was my responsibility as a child that had already been abused to prevent it happening again.

This same organisation documented in my notes on discharge that I was 'low risk' of future CSE as I had 'built resilience in sessions'... 'I now understood the dangers and can make more informed choices in the future.' It also states that because I came from a good family home, that my parents both had good jobs and that I didn't present as 'over sexualised', I was low risk. Unfortunately, my abuse continued.

The passage from Faye contains all the assumptions discussed in this chapter. Faye received specialist CSE services that positioned her as risk-taking, vulnerable and in need of six sessions of education. Despite the view of the professionals that the education had prevented her from being abused in the future, her abuse continued because the education was not enough to protect her from adult sex offenders. She was not in control of the abuse.

Herein lies the assumption – that an educated girl who is taught about abuse, grooming and violence can use the education to protect herself from abuse, grooming and violence. Whilst education is important, it is not protective when a girl is being assaulted, abused, raped and trafficked.

It is not common practice in any other form of child harm to educate the child about the form of harm and then expect them to be able to exit the harm or reduce their own harm.

For example, educative approaches are not used in intrafamilial child sexual abuse, physical child abuse or neglect. Children who were being neglected, physically abused or sexually abused would not receive six sessions of education on those topics to 'reduce their risk' of being neglected or abused.

Abuse of children is a form of oppression. Therefore, it is interesting to draw parallels with other forms of oppression to consider whether we would utilise the educative approach in other areas. Consider, for example, if we decided to educate Black children about racism and then insisted that those children could now protect themselves from racism and racially aggravated assaults, because they had the knowledge, they needed to identify racism and stop it. Most people would agree that this approach is not only ridiculous, but harmful. It would leave the child in an oppressive or abusive situation whilst the onus was on them to learn more about protecting themselves.

It would not be ethical or effective to educate an oppressed or abused group of children about the concept of the abuse or oppression and then expect them to protect themselves from it. These approaches ignore the power dynamics in society and those created by the offender. Instead, educative approaches focus on upskilling and teaching the child about the form of harm they are being subjected to with the hope that they will either escape, disclose, identify it or acknowledge it.

The protection of girls and the prevention of CSE as a form of sexual violence has been hindered by issues of definition, the conceptualisation of risk and vulnerability, the positioning of the girl as the problem and the solution to CSE – and the misunderstanding of the use of education as a preventative method.

All these problems serve to erase the actions, decisions and motivations of sex offenders and cause professionals to focus on the behaviours and characteristics of the girl, leading to the acceptance and utilisation of rape myths and victim blaming in practice.

Whilst focus remains on what the girl could have done differently, how the girl could behave better, how the girl could reduce her own vulnerabilities and how the girl could be educated more about relationships and grooming – the action of the offender who chooses to abuse, rape and traffic girls is ignored.

Girls subjected to CSE are victims not only of serious crime, but also of breaches of their human rights. Instead of positioning the girl as the cause and solution to CSE, she should be regarded as an innocent victim of a serious crime that was deliberately perpetrated by sex offenders to harm her as a child.

This shift in thinking would also require a dramatic shift in definitions and conceptualisations. Specifically, it would require the removal of the concept of 'exchange' from all definitions, theory and practice in CSE.

At no point should the rape, abuse, assault, grooming and trafficking of children be framed as 'a form of exchange in which the child gets something they want or need'. Further, radical change in practice and assessment would need to occur to remove the assumptions that girls can control their own 'risk' and 'vulnerability' to sexual violence perpetrated men and boys.

Together, theory, practice and policy need to reflect on the messages we give to girls when we ask or force them to change their own character or behaviour – and tell them that this will protect them from sexual violence.

The depressing message of this chapter is that all the victim blaming messages and misogyny that we lay at the feet of adult women is also put on girls in childhood when they are subjected to male violence.

15.

Talking to women about victim blaming

The best way to explore the victim blaming of women is to talk to women who have been blamed for being subjected to male violence. That seems an obvious assertion, but the majority of research on the exploration of victim blaming is quantitative in nature. Rather than talking to women who have been blamed, we have been counting prevalence or conducting quantitative surveys.

Victim blaming and self-blame of women has been shown to be influenced by and constructed with language and discourses about women, sexual violence and blame (Klein, 2013). Relativist approaches to language propose that language constructs reality, meaning that the words we use to express our ideas and discourses about ourselves and the world can give us clues to the power dynamics, constructions, positions and dilemmas in social issues (Klein, 2013; Wetherell, Taylor & Yates, 2014). Whilst this method is rare (Maier, 2013), one example of the way language has been examined in sexual and domestic violence includes the edited series by Klein (2013, p1) who argues that language should be explored and analysed because, 'language use, for better or worse, shapes the process of perceiving, interpreting and responding to abuse.'

The argument Klein is proposing here is that the way we talk about victim blaming, sexual violence and abuse of women will shape the way we respond to it (individually and collectively).

If our language minimises it, we will minimise it. If our language trivialises it, we will trivialise it. If our language constructs it as a hyperbolic issue that feminists moan about, we will treat it as a hyperbolic issue that feminists moan about.

And if we construct male violence as women's fault, we will hold women responsible for rape, sexual violence and abuse.

Previous research has suggested that victim blaming and self-blame can be explained by rape myth acceptance, belief in a just world, attribution bias or hostile sexism towards women, with many studies seeking to explore correlations and relationships between scores on psychometric measures of these factors (Anderson, 1999; Maier, 2013). However, studies which centre the talk of women as they construct their own thoughts about why women are blamed for sexual violence and why women might blame themselves for sexual violence are rare (Klein, 2013; Maier, 2013).

This chapter contains the results to one of my studies which used open-ended, semi-structured interviews to explore the way women construct victim blaming and self-blame of women subjected to sexual violence in their talk.

This was not specific to their own experiences of sexual violence or blame but included their ideas on why victim blaming was so prevalent, what led people to blame women and what led women to blame themselves for sexual violence perpetrated against them by men.

The research question was:

> How do women use language to construct their understanding of victim blaming and self-blame of women who have been subjected to sexual violence?

I wanted to make sure that I asked questions that would give women the space to discuss their own opinions on the victim blaming of women, why they were blamed, why women blame themselves and what we could do differently. Surely, women who have been subjected to male violence are the experts of their own experiences of being blamed for male violence.

I found a lot of the previous research to be oversimplified. Women were described as fairly basic thinkers who believe and take on narratives from society without any real interrogation. It was assumed that women blamed themselves for sexual violence because they had internal issues such as low self-esteem. There is much talk in the existing literature about the way women 'absorb' messages from society without ever criticising or challenging those messages.

I wanted to find out if that was true – and whether women really were blindly accepting victim blaming and self-blame narratives.

By utilising a critical discursive analysis, this chapter presents the discursive tools used by women as they negotiate explanations of victim blaming and self-blame of themselves and other women.

A discursive tool is a concept from critical discourse analysis which describes a way that language can be used to construct our understanding of people, events, concepts, ideologies and issues in society. In critical discourse analysis, there are three key terms:

Interpretative repertoire

A collection of widely used metaphors, phrases, terms and ways of talking about a specific issue. The building blocks of conversation, they are a selection of commonly recited or replicated linguistic resources that are available, and utilised by people when they speak (Edley, 2001; Potter and Wetherell, 1987).

Examples of common interpretative repertoires about women:

- Women are terrible drivers
- Blondes have more fun
- Women belong in the kitchen

Sometimes, interpretative repertoires are described as a set of well-used narratives that are always available. Sort of like being able to take out a well-used, well-read book from a huge library of social narratives.

We tend to find that when people talk about specific social issues, they employ interpretative repertoires to construct their understanding of that social issue. People get their interpretative repertoires from years of socialization. They include phrases, sayings, stereotypes, myths and common discourses. It is of interest to explore which repertoires people employ, how they use them and when they use them.

Ideological dilemma

A widely employed set of phrases, explanations or understandings about an issue, embedded in an ideology, set of values, beliefs or culture that become fragmented, inconsistent or contradictory when people talk about them. Often described as 'common-sense explanations' that contradict other dominant 'common-sense explanations' of the same issue (Edley, 2001; Billig et al. 1988).

Examples of common ideological dilemmas about women:

- Women should be able to wear whatever they want, but they should also know that if they wear that skirt, they will attract the wrong attention
- We should support women to become sex workers because it is a legitimate career, but I would never let my own daughter do it

- Women should be sexy, but not too sexy because then they are just asking for it
- Women are equal to men in society, but women also need to learn their place and know that men are better than them at a lot of things

Hopefully you can see from the examples that an ideological dilemma is where someone talks in a contradictory way. Usually, this reveals two (or more) competing ideologies or discourses that the person is employing simultaneously whilst speaking.

This is of great interest when analysing speech and written word because it gives the opportunity to explore complex social narratives which often overlap, contradict or oppose each other.

Subject position

The way language and the speaker locate themselves and others in conversation and construct identities of people and organisations in relation to others in hierarchies of social position, power and control (Edley, 2001).

When we speak about something, we always position ourselves in relation to others. We might position ourselves as a victim of male violence, or a survivor of male violence, for example. Positioning ourselves as a victim when we talk might construct us in a different way to if we positioned ourselves as a survivor.

When talking about social issues such as male violence, we might position men as being conscious oppressors, as colluding with oppression, as being passive supporters of oppression, as turning a blind eye to oppression, or as being completely ignorant to the role they play in a patriarchal society. The different ways we would position men in the subject of male violence would change the way we understood and responded to male violence. Therefore, the third discursive tool of interest is the subject position – and the way the speaker positions themselves and the people they talk about in relation to others.

Using these discursive tools to analyse the 10 interviews was particularly useful to deconstruct the existing understanding of women as simple thinkers who absorb victim blaming and self-blaming messages from society without a second thought.

When I analysed the extracts in this chapter, I instead found that women constructed victim blaming and self-blame with multiple competing interpretative repertoires from society and support networks. Their talk often engaged ideological dilemmas about being positioned as to blame for sexual violence, whilst 'feeling' that they were not to blame. Talk was complex, nuanced and multi-faceted, suggesting that women do not simply 'absorb' discourses about victim blaming and self-blame from society, but interrogate victim blaming and self-blame as they talk about it. They are certainly impacted by victim blaming and self-blame discourses, but as this chapter will show, they do not simply accept them to be true.

The sample for this study was ten women aged 19-76 years old, living in the UK, who had been subjected to sexual violence and were accessing support services. The sample was self-selecting from three sexual violence services in England, and all women must have been subjected to sexual violence since the age of 13 years old. The women were from a range of ethnicities, including South Asian Pakistani, Black Caribbean, Polish and White British.

They had a range of life experiences, such as being a stay at home parent and wife, being retired, being unable to work due to disability, currently studying at university and careers including a nurse, counsellor, professional ballet dancer and teacher. Women who participated also spoke about their religious beliefs, including Islam, Christianity, Catholicism and Atheism. All women were accessing sexual violence support services at the time of participation and had self-referred to the organisation to seek help.

Learning from feedback

As part of the commitment to centring women's voices throughout this research, all women were contacted when the transcripts were being analysed to invite them to read through the initial findings and themes before they were written up for this book. All ten women were contacted with copies of the findings and five of them replied to give their thoughts about my interpretation of their talk.

All women agreed with the findings and said that taking part in the study and reading the findings had been a valuable experience.

One woman said that she was happy that someone was presenting research about women's experiences of victim blaming and self-blame as she felt it was under researched and not talked about enough. All five women said that they felt their thoughts were accurately represented.

One of the first things I did was to explore how many women answered in a similar way to each other. Below is a table which contains the most common themes in the speech, how many times it was said across all 10 interviews and how many individual women talked about it.

Each of the discursive tools contained within the table are then discussed with real extracts from the interviews with women.

Key discursive tools used by women to talk about victim blaming and self-blame

Discursive tool	Occurrences in speech	Number of women using this discursive tool
Rape myths and stereotypes	23	10 (100%)
Women must have done something wrong to deserve sexual violence	8	5 (50%)
Women should change something about themselves to protect themselves from male violence	21	6 (60%)
Knowing the sexual violence is wrong but not being able to stop it	20	4 (40%)
Questioning whether she is truly to blame or whether she is overthinking it	15	3 (30%
Knowing logically that she is not to blame but still feeling to blame	17	8 (80%)
Women positioned as responsible for men's behaviour	19	6 (60%)
Women positioned as victims of a misogynistic society	10	5 (50%)

Findings are presented as interpretative repertoires, ideological dilemmas and subject positioning in the language of the women. However, important consideration must be given to the fact that ideological dilemmas and subject positioning of self and others are often influenced by and interlinked with interpretative repertoires and so presenting them as separate artefacts in language is not always helpful.

Rape myths

The most common interpretative repertoire utilised by the women was rape myths. As a set of commonly held beliefs available to society, when women were asked why women were blamed or why women might blame themselves for being subjected to sexual violence, one of the most common constructs used to explain victim blaming was with a rape myth. Rape myths were used by women to explain why observers and others blamed women but were also used to explain why women blamed themselves.

Extract 1

RESEARCHER: *Why do you think some people blame women who have been subjected to different forms of sexual violence?*

AMY: *That they are dirty. Um, but yeah, I think that's the ultimate thing they think, is like, oh, they must be dirty, or they flaunt themselves, or – I don't know. From my experience, yeah, I think that's, that's what I think people think. But, um, they, like, say, oh, it's how they've dressed, or it's cos they wear too much makeup, cos they're overconfident and they're quite flirtatious. Um, yeah, I'd say that's what people think (laughs).'*

RESEARCHER: *Yeah, I see.*

AMY: *Um, so yeah, I think, er, we blame ourselves for strength, like lack of strength. From my experience, strength, um, body size maybe, how I look, maybe too confident, I think that might've attracted the wrong people and – I don't know. Like they're the only ones that can think of.*

Extract 1 was fairly typical of the responses from all women, who described numerous rape myths in their answers. Women were able to recount almost every commonly held rape myth belief and positioned the interpretative repertoire of the rape myth as being used by 'them' and they' (meaning external people, society, family and friends) but also used them to describe their own experiences of rape and sexual assault.

Extract 2

JANE: *It's more of a, erm, you know, "You could have led them on," or "You got drunk," or, "It's not their fault, how were they to know?" Or, "They couldn't control themselves because of what you were wearing."*

Extract 3

DANIELLE: *Um because we are all classed as the same and we are all slappers and all classed as going out in little dresses and because the way you look, you attract that and that's why a man does it*

All women discussed the rape myth that blames women for being raped or sexually assaulted due to wearing revealing clothing. This rape myth, along with the many others discussed, were used to construct women understanding of why people blame women, but also why women blamed themselves, as seen in Extract 1. Women also appeared so aware of the rape myths and stereotypes used by society and authorities that they were comparing their own rape experiences against the known rape myths to assess whether they would be taken seriously or not, something that has been repeatedly found in previous research (Campbell and Raja, 2005).

In Extract 4, Sasha frames her rape as a 'best case scenario' and 'as good as you are going to get' because she understood that her rape fitted the 'real rape' stereotype or 'classic rape' as suggested by Williams (1984) and that people would be more likely to perceive what happened to her to be a rape.

Extract 4

SASHA: *…um, so I've experienced a number of different, um, rapes, I guess, um, and one was your kind of, I guess best case scenario in some ways, in that there were witnesses, a stranger jumped out of nowhere, um, he was an illegal immigrant. So, you know, on the face of it, that's as good as you're going to get as a* *victim, um, to any kind of experience in terms of how people are going to perceive that.*

As an interpretative repertoire, rape myths were influential in the women' understanding of themselves and others, in which they knew they would be measured against and blamed using the rape myths which position them as lying or deserving of sexual violence (Payne et al., 1999). For some women, they had accepted rape myths and applied them to themselves, whereas other women only talked about them as being held in wider society and being applied to women from a distance.

Women must have done something wrong to deserve sexual violence

An increasingly dilemmatic interpretative repertoire employed by women was the commonly held belief in society that women must have done something wrong to deserve sexual violence, which is linked in part, to one of the commonly held rape myths that women deserve it or did something which led the perpetrator to commit sexual violence offences. In addition, this theme may be related to BJW (Lerner, 1980). The way this interpretative repertoire was applied to construct victim blaming and self-blame varied. Some women used it to talk about the way they felt about themselves and some women used it to talk about beliefs held by others in society that would be applied to women who had been subjected to sexual violence. In extract 5, Phoebe talks about the response from others and the way 'they' would look for something the woman did wrong which led to being raped.

Extract 5

PHOEBE: *They're just like, well you know, she – she must have wanted it. She must have done something to deserve it. She must have sought it out, um, you know, just that, that whole stereotypical response that you tend to get.*

Here, Phoebe's talk is a list of words that represent discourses about women subjected to sexual violence: that they want it, deserve it or sought it out; but this is also accompanied by an acknowledgement that they are stereotypes. However, when other women utilised this interpretative repertoire, they talked about applying it to themselves before realising they did not wholly believe they did something wrong to deserve being raped or abused. As demonstrated in extracts 6, 7 and 8, all women who discussed this commonly held belief who had initially applied it to themselves (sometimes for decades); eventually questioned whether they really had done anything wrong.

Extract 6

SAMMI: *I questioned everything. You know, "Is it because I look older? Is it because I'm different to my sisters? Is it because I was um a quieter one than my two sisters? Is it because I wasn't close to my Mum, my Dad wasn't around, and I desperately wanted a Father figure in my life?" I looked at everything. So, I think for me that's when the penny dropped, because up until then I did used to think I must've done something wrong.*

Extract 7

JANE: *I was blamed that, you know, it was my fault, I was hanging around him too much, I was leading him on too much. And it's like, well not really! I used to play cards with you because you had no-one else that would hang out with you. It was like, well apparently, I was 'leading him on' and I was 'naïve because I was very young' and I 'didn't realise what I was doing.'*

Extract 8

MAY: *That sort of thing doesn't happen to people and if it does happen to you, you must have been asking for it. And I don't think at seven when it first happened, I was asking for it!*

This interpretative repertoire was of interest because whilst it was utilised by almost every woman as they explained victim blaming, they also accepted that it was not true – either for themselves or for others. Most of the women talked in past tense whilst applying it to themselves, but their explanations of this interpretative repertoire were entwined with present tense rebuttals of this commonly held narrative about sexual violence; suggesting a change in the way they constructed their blame over time.

An example of this is Extract 7 in which Jane gets part way through the explanation of why she was blamed for being raped before exclaiming 'Well not really!' before returning to the reasons why she was to blame and adding in the word 'apparently' and beginning to talk in quotes. In Extract 8, May talked in a similar way in which she began the sentence by describing herself as 'asking for it' right before stating 'I don't think at seven (...) I was asking for it!'.

As the interpretative repertoire was used in speech, women started to employ contradictory discourse about women doing something wrong to deserve sexual violence – and began to reject this interpretative repertoire, therefore contributing to an ideological dilemma about victim blaming. This resulted in a simultaneous construction of blame as being about women who do something wrong to deserve sexual violence whilst also rejecting this explanation, especially when it was applied to themselves.

Women also talked about doing 'everything right' and 'still' being raped or abused.

Extract 10

JANE: *If I'm not, if I'm, if I have not done a thing wrong, why do people keep coming for me? Why can't they just move on to someone else? I know it's horrible to say*

RESEARCHER: *Yeah, I, I get it, yeah.*

JANE...*but you do, but it is just something that goes through your mind at first and it's like, you know, "Why do they keep coming back for me then if I've done nothing wrong? So, what these guys have been saying must be true. They must be right, and I must blame myself, because I have done something wrong. But then I don't know if I'm one of them people because I can't see myself doing anything to lead anyone on...*

Sasha discussed the contradictory discourse that even if a woman did everything right or avoided danger or risk, there would still be a chance that they will be raped or assaulted. This contradicts the interpretative repertoire that women should change something about their character, behaviour or appearance in order to protect themselves.

Extract 11

SASHA: *cos you feel like there's an element of well, you know, you should look after yourself, but then you suddenly realise that actually if it wasn't you, it would be somebody else and all you're doing is protecting that, that one person, effectively, and*

226

essentially you're not even really protecting them because it could have happened no matter what they were wearing or what they were doing

This theme presented evidence of a commonly used interpretative repertoire that women must have done something wrong to deserve sexual violence, but also the emerging evidence of an ideological dilemma in which some women began to question whether they had done something wrong to deserve the rape or assault. This theme could relate to the interplay between rape myths and BJW, in which women are employing interpretative repertoires from societal rape myths and the belief that you get what you deserve in life, before interrogating these interpretative repertoires and concluding that these initially held beliefs cannot be right.

Women should change something about themselves to protect themselves from sexual violence

One of the most frequently utilised interpretative repertoires to construct their understanding of victim blaming and self-blame after sexual violence was the commonly held belief in society that women should change something about themselves (e.g., their behaviour, character, appearance, beliefs) to protect themselves from sexual violence. Originally theorised by Janoff-Bulman (1979), it is commonly believed that self-blame and making behavioural changes may be an adaptive coping mechanism which increases feelings of control for the woman (Frazier, 1990; Frazier, 2005). However, as the data were analysed, it became clearer that women were challenging the discourse that they should change something about themselves.

Women tended to employ this interpretative repertoire when talking about themselves and their own self-blame, rather than talking about external people utilising this interpretative repertoire in their reasons as to why others blamed them. Women talked about the need to change something about themselves in order to protect themselves from sexual violence.

In Extract 13, changing the self is framed by Sasha as a 'self-protective element' and a 'normal human defence mechanism' in which women try to work out what they did that led to being raped, and then try to change it so it doesn't happen again, which is similar to the theories surrounding counterfactual thinking, perceived control and even Janoff-Bulman's work (1979).

Extract 13

SASHA: *I think there is a really strong self-protective element to blaming yourself and it kind of rationalises things, it means if you don't do it again, it won't happen again. And so, I don't think it's – really, I don't think it's wholly external. I think it's a – I think it's a normal human defence mechanism, like trying to work out what it was that led up to disaster, then not doing that again. It's almost like a superstitious thing.*

Jane and Amy talked in past tense whilst describing normal, everyday behaviours they used to enjoy or feel comfortable with that they had changed since being blamed for sexual violence. They constructed their behaviours as problematic and talked about closing themselves away or becoming more conscious. Arguably, these constructions of changing the self as protection from sexual violence were more in line with contemporary findings that self-blame is maladaptive and impacts on social interactions and wellbeing of women (Miller et al., 2010).

Extract 14

JANE: *I can be quite friendly and huggy. I've closed myself away a bit more now, but I used to go up and hug all my best friends.*

Extract 15

AMY: *It was just cos I enjoyed dancing and feel good about myself when I dance. And I still do now, to this day. I'm a bit more conscious of when I dance and teach, cos I'm a dance teacher. But now it— I couldn't have helped my body shape. It was just how I grew. So, yeah.*

However, Danielle talked about a professional who directly told her she was to blame for being raped by a stranger who had drugged her after a ballet show. The words of the psychologist from whom she sought help for trauma, caused her to change many things about her life as she believed the psychologist was right – that she should change her appearance, career and behaviour in order to protect herself from sexual violence.

Extract 16

DANIELLE: *Yes so basically um I went to see a psychologist when I came back to England and he said, 'Look at yourself – you're a professional dancer, you are tall, beautiful and blonde – what did you expect?' And that's exactly what he said to me, so I walked out of that room and I changed my whole life. I mean I have only just started going back to my natural hair colour, but I dyed my hair black!*

RESEARCHER: *Did you?*

DANIELLE: *Yeah, I changed everything, and I thought if I could block that bit of my life away then it didn't happen, and I wanted to cover it all up so I could pretend it didn't happen*

RESEARCHER: *So that psychologist had a massive impact on you?*

DANIELLE: *Massive.*

RESEARCHER: *Do you think you were consciously thinking 'right, he must be right, I am going to change' or…*

DANIELLE: *Yeah, I agreed with it – I thought I agreed with it and I changed everything about myself. And I guess that's where some of the changing of yourself like your hair and your life – it was about protecting myself. Yeah. I didn't get as much attention from guys at all when I had black hair. I stopped dancing too. I opened a dance school for a few years and then I stopped.*

In Danielle's experience, the psychologist was the first person to construct a narrative in which Danielle was to blame. Before the appointment, she had never considered herself to blame (she was unconscious as she had been deliberately drugged by the perpetrator). However, once the psychologist had applied this interpretative repertoire to her experience, Danielle agreed, repositioned herself as to blame for being raped and in need of characterological and behavioural change.

This interpretative repertoire was featured in the answers of every participant. All women who took part in the study talked about making changes to themselves in order to protect themselves from future sexual violence, thereby positioning themselves as at fault for the rape or assaults they endured. Whilst discussing this interpretative repertoire, there was rarely mention of perpetrators or any other reasons for the sexual violence, other than their own behaviours, characters or appearances. Only one participant pointed out that irony of women being told to change something about themselves rather than perpetrators of crime being held responsible.

In Extract 17, Sasha compares the responses to terrorism to the responses to the rape of women and points out that women who are victims of sexual violence are asked to change themselves to protect themselves from crimes, whereas in terrorism crimes, the response is that no one should have to change themselves, to live a life free from crime and harm.

Extract 17

SASHA: *When it comes to rape, then it's like it's almost the complete opposite reaction, um, that we should change our behaviours, that we should change how we act so that we don't experience sexual violence, but the response to terrorism is usually one of, um, and that we should carry on as we were (laughs) and that, you know, people shouldn't stop us from being free!*

However, this interpretative repertoire appears to contribute to a significant ideological dilemma when women talked about the changes they made to their lives, bodies and characters feeling punitive or affecting their freedom.

As Sasha said, other victims of crime are not expected to change their lives in the way the women were describing and whilst all women accepted that they did change something about themselves to try to protect themselves from sexual violence, they often questioned whether it was fair or whether it was affecting their lives. Jane spoke of the blame stopping her from going outside, being sociable and leaving her bedroom, before suggesting that the self-blame also stopped her from seeking support.

Extract 18

JANE: *Erm, well it definitely has stopped me going outside and being sociable. I literally lock myself in, not just in my house, in my bedroom. It had to be my bedroom because that's where I felt safe. But if I didn't blame myself and I wasn't blamed so much by them who did all of that, I don't think I actually would have just gone and hid myself in my bed. I think I would have – sorry I'm starting to choke up a bit – sorry. I think I would have come and got a counsellor a lot sooner. A lot sooner.*

Amy and Demi discussed the psychological changes after they were raped as being a constant state of hypervigilance when they meet new men. They both talked about two competing narratives: the need to be cautious and to keep themselves safe versus having a normal, safe interaction with men they didn't know. Both highlighted positive interactions with men, but also an immediate sense of protection from danger.

Extract 19

AMY: *So, I dropped him off and it was fine, anyway. But that could've been something really serious and I thought, oh my god. And I was kicking myself after, for a few days after. I really upset myself, thinking, how did I let my – let this person come? Why did I be that friendly again? That, that was like a big no-no. I should've not even got that far for him to come to my house and know where I live. So I thought, when I was talking and having a nice, it was even a laugh – and I don't remember the last time I laughed – I thought, oh, it's nice to have a nice chat with a man and just have a nice conversation. So, I think I was maybe a bit too comfortable.*

Extract 20

DEMI: *When people, when like a guy gives you a compliment or anyone just gives you a compliment, you can think, 'Ah, they've just complimented me. I feel good in what I wear now.'*

RESERCHER: *Yeah.*

DEMI: *And they, I, forget to think what that compliment could mean... and if they follow you home.*

This theme presented a set of competing beliefs, impacts and feelings about self-blame and changing the self after sexual violence or in order to protect the self from sexual violence. Initially positioning themselves as to blame and in need of change to protect themselves, women also argued against and challenged the discourse that recommended they should change themselves or monitor their own behaviour. Contrary to theories that behavioural self-blame and changing the self could be an adaptive coping mechanism (Janoff-Bulman, 1979), women constructed this narrative as stressful, confusing, unhelpful and causing them a great deal of worry about whether their behaviours would lead to more sexual violence.

Knowing the sexual violence is wrong but not being able to stop it

This ideological dilemma was discussed by almost all women. It was presented in the discussions as a contradictory narrative of knowing that what was happening to them was wrong, abusive or violent but not feeling able to stop it from happening. Therefore, when discussing self-blame and victim blaming, women talked about the blame coming from knowing they were being abused or raped, but not doing enough to stop it. This contradicts the commonly held interpretative repertoire that women who are raped or abused did not know what was happening to them, and they therefore require information or education to protect themselves (Jago and Christenfield, 2018). Conversely, all of the women interviewed said they knew that what was happening to them was wrong but positioned themselves as powerless or not 'confident' enough to stop the offender.

May positioned men as 'in the right' and repeatedly positioned herself as having 'no worth' for 'allowing' the sexual abuse perpetrated by her stepfather, which she does report saying no to, despite manipulation.

Extract 21

MAY: *Yeah, yeah. My stepfather wanted to sleep with me, he promised he would point the house outside, if I would – so I did manage to say no to him, but it makes you feel as if men are in the right and you should do what they say and if you don't, um, you've got no worth, you feel as though you got no worth cos you let it happen and it's so stupid but it's your fault that you have no worth cos now you allowed it to happen.*

Demi also discussed being made to feel powerless due to manipulation and then being forced to perform sex acts she didn't want to do. Even after the rapes, Demi positioned herself as having no choice and losing confidence. Confidence became a recurring theme in which women talked about knowing they were being raped or abused but not having the confidence to stop it – or in Jane's case, disclose to others.

Extract 22

DEMI: *And then, sort of, so – and then because of that I kind of lost confidence and I didn't feel like I was wanted, so I didn't really want to have sex. I suppose, er, I didn't. And then I didn't really have a choice after a while, because I think it was like, "Oh I don't want this. I have to do this to keep him, to keep him here." And then it got to a stage where he was saying, "I will leave you if you don't do this." And so, I had to, you know, I, I, I like never have wanted to have anal sex in my life, it wasn't something that I want, I have ever wanted. But then I think you know where I was at the time, I don't think that would have – I wouldn't have left, I wouldn't have left.*

Jane positioned herself as a 'freak' with no confidence, who blamed herself and that no one would believe her disclosure, despite her knowing she was raped. She said that her lowered self-esteem made the self-blame worse which led to her positioning herself as a freak.

Extract 23

JANE: *And obviously being picked on lowered my confidence and my self-esteem went really low, like quite low after that compared to what it was before. I just made it worse, so I was less likely to speak out anyway because now I had no confidence. That made me think even worse that it was my fault, because it's like, "Oh maybe I am to blame because I'm a freak," so, "No-one likes freaks, no-one's gonna believe freaks."*

And even when some women spoke out about being raped as teenagers, their knowledge of the rape and their confidence to disclose was met with further manipulation and threats. Amy reported knowing that her friend's stepdad had raped her, but his wife told her they would kill her, or her friend would be taken into local authority care if she ever told anyone, which stopped her from disclosing.

Extract 24

AMY: *He was my friend from school's stepdad, and I told the mum. But the mum said, if I tell anybody, that, um, they would either kill me, or my friend will get put into care. And obviously now I'm like, that will never have happened. But as I say, I couldn't do anything.*

It became clear in the narratives of all the women, that they had said no and that they had known they were being abused or raped at the time of the offence, but constructed themselves as unable to say no, or unable to stop the perpetrator. In Phoebe's experience, she repeatedly said no and pushed the perpetrator away as she woke up and was ignored. Phoebe echoed the words of Amy and said she couldn't do anything to stop him, despite knowing she was being sexually assaulted in her hotel room.

Extract 25

PHOEBE: *But I remember then, actually in the room, we were just chatting on the bed, and, you know, he, he was touching me with his hands, and I was pushing his hand away, going no, no, no, I've just woken up, I don't want that. But he kept doing it, so in the end I just stopped fighting it. Um, so, you know, he was just touching me with his hands, you know, fingering me and stuff like that. Um, and I remember thinking then, I felt quite uncomfortable about it but felt like I couldn't – I couldn't do anything.*

Further to a feeling of not being able to do anything about a rape or assault, Sasha positioned herself as being stuck in a 'contract' with the perpetrator and there was no way of getting out of the situation. Despite knowing the situation had become dangerous and she did not want the sexual intercourse, Sasha presented a contradictory narrative of simultaneously knowing she didn't want sex but also felt the perpetrator was entitled to it because she had 'led someone on'.

Extract 26

SASHA: *what's acceptable to you, um, and also um, kind of in the moment labelling something as inappropriate because you're so used to kind of assuming that you've done something to get you to that stage, you think – you know, you kind of feel like you've signed a contract almost or like there's not getting out of this or, um, you've led someone on this long, so this is going to happen and you don't feel so able to say actually, you know, this shouldn't go any further. I need to leave.*

Together, this theme presented a contradictory interpretative repertoire about whether women know what sexual violence is as it is happening, and whether knowing they were being raped or assaulted would help them to stop the perpetrator. Women positioned themselves as powerless, not able to do anything to stop the perpetrator and lacking in confidence. This was particularly of interest considering that all women described saying 'no' repeatedly to the perpetrator before being manipulated or overpowered. This challenges previous research that found that when women did not fight back or assert themselves, they were less likely to acknowledge that they were raped or sexually assaulted (Donde et al., 2018). Here, it seems that women knew they were being sexually assaulted or raped, acknowledge it as such but were unable to prevent the perpetrator assaulting them.

Questioning whether she is truly to blame or whether she is overthinking it

When women discussed victim blaming and self-blame, there was a distinct ideological dilemma that presented repeatedly – and was talked about by almost all women. They talked about a feeling of over-analysing themselves or overthinking the victim blaming and self-blame, to a point where they become obsessed with it. Those women who were blamed for sexual violence perpetrated against them used a competing narrative in which they applied the interpretative repertoires of rape myths and of changing themselves to protect themselves from sexual violence. However, whilst they applied the interpretative repertoires, the women also talked of overthinking the rape or abuse which had led to over-analysis of self and an impact on their lifestyles and wellbeing. This theme again presents evidence that self-blame is not an adaptive or positive coping mechanism as presented by Janoff-Bulman (1979) and supports more contemporary research that self-blame and counterfactual thinking in such cases is unhelpful and potentially harmful (Frazier, 1990; 2005).

Danielle and Amy both used the word 'over-analyse' whilst talking in questions about themselves and the blame.

Extract 27

DANIELLE: *That would never happen to me again? I don't know? Maybe I over analyse it all? I do self-blame because I think it's looking back on things that happened and you think 'if I hadn't have done that then this wouldn't have happened' and it think it's this over-analysing that I do*

Extract 28

AMY: *And I still do now, to this day. I'm a bit more conscious of when I dance and teach, cos I'm a dance teacher. I always think, oh, is it cos of my body shape or size? You know, big boobs? (laughs). I don't know. I, I always— And even constantly to this day, I still overanalyse myself.*

RESEARCHER: *Yeah.*

AMY: *I don't think I'll ever not do that now.*

Jane talked of the questions she asked of herself based on rape myths and the interpretative repertoire that she should change something about herself to protect herself form sexual violence. She described it as 'over thinking', as did Amy and Demi. Amy described the overthinking as affecting her mental health, as she is constantly having to think and over-think the motives, actions and behaviours of herself and others, in order to stay safe from sexual violence.

Extract 29

JANE: *And everywhere I went I was like, "Hi," because if I knew someone I was like (gasps), "Oh no, what if I just smiled?" Or, "What if my skirt's a little bit too short?" "What if I need to wear a higher top," you know. "Should I wear my hair up or should I just wear it down straight, so it doesn't look too bouncy or flirty." I got to the point where I thought my nails, my shoes and my hair between them looked flirty, let alone my...my outfit. I was always over thinking.*

Extract 30

AMY: *Yeah. Sometimes it annoys me cos I feel like I'm always questioning people's motives or why they wanna be nice or... why are they aggressive, anything. Anything we say or do, I have to – I think, mentally, it drives you insane (laughs). Mentally, I think it gives you – Well, I'm sure I've got mental health (laughs) – Like it makes your head just go crazy, like you're over-thinking everything.*

This ideological dilemma revealed an active interaction with victim blaming and self-blame in which women did not passively accept self-blame, but did use it to question the decisions, actions, characters and motivations of themselves and others. The dilemmatic exchange between applying interpretative repertoires and rape myths to themselves but also constructing the constant questioning of themselves was reported to be exhausting and all encompassing, which appears to have negative consequences for their mental health and day to day lives.

Knowing logically that she is not to blame, but still feeling to blame

Within the conversations with all women, there were constructions of self-blame as being accepted but also not accepted at the same time. Women talked about knowing 'logically' and 'consciously' that they were not to blame or called their self-blame 'not logical' but described the self-blame as something deeper than logic or conscious thinking. It appears that women were struggling against the interpretative repertoires about blame which was resulting in a contradictory narrative in which women positioned themselves as not to blame but still 'feeling' to blame. The discussions became an uncomfortable construction of self-blame as being something that was deep within them, but not accepted as fact.

Extract 31

SASHA: *Um, I think – yeah, I think honestly yeah. I think if you asked me like consciously do you blame yourself, then I always say no but, um, I think it's a bit – it's kind of a bit more subtle, it's a bit deeper than that. Um, I think it does kind of – I don't really know how to describe it.*

Extract 32

RESEARCHER: *So, do you blame yourself less now?*

MAY: *Not. No. When you have lived with something like that for so many years its really difficult to change your way of thinking and you think you have but you haven't and it's still there because logically it doesn't make sense that you think that way, but you do. Yep.*

However, Amy described the feeling as being inverted. A feeling that on the surface, she thinks it was her fault for being raped – but that 'deep down' she knew it was not her fault. This theme presents a contradictory, almost dichotomous, relationship with self-blame after sexual violence.

Extract 33

AMY: *Now, I don't know. I still, it's still in my mind but I'm still not a hundred per cent convinced that it wasn't all of my fault (laughs). As much as I say it, that I think it's my fault, I know deep, deep, deep down that it's not my fault.*

RESEARCHER: *Hmm.*

AMY: *But unless something in my head just says, "Well, if you did this differently, then it may not have happened", or what-ifs. But you can be what-iffing it forever (laughs).*

Some women talked about their experience of being directly blamed by family members and initially accepting the blame or reasoning behind why they were raped or abused, before questioning their narrative. Sammi and Phoebe spoke of a realisation that occurred that they were not to blame for being raped, but both also talked back and forth between questioning the blamer and questioning themselves. The movement in the speech between questioning themselves and the person who blamed them was notable, in which women positioned themselves as victims of blaming from family and then repositioned themselves as assertive. However, both women were assertive in their heads, but did not challenge the blamer out loud.

Extract 34

PHOEBE: *and what my mum said, it sort of stayed with me for years. What my mum said to me is, she said, 'Oh she hasn't – she hasn't been raped, she's just had a nasty experience!' Um, and that, you know, I found that quite confusing because then I thought well actually then, have I? But I know – I know that I was crying. I know that he like, he hurt the top of my legs. I said no I didn't want to, um, and, you know, I think, you know, did my mum genuinely think that? So, what it did for me, was it reinforced in me really, that because of possibly my mum's perception of me being a bit of a slag, um, it kind of like, 'Well, you know, what do you expect?' type thing. And so, kind of reinforced really that I had… it was something that basically, chalked down to experience, not complaining about and just, you know, get on with it.*

Extract 35

SAMMI: *Uncle suggesting that I was a very flirtatious child, and could that possibly be a reason for why things had happened? And at the time I wasn't kind of aware, you know, I was 13, I wasn't kind of aware. But looking back on it now, I think that that is absolutely abhorrent to think that a child from five to thirteen years old can flirt with an adult and that is the reason why she deserves to be sexually abused. That's just, you know, shocking*

Discussions with women also included a further contradiction in the self-blame narrative in which women talked about blaming themselves, but not other women who had been subjected to the same violence.

Extract 36

MAY: *And in the same way, you still feel the same and you feel guilty, but would you blame a woman who went through the same thing as you? No!*

RESEARCHER: *No?*

MAY: *Because they are not me! (laughs) I know it sounds stupid.*

This theme (like the one before) presented self-blame after victim blaming to be diverse and dynamic – with women as active agents wrestling with the blame and using reason and logic to try to understand it rather than passive vessels which accept victim blaming to be true and then apply it to themselves. This theme also seems to present self-blame after victim blaming to be existing at two levels – a conscious, logical level and a deeper, emotional level that women described as difficult to explain or 'stupid'. This is a particularly important finding as many of the therapeutic interventions to challenge self-blame focus on cognitive restructuring, CBT or approaches that encourage the person to think differently about the sexual violence by breaking down rape myths or faulty beliefs (Jaycox, Zoellner & Foa, 2002, p.893). However, this is unlikely to be effective if women already agree that they 'know' they are not to blame but still 'feel' to blame.

Women positioned as responsible for men's behaviours

This subject position was the most frequently used by the women when discussing why women were blamed or why women blame themselves for sexual violence. Women positioned women as responsible for men's behaviours or talked about the way society had put them in that position as woman – in which others had held her responsible for the behaviours and responses of men. However, when talking about 'men', they were not just talking about perpetrators or men they deemed to be a risk to them – they also talked about being responsible for the reactions of their male family members when they learned that they had been raped.

Extract 37

DEMI: *When I've spoken to, um, someone, my mental health nurse about it she, she said, "Well are you going to go to the Police?" And I said, "Well, um, no." And then there was this sort of, "Well what if he does it so someone else?"*

RESEARCHER: *Oh no.*

DEMI: *Yeah. (Laughs) I thought— "Yeah, as if his behaviour is my responsibility!"*

Phoebe discussed national public awareness campaigns that also place responsibility on women, positioning them as the receiver of the messages about sexual violence, rather than perpetrators.

Extract 38

PHOEBE: *And I think even when there is big things from the police at certain times of the year, you know, like Christmas, around; all women make sure you've got enough money to get home, make sure you know, know who you're getting in a taxi – with – so I think it tends to place the responsibility on women for controlling… controlling men's behaviour in the main*

This discourse of women being repeatedly positioned as responsible for the behaviour of men who have raped and abused them was brought up by May, who asked rhetorical questions about why no one was asking questions directly to perpetrators of abuse and violence.

Extract 39

MAY: *But I've never understood why, we place you know, so much emphasis on women who are predominantly, you know, the, the victims in this, as opposed to actually asking the questions of, well why do those men rape in the first place? Why do they continue to beat their partner? My worry would be that, you know, is there something that makes it feel like again, that women can control that, you know, and they, they can't, it's absolutely... it's never their fault. It actually never rests with it being our fault.*

Sasha talked generally about feeling responsible for rape even when no one had told her so. She positioned herself and her own safety as second to the perpetrator's wants and need – to the point where Sasha apologised to one of the men who raped her because he complained that she didn't enjoy it.

Extract 40

SASHA: *I feel – I feel like it's getting better, but there's still this element of, um, I guess even when it's not kind of overtly blaming somebody, that there's an element of that you should take responsibility for what happened. So, you become more vulnerable because you're so used to kind of taking responsibility for that other person's actions, that you – it's almost like you think about them before you think about yourself and your safety*

RESEARCHER: *Yeah, I see what you're saying*

SASHA: *Um, and so I guess that is that kind of – that's when you take responsibility for something that is way beyond your control and, and after what, what was actually a rape, I texted him to say I was really sorry that I didn't enjoy it and that, um, it wasn't his fault that I just wasn't into it. I was like, 'Like, why did you apologise?' Um, and I guess that's taking that responsibility to its extreme, is to say sorry for, um, getting raped*

The positioning of women as responsible for men's behaviours extended past the perpetrator and towards husbands, boyfriends and fathers. Demi and two other women positioned themselves as not only responsible for the rapes, but responsible for the impact their disclosure would have on male family members. They did not discuss the same concern about impact on or responsibility for their mothers, or female friends or sisters. Demi told her mum and friends, but never told her Dad as she felt responsible for his reaction.

Extract 41

DEMI: *I feel also that, I don't, I, I'm worried that it will cause other people pain. You know, I can't imagine telling my Dad that something like that's happened to me. I just feel like I don't – he – it would hurt him, and I don't want to hurt him, and I don't want him to have to think about it. Um, so I'd rather just keep all the pain to myself.*

This theme was based on subject positioning in the talk about victim blaming and self-blame of women. It demonstrated that even when women were not directly blamed by someone, they already felt a sense of responsibility from their upbringing and from society that positioned them as responsible for the actions of men – and even the emotions and responses of men. This theme is linguistically of interest, as it was the only theme that utilised the term 'responsibility' instead of blame. Women applied the word 'responsibility' to construct and sometimes reject, a positioning of them as in control of the actions, reactions, behaviours and motivations of men. This finding is particularly significant considering the debate in the literature about the conflation of words 'blame' and 'responsibility' (Critchlow et al., 1985; Shaver and Drown, 1986).

Women are positioned as victim of a misogynistic society

The final theme was a subject position in which women were positioned as secondary victims of a misogynistic society that did not treat them fairly. Women discussed victim blaming as a symptom of a society that discriminates against and attempts to control women through culture, media, gender roles and societal norms. All women talked about this subject position.

Phoebe positioned women as treated badly due to social messages and attitudes towards women, and Sasha positioned women as being treated unfairly in contrast to men, who are not expected to curb their sexuality or behaviours.

Extract 42

PHOEBE: *I think, because we do live in quite a patriarchal society. I think you've got a lot of misogyny that comes around, um, magazines, social media, so I think you know, the attitudes to women, um, are not in the main very healthy. It's not just about the sexual assault stuff I guess, it's around the traditional roles that women have, and you know, what are those messages that people pick up there. Um, you know, and how they treat women in general.*

Extract 43

SASHA: - *I think what feeds into that is this idea of, um, I guess how autonomous women should be and how they should be well-behaved. I think that really fits – kind of feeds into that and so it makes it easier because we don't, we don't expect men to do the same thing, even though they do get – there is sexual violence against men. Um, there isn't that same pressure that they should somehow, you know, curb their sexuality or their behaviour or how they dress, um, and I think that's to do with just how easy women, er, and their role in society.*

Demi and Amy both related victim blaming to a punishment for women and girls being sexually active in a society which objectifies and abuses women but does not see them as independent sexual beings. This is an interesting finding when considered with the findings from the BOWSVA study which found one of the seven components of victim blaming to be 'the sexually active woman', who deserves much more blame for sexual violence perpetrated against her, simply for being sexually liberal or enjoying sex.

Extract 44

DEMI: *Yeah. But I'm also, well, I'm also convinced that we still have a massive problem with women being sexual beings. And so, there's this you know, if a woman has gone out and had a one-night stand and is assaulted on her one-night stand, then it's her fault because she shouldn't be having a one-night stand. Not that a man shouldn't be behaving in that way. Um, and so I think that there's a lot tied up around women's sexuality.*

Extract 45

AMY: *But then I think I was partly to blame because — Not blame, but, okay, maybe, because, um, he heard that I had a boyfriend…and because I had had sex and I was young. I wasn't sixteen. Is that, is that the law, sixteen or eighteen?*

RESEARCHER: *Hm-hm, yeah, sixteen.*

AMY: *And I was nearly sixteen (laughs), so I was like, oh, this is probably punishment because I wasn't sixteen yet. That's what I thought in my head.*

Jane and Sasha positioned victim blaming as a way in which women were unfairly blamed for behaviours, characteristics and appearances that would be acceptable for a man in the same community.

Extract 46

JANE: *Men can go around with their tops off, half naked, topless in small shorts – it doesn't matter, they wear what they like. Women walk around in shorts and a little tank top, and they were asking for it if they get caught up a back street.*

Extract 47

SASHA: *it becomes even more clear that, that women are being constrained and being told to live life less than, than men because of the kind of threat that's around um, but I think because of how we're immersed in this society that blames women and sees women more in a certain way that it makes it so much easier, um, to then blame yourself even for the most obvious examples*

This theme is an important inclusion as all women who took part in the study positioned themselves and other women, as victims of an inherently unfair, misogynistic society in which their behaviours, appearances, characters and lifestyles were under constant scrutiny when compared with the men in their communities or families. When asked why they thought women were blamed for sexual violence, all answers contained a construction of a harmful, woman-hating society that judged, blamed and hurt them daily. They also constructed men as unanswerable to the same standards or judgement and often compared themselves to men when positioning themselves as affected by misogyny. In the talk, they used the comparisons with men's lives to construct a gap in justice and fairness in the way women were blamed for sexual violence.

The results presented eight key themes that provide insight into the way women construct victim blaming and self-blame of women through talk. Through the use of interpretative repertoires, ideological dilemmas and subject positions, women employed a complex and dynamic range of discursive tools to discuss victim blaming and self-blame in often contradictory and dichotomous ways.

As the most dominant interpretative repertoire, victim blaming, and self-blame had strong links to common rape myths and gender role stereotypes utilised in society. Women discussed every rape myth in the updated IRMAS subscales 1 (she asked for it) and 3 (It wasn't really rape) but did not mention or utilise any of the common rape myths from subscale 2 (he didn't mean to) or subscale 4 (she lied) (McMahon and Farmer, 2011). This is important because whilst the use of rape myths was frequent in the talk, none of the women positioned the perpetrators as not meaning to hurt them and they did not position other women as lying about rape or sexual assault. They did, however, use the remaining rape myths to talk about why other women were blamed, why they were personally blamed and why they blame themselves. Rape myths recurred in the talk, with women using the commonly held myths to question themselves, their appearance, character and behaviour before, during and after they were raped or assaulted (Payne, 1999; Peterson & Muehlenhard, 2004).

In line with findings from others, the women in this study were aware of a 'perfect victim' stereotype arising from the powerful rape myths and victim stereotypes – and they did measure themselves against them (Campbell et al., 2001; Kahn et al., 1994; Koppelaar et al., 1997; Mont et al., 2003; Ryan, 1988). Women talked about a hierarchy of victimhood in which they were measuring and positioning themselves against commonly held beliefs to assess whether they were a 'real' victim of rape or not. This is not necessarily because women did not believe they had been raped or abused, but seemingly because they were assessing whether others would see their culpability in the same way.

Sasha described her rape as 'as good as you're going to get' to mean that her rape and rapist fit all the ideal stereotypes of a 'real' rape in the interpretative repertoire that she hoped would protect her from blame. She was attacked in broad daylight, by an illegal immigrant who jumped out of a hidden space and raped her in the street in front of witnesses. She recognised that this rape fit a specific stereotype of rape and thought this would remove the victim blaming she may have faced. However, she then told how she realised she was not the 'perfect victim' when the police learned she had been raped before, that she had been drinking before the offence occurred and that she had mental health issues. She recognised that she was being constructed as the non-credible victim and being measured against the commonly accepted rape myths and victim stereotypes, she had heard before.

Other women discussed how aware they were that the societal narratives about women's sexuality had positioned them as either deserving or sexual violence or deserving of some sort of punishment for being sexually active, dressing in revealing clothing or having multiple partners. In keeping with the findings from Chapter 5, women in this study discussed the dichotomous expectation on women to be sexually available, to be sexy and attractive and to want sex with men – but that these wants and desires would result in more victim blaming because society had a problem with female sexuality and sexual pleasure. This echoes the arguments of Ringrose (2013) and Duschinsky (2013).

Women did wrestle with whether they deserved to be raped and abused, often concluding that they didn't know if they deserved it or not – or using an ideological dilemma which kept them stuck between feeling that no women deserved to be raped or abused, but often wondered whether they were subjected to sexual violence as a punishment because they had done something wrong. This bore strong similarities to the way BJW was theorised by Lerner (1980) and in the way Janoff-Bulman (1979) had theorised about characterological self-blame, in which the women had begun to consider if their personal characters or something about them was causing them to deserve sexual violence.

All women experienced victim blaming and self-blame and described the profound impact this had on them, most often resulting in them changing something about themselves. Janoff-Bulman (1979) argued that self-blame could be adaptive and positive because it could help women subjected to sexual violence to feel more in control by changing something about themselves to avoid future revictimisation. However, this assertion was not supported by the current study, as although women did blame themselves, and they did try to change something about themselves, this did not make them feel more in control or empowered. They described years of questioning themselves, over-analysing themselves, over-thinking their experiences, decisions and characters, but they did not describe a feeling of control. In fact, two women described it as feeling like they were 'going crazy'.

Women also did not appear to believe that the changes they made would protect them from further sexual violence. This finding is important both for research and for practical applications in the world. Women are often told to change something about themselves, to become more aware, to educate themselves or to learn to spot the signs of a rapist or abuser. Despite all women in the sample applying this interpretative repertoire to their own lives and even following the explicit advice from family, friends and professionals to change something about themselves, this was constructed as dilemmatic because women did not believe it would protect them from sexual violence despite making the changes.

Women who had been blamed for sexual violence made significant changes to their lives that were either perceived as related to the offence (stopped drinking in bars) or were not related at all to the offence (quit job as a dance teacher years later) but felt protective or relevant. Women often accepted the interpretative repertoire for long periods of time before it became dilemmatic, with some women making life changes for years before realising that they were not protective – or spending decades trying to protect themselves better whilst still being abused by partners or family members. Women therefore had a complicated relationship with the discourse that women should change themselves to protect themselves from sexual violence. Although they did accept this to be true and they did make changes, in the interviews they constructed this as a contradictory and complex issue in which they had slowly come around to a new understanding that the messages they had been given were wrong, they had not protected them, and they had restricted their lives.

Looking past the rape myths, many of the other findings were highly dynamic and dilemmatic. Women did not construct victim blaming or self-blame as passively absorbed from society or from their support network, rather, it was more complicated. Women did talk about messages in society, media, policing, law, communities and culture and did apply them to themselves, but they also rejected them. Whilst women positioned themselves as to blame for sexual violence and some even directly said that they still felt they were to blame for rape, assaults and abuse, they simultaneously stated that they 'knew' they were not to blame. There was a clear dilemma for women between 'knowing' and 'feeling' self-blame.

It appears that women constructed self-blame as existing on two competing levels. Women described a difference between feeling to blame for sexual violence and knowing whether they were actually to blame for the offence. This suggests that despite the harmful victim blaming the women experienced, and the self-blame they still felt years later, there was a level of reasoning that rejected those narratives and constructed the perpetrator as to blame for sexual violence. However, this created a dilemma in the talk, in which women said they knew they were not to blame, but still felt to blame. The phrase 'deep down' was used repeatedly, as though women were alluding to a feeling of self-blame that was much deeper than logical, rational thoughts about sexual violence perpetrator and victim roles.

Women positioned themselves as to blame for sexual violence by labelling themselves unassertive or lacking in confidence, which supports previous arguments by Livingston et al. (2007) and Macy et al. (2006) that women who are not assertive blame themselves for sexual violence. Further, low assertiveness of women is argued to be related to repeat sexual victimisation (Greene & Navarro, 1998). One of the main reasons given by women for blaming themselves was because they knew they were being abused or raped but felt that they could not do anything stop the perpetrator. However, this self-blame for lack of action contrasted with descriptions that indicated that every woman interviewed did do something to try to stop the perpetrator, despite feeling that they didn't. Women reported that they said no repeatedly to the perpetrator, tried to talk their way out of situation, tried to appease the offender, pushed him away and resisted – but they still also positioned themselves as not having done enough to stop him. They talked frequently about not having the confidence to have stopped the perpetrator, and as they spoke, they often finished sentences with the phrase 'there was nothing I could do', as they positioned themselves as powerless to the offence.

This has important implications for sexual refusal assertiveness research and programmes, because the premise of such research and programmes (Kitzinger and Frith, 1999; Women & Equalities Committee, 2016) are based on the view that women were raped because they did not assert themselves, did not try to stop the offender or did not say 'no' clearly enough (which is a rape myth used in the U-IRMAS). However, the current research suggests that the women interviewed all tried repeatedly to stop the offence but seemingly due to the rape myths and interpretative repertoire that they should have done something differently or more radical to prevent the offence, the women still reported feeling that they didn't do enough.

Finally, women positioned themselves as victims of a misogynistic and patriarchal society that simultaneously objectified, sexualised, controlled, judged, discriminated against and mistreated them. They were very aware of the social constructions of women's gender roles and how they were 'supposed' to behave, appear and live their lives. Women described victim blaming as a symptom of a misogynistic society that repeatedly provides hostile messages about women through the media and does not hold men responsible for their sexual or violent offences towards women. Victim blaming was explained using contrasting experiences for men and women in which women were positioned as more harshly judged for every day behaviours or experiences than men.

Reflexive comment

Conducting this study was a humbling experience and provided several learning curves for me. I was struck by how complex the narratives were, how informed the women were about the origins of victim blaming and how clearly they saw and labelled misogyny. The women I interviewed understood rape myths and could easily identify sources of victim blaming, sexism and misogyny that they felt had influenced the blame and self-blame they experienced. It struck me that the women I interviewed understood and articulated the dynamics they live in, they named male violence confidently and they also called out victim blaming as and when they saw it. This means that I must have been holding some pre-existing belief that the women I interviewed would not be able to explain the origins and motivations for blaming women, which surprised me.

This confronted me with my second learning curve – that women were not passively absorbing victim blaming, self-blame or misogyny from society and support networks. Their descriptions suggested that they were wrestling with it, fighting it, interrogating it, challenging it and resenting it. Despite this messy process, they did blame themselves. However, they did not do this in a one-dimensional, linear, passive way. They blamed themselves but simultaneously told themselves that they were not to blame. They changed something about themselves but simultaneously knew that changing themselves would not protect them from sexual violence. They questioned their behaviours and characters, but they also criticised themselves for doing this. Clearly the connection between self-blame, acceptance of victim blaming, and rape myths was much more complicated and fraught than I had been led to believe by the literature.

By centring the voices of women and exploring the discursive tools they used to construct victim blaming and self-blame, this study has highlighted that women have a complex, challenging and active relationship with victim blaming of themselves and self-blame. Rather than positioning themselves as passively and naively accepting rape myths, victim blaming, self-blame and misogyny due to lack of understanding or awareness – women actively interrogated, criticised and attempted to reject blame for sexual violence perpetrated against them. Despite this construction of self being hopeful and active, women were simultaneously aware of how others perceived them to be to blame for sexual violence and utilised the interpretative repertoires in society to compare their sexual violence against the victim blaming messages and rape myths they knew they would encounter.

This section will discuss how the findings from this study influenced the aims of the next study. The study reported in Chapter 16 is a qualitative semi-structured interview study that seeks to explore the way professionals construct the victim blaming and self-blame of women after sexual violence. This study was designed to use the same questions as the study contained within this chapter, to explore whether professionals working in sexual violence had a similar way of understanding and constructing victim blaming and self-blame as the women whom they are supporting.

In this chapter, the findings suggested that women were dynamic thinkers who understood the origins of victim blaming, challenged and rejected victim blaming whilst also believing and applying it to themselves. It was therefore important to take the findings from this chapter and explore whether the professionals working with women subjected to sexual violence also perceived women as dynamic, informed thinkers who could hold conflicting, simultaneous interpretative repertoires and dilemmas. The way professionals use language to construct women, self-blame and victim blaming may be important to practice and the experiences of women subjected to sexual violence.

16.

Talking to professionals about victim blaming

To build on and support the previous study exploring the way women construct victim blaming and self-blame through talk, this study sought to explore how professionals working directly with women subjected to sexual violence would construct the same issues.

In the UK, support services for women subjected to sexual violence are predominantly provided by the charitable sector. Services include helplines, advice and counselling services, Independent Sexual Violence Advocate (ISVAs), victim support services, domestic and sexual violence refuges and peer support services (Du Mont et al., 2003; Maier, 2013). Professionals working in the sectors that support women subjected to sexual violence have been shown to accept rape myths and victim blaming beliefs at around the same rate as the general public (Martin, 2005; Sleath, 2011). Older qualitative research found that rape victim advocates held beliefs that rape was a crime of power but did endorse the rape myth that men who rape women are sick or mentally ill (Andersen & Renzetti, 1980).

Despite these professionals working in this sector, there is little qualitative research exploring how professionals understand victim stereotypes, self-blame and victim blaming of women subjected to sexual violence (Maier, 2013). Research about victim blaming of women tends to focus on quantitative, self-report measure studies which led to calls for more naturalistic, conversation-based research (Anderson, 1999). Of the small number of qualitative studies with sexual violence support professionals, the focus tended to be on service delivery or barriers to collaboration with other services (Campbell, 1998; Maier, 2013; Payne, 2007).

The second issue to explore is whether and how professionals could work with women to support them to understand that they are not to blame for sexual violence. Victim blaming and self-blame of women has been shown to be influenced by and constructed with language and discourses about women, sexual violence and blame. Relativist approaches to language propose that language constructs reality, meaning that the words we use to express our ideas and narratives about ourselves and the world can give us clues to the power dynamics, constructions, positions and dilemmas in social issues (Edley, 2001; Wetherell, Taylor & Yates, 2014).

Given these issues, the current study sought to explore the way professionals working with women subjected to sexual violence described and constructed victim blaming and self-blame.

Secondly, the study sought to explore how professionals talked about their role in helping women to reduce feelings of self-blame and the harm caused by victim blaming. This study sought to listen to professionals working with women subjected to sexual violence, and to present the discursive tools utilised to construct victim blaming and self-blame of the women they support.

By employing a critical discursive analysis again, this study aims to answer the research question:

How do professionals use language to construct their understanding of victim blaming and self-blame of women who have been subjected to sexual violence?

The sample for this study was eleven professionals working in sexual violence support services, working with caseloads of women who had been subjected to sexual violence and abuse.

Professionals came from three different sexual violence support services in the Midlands, UK. Whilst all professionals supported women after sexual violence, they took on a variety of roles including counsellors, psychotherapists, addiction counsellor, ISVA (independent sexual violence advocate), counselling managers and CEO of rape and sexual violence centre.

All professionals were female except one who was a male counsellor working with women who had been raped or abused and developed addictions. There was no stipulation for professionals to be female, but only one male applied to take part in this study. Having one male participant does present an important challenge for this study, especially as some could argue that he has a different perspective as a male who is not subjected to the same experiences as females in the workplace or in his life. However, his responses were not noted to be particularly different from the responses of the female professionals in this study and he did not appear to demonstrate any divergent views to any of the other professionals.

Eight professionals took part in the study in face-to-face interviews and three chose to take part over the phone due to their schedules.

Interviews varied from around 35 minutes to 75 minutes and were based on the questions set out in the semi-structured interview question schedule.

The same analytic steps were followed as described in the previous chapter. Data was transcribed, anonymised and all names were replaced by a pseudonym.

Professionals were also invited to give feedback on the findings and chapter written here before it was submitted. All professionals were contacted by email with copies of the findings from discourse analysis and a final draft copy of this chapter. They were given a month to submit any written feedback if they wanted it to be included in this chapter. Out of eleven professionals, seven wrote back with feedback reported below.

Learning from feedback

Professionals replied with a wide range of responses to their interviews and the findings from the study. All thanked me for the work and expressed interest in taking part and the added opportunity of being able to read the discourse analysis findings and a copy of this chapter. One woman wrote back to say,

> 'It made interesting, but quite honestly surprising reading. I actually felt really sad to read the professional perspectives of victim blaming. It reads almost that professionals have very little in the way of hope for the women we support.'

This response was shared by another professional who wrote:

> 'It was clearly a really difficult topic with many contradictions that you must have struggled with- we didn't present you with a very straight forward and coherent set of responses did we!?'

The feedback I received from professionals sparked long conversations about how we could move forward and change practice to ensure women and girls were getting the best service from professionals who may feel that deconstructing feelings of blame is difficult to do. It was an important and enlightening process to talk to professionals about their interpretation, of my own interpretation of their talk. All professionals felt that they were fairly represented, but most expressed surprise at some of the findings from others and when grouped together.

Results

This section will present the results from the critical discourse analysis to answer the research question:

How do professionals use language to construct their understanding of victim blaming and self-blame of women who have been subjected to sexual violence?

The secondary research question:

How do professionals talk about supporting women who blame themselves for sexual violence?

Key discursive tools used by professionals to talk about victim blaming and self-blame of women

Discursive tool	Occurrences in speech	Number of professionals using this discursive tool
Rape myths and stereotypes	17	11 (100%)
Women who cannot deconstruct self-blame must have childhood traumas	15	7 (64%)
Women positioned as passive and helpless to absorbing victim blaming into their own belief system	18	11 (100%)
Family are positioned as the most important factor in victim blaming and self-blame of women	21	11 (100%)
Telling a woman that she is not to blame does not mean she will feel a reduction of blame	19	11 (100%)
Direct versus indirect challenge of self-blame	14	9 (82%)

Findings are presented as interpretative repertoires, ideological dilemmas and subject positioning in the language of the professionals (IR, ID, and SP, respectively). Multiple codes could be applied if sentences or passages contained multiple discursive tools. However, important consideration must be given to the fact that ideological dilemmas and subject positioning of self and others are often influenced by and interlinked with interpretative repertoires and so presenting them as separate artefacts in language is not always helpful.

Rape myths

Rape myths were discussed frequently by all professionals, who cited rape myths as the main reason they believed women were still being blamed for sexual violence. As a dominant interpretative repertoire, professionals quickly and frequently gave examples of rape myths affecting the women they work with and affecting other parts of practice such as law, health care and therapy. Professionals gave hundreds of examples of rape myths being used in the lives of the women they were supporting.

Extract 1:

GEORGIA: *There is quite a lot, you know, if you wear – wore certain colour shoes or if you wore short – a short skirt or all that usual stuff; you wear too much make-up. And then you go out drinking and that, then, you know, what do you expect?*

Extract 2:

SARA: *Erm, but I think in general there's this kind of culture of focussing on women were wearing, whether they were drinking alcohol at the time, what their sort of history has been of sexual relationships, whether sort of put themselves in a vulnerable position. And so, I think there's like a real culture of trying to explain it away.*

Extract 3:

SAMMI: *And I think that it is easy to say, "Well she should have kept her legs crossed," or, "She should have fought more," or, "She should have screamed." And again, if you don't have that understanding of perhaps how the body responds to that, you know, that fight/flight response, then yes it's very easy to say well,*

"You know, she should have fought him off," or, "She should have screamed louder."

Professionals spoke about rape myths, generally in third person, as if they were talking about what they had heard others say about women. They construct the use of long lists of rape myths as a cultural or societal issue and whilst they distanced themselves from that culture or society, they talked about the way women they worked with would employ the same rape myths when deciding whether to tell their family or friends what had happened, supporting existing evidence (Mont et al., 2003; Campbell et al., 2001; Ullman, 2010) .

Extract 4:

MADDY: *Societal (sighs) responses I've encountered are quite negative. I think that's a massive, massive problem that we've got, um, just through the myths and stereotypes that are just rife within society. And so many people that I work with actually don't tell the nearest people to them because of those myths and stereotypes, that they won't be believed. And – or they are gonna think it's their fault and – and, you know, they've asked for it, so to speak.*

Maddy was not the only participant to describe rape myths as a 'massive' problem. In fact, every participant situated rape myths and victim blaming of women as coming from 'society'. Often, professionals would separate themselves from the construct of society in their talk and talked in third person about the society that uses rape myths and stereotypes – positioning society as the problem, positioning themselves as outside of that problem. Professionals described victim blaming as being used by people from the rest of society, outside of the field of sexual violence support.

Extract 5:

FAY: *I think there is a large proportion of society though who are at one end of – of the scale which would give a, um, a response which is blaming, unsupportive, um, cruel, um, (…). Some of them are all formed – most of them, all of them, are formed around the myths of sexual violence.*

Extract 6:

JULIANNA: *Er, I think society at large don't like to think that people are, are, are capable of conscious acts like that.*

Extract 7:

ROB: *Almost saying, well she asked for it, and that, that kind of – you know, putting yourself in a vulnerable position – I just think, you know, society infects everything with that general view.*

Professionals positioned themselves as different and separate from the society that used rape myths to blame women for sexual violence. Society is constructed as a judgmental, uneducated, all-encompassing force that could influence millions of people to accept the rape myth discourses in order to blame women. In extract 7, Rob describes societal rape myths as 'infecting' everything with a general view that women 'ask for it' or put themselves in positions where they are sexually harmed.

Women who cannot deconstruct self-blame must have childhood traumas

One of the most frequent themes in the data was an interpretative repertoire that was utilised by 7 of the 11 professionals. This common narrative was an explanation about women who struggle to let go of, or challenge self-blame, which the 7 professionals put down to the woman having childhood traumas that left her weaker, with lower self-esteem or lower self-worth which meant she was unable to deconstruct the victim blaming being put towards her, and the feelings of self-blame she had about herself. Charlotte went further and positioned women who could not challenge victim blaming or feelings of self-blame as not sophisticated or mature enough to realise what was happening to them, which strongly contrasts with the findings from the previous study with women themselves (Chapter 5).

Extract 8:

CHARLOTTE: *They're not sophisticated enough, they're not mature enough to recognise what has happened to them. So, it's – again it's a really subtle process. So, I think in – in people who've been abused in childhood, it's really easy to see how the* blame gets shifted to them, um, through the process of grooming, um, and then they're not able to get out of it

Extract 9:

TERI: *So, is it, is it possible with everybody to turn that off completely for life? No, I don't, sadly I don't think it is, I think you will always have people that will always feel that it's – they have some connection to, to the abuse in some form. And I think probably more so in the people that have been abused from a very young age or the people that have, um, been groomed*

Professionals positioned some women as beyond help if they were abused in childhood – positioning the belief of blame as so deeply embedded and accepted by the woman that it would be very difficult for anyone to challenge it or reduce it. Teri frames some girls who have been groomed in childhood as having a 'connection to the abuse' and that they will 'always feel' that way (blame themselves for sexual violence). Whilst this does not directly blame the women for sexual violence, it does position them as being 'connected' and unable to 'turn it off', which positions them as unchangeable or helpless.

Extract 10:

JULIANNA: *the person has then become accustomed to, this, this is what happens and there is no way to fight it or um – so they just have a very strong belief, I think they are conditioned to accept that's just, that's just my lot in life.*

Extract 11:

SARA: *I think it's so evident to me that people who had sort of really, really difficult early childhoods and relationships and sort of very difficult relationships where they haven't been valued it's so much more difficult, erm, to work through those beliefs about themselves than it is with someone who's got a different kind of foundation.*

Extract 12:

MADDY: *It's a really difficult one that is, because if they don't have kind of – if it is just them telling themselves that, "Well, I deserved that" then (pause) my experience tells me that well, that person's self-worth is so very small to begin with so there must have been something either missing or something that's happened before that.*

Maddy's account bore striking resemblance to that of Jane in the previous chapter, who talked about her self-esteem being so low that she sometimes believed she was to blame and positioned herself as a 'freak' who no one would believe. However, Jane stated that the sexual violence eroded her self-esteem whilst Maddy positioned women who blame themselves as already having something 'either missing or something that's happened before'. This supports work by Maier (2013) that professionals can successfully break down some myths about victims (by talking about rape myths openly and critically) but can still hold other victim blaming beliefs.

There were no other explanations offered by the professionals to account for why some women might struggle to deal with feelings of self-blame. When asked whether there were some women who found self-blame difficult to shift, all professionals who discussed this topic unanimously answered that it would be the women who were also abused in childhood. This was an interpretative repertoire that was utilised and discussed in the same way across 9 professionals, suggesting either that women who were abused in childhood do seem to struggle much more with reducing feelings of self-blame as suggested by some research (Filipas & Ullman, 2006; Messman-Moore & Long, 2003), or that professionals have constructed those women to be more accepting of victim blaming and self-blame because they have suffered from it for much longer. In extract 12, Maddy describes women who cannot reduce their feelings of self-blame as having 'something missing or something that's happened before'. In turn, this meant that professionals were constructing some women as better at reducing feelings of self-blame than others. This finding is of interest, as some professionals have constructed women as traumatised victims, trapped inside a belief of self-blame that they cannot get out of.

Women positioned as passive and helpless to absorbing victim blaming into their own belief system

This theme contained two competing subject positions of women as simultaneously passive, helpless and powerless to absorbing victim blaming beliefs but also strongly resistant to absorbing counter-narratives and beliefs. Within the talk, this created an ideological dilemma for professionals who frequently described self-blame as a feeling that women absorb from society without any interrogation but also identified hat the same women were resistant to new beliefs from the participant.

When talking about where self-blame comes from in women who have been subjected to sexual violence, professionals constructed women as passive, with the words 'internalise', 'absorb', 'accept', 'adopt', 'automatically take on' and 'believe' used frequently. Women were constructed to be highly influenced by others and not able to challenge or confront victim blaming, which they believed completely.

Extract 13:

MADDY: *In the beginning stages of therapy they absolutely believe whoever's told them so that they – that is – now become their belief.*

RESEARCHER: *Right okay. Yeah.*

MADDY: *So, they've kind of opened up to their sister or whoever. They've reflected that, that they shouldn't have put themselves in that position and it is their fault, then they adopt that.*

Extract 14:

GEORGIA: *I think at the time she had no other option other than to, obviously this is my mum telling me 'I'm bad, I'm doing the wrong thing.'*

Extract 15:

TARA: *But over the years what I have seen is more that people do tend to soak up those messages. It's somehow, it's that way their brain works isn't it?*

Further than this, professionals positioned women as naïve absorbers of other's beliefs, in which they will quickly adopt another point of view or perception of blame without argument, because they have low self-worth.

Extract 16:

GEORGIA: *So, their – their self-worth is based on what other people tell them they're worth.*

RESEARCHER: *Yeah.*

GEORGIA: *So, they haven't really, um, developed their own sense of who they are, and they haven't any sense of value for themselves other than what other people give them. So that's, um, they're always dependent on the opinion of others.*

Extract 17:

JULIANNA: *And very often they internalise that, I lied so I deserved it, so it's all my fault. (Sighs) Sadly it's not hard to convince someone that they are too blame, um, it can be done really quite subtlety without the words; it's your fault, you caused it.*

However, despite the frequent positioning of women as passive to the internalisation of new narratives or beliefs about blame, the same professionals also positioned women as being strongly resistant to new beliefs that counter self-blame, presenting evidence of an ideological dilemma about the passivity and agency of women.

Extract 18:

MADDY: *Absolutely, yeah. And I guess it's (pause) it's a time game with them, because, you know, um, you – you work with – with your client at their pace as well, so with those that are really kind of – I guess (sighs) just in that bubble of self-blame and they are resistant to even entertaining the idea that it actually might not be, it lengthens the work. Makes it twice as long.*

Extract 19:

JULIANNA: *Yeah, I think there are, there are clients like that who are completely closed to the thought that, you know, it could be anyone else's responsibility*

In Extract 20 below, Fay describes the way women might challenge her when she is trying to convince them that they are not to blame and that they defend their beliefs. This is very different from the construction of women as being helpless and powerless to new beliefs and perceptions of sexual violence. Women subjected to sexual violence are described as passively, automatically taking on a new belief but also defensively and actively challenging a second new belief.

Extract 20:

FAY: *And really, you know, get going on high level challenge, um, so timing is important. I suppose, um, wh- you've got to look at if you're challenged in defence, if it's a part of a person's defence, that there needs to be something else in place that they can draw on because a defence is a strategy.*

This theme suggests an ideological dilemma in which women are positioned as both passive and active in constructing their beliefs about self-blame. This could be due to the strengths of the messages, in which victim blaming and self-blame of women is possibly a more powerful and common narrative and so more readily accepted by the women – but the counter-narrative that it was not their fault is possibly more uncommon and less readily accepted by women. It could also be that when professionals describe women as passively absorbing self-blame and victim blaming from others, they assume that the process was quick and passive, rather than being a difficult, complex process in which her beliefs are changed or confirmed, or both. Arguably, if professionals had initially constructed women as passive, defenceless and easy to convince of new beliefs about themselves, this theme may present discourses of frustration when women do not accept their new, more positive beliefs, being presented to them by the professionals.

Family are positioned as the most important factor in victim blaming and self-blame of women

This theme was one of the most commonly utilised interpretative repertoires and ideological dilemmas in the study, with all professionals positioning the family unit as being the most influential and pivotal factor that would influence self-blame and the acceptance of victim blaming. However, the discussion around the support network of family and friends became more complicated, with professionals describing the support network as the most important part of the help and recovery a woman might need, even though every participant described the family as being the main source of victim blaming and feelings of self-blame. So, whilst the family were described as causing harm to the woman (which supports findings from Campbell et al. (2001) and Kalra and Bhugra, 2013), the family were still positioned as the most important factor for the woman's support and recovery.

All professionals positioned the family as a key source of victim blaming and feelings of self-blame for women subjected to sexual violence.

Extract 21:

RESEARCHER: *Where do you see victim blaming coming from?*

MADDY: *From – from everybody around them really. Everybody around them. Their entire support network and I do think that because it's not supportive at all. Um, but that's who they will turn to naturally and then they get, "Well, why on earth would you have done that?"*

Extract 22:

GEORGIA: *Often the families blame the victim and it seems to be a lot of the blame isn't around so much that they caused that to happen although there is some – some feeling of that happened to you so now you are the (pause) the – the raped person in the family.*

RESEARCHER: *Yeah. Yeah.*

GEORGIA: *Um, but more to do with now that you've brought this to light, especially if the perpetrator is a family member, now you've brought this to light you've disrupted the family.*

RESEARCHER: *Ah okay.*

GEORGIA: *So, there's blame around the impact.*

Extract 23:

SAMANTHA: *Police got involved, you know, by bringing it out in the open you've brought shame on the family.*

Professionals described the way the family responded was not what the woman had expected and the lack of support or the direct victim blaming was a shock and disappointment. Professionals described the family as a source of great harm when they blamed the woman for sexual abuse or rape, and positioned the women as expecting her family to be the ones who would protect and support her. This mirrors previous research findings (Campbell et al., 2001; Ullman, 1996; 1999).

Extract 24:

GEORGIA: *their family don't – don't accept them so if the family don't accept them then who can? Then how – but they're almost like the – the safety net, aren't they? They – they're at the bottom of the – well, the last resource that you know that you can rely on them for that sort of – that sort of glimmer of hope.*

RESEARCHER: *Yeah.*

GEORGIA: *And it's almost like you could go go through everyone else…but you know that they'll catch you. If they don't catch you then – then why – why do you care what happens?*

RESEARCHER: *Yeah.*

GEORGIA: *And I'm sure there are – they'll be other people out there but the – what the expectation is that they would be the strongest.*

Despite the way the family was constructed as the main source of victim blaming, they were simultaneously but tentatively, constructed as the main source of support and safety. As in extract 24 when Georgia positioned the family as 'the last resource' and 'a glimmer of hope', in extract 25, Teri describes the family as a support network that we all need:

Extract 25:

TERI: *But working with so many people that haven't told anybody in their life is really hard because then they don't have that support network that we all need.*

This is particularly interesting because it supports findings by Ullman (1996; 1999) who found that when the family network was negative, it had a negative impact on women, but that women still disclosed to the family more than any other group. This presents a dilemma for women, who may expect their families to be supportive and disclose sexual violence to them but are frequently blamed and ostracised, not only for the sexual violence but for the reputation or perception of the family network (White & Rollins, 1981; Mason et al., 2008).

Telling a woman that she is not to blame does not mean she will feel a reduction of blame

All professionals talked about the process of challenging victim blaming and self-blame of women as an ideological dilemma. Throughout the talk, professionals described their methods and approaches to challenging victim blaming and self-blame, often caveating their sentences with a competing belief that telling a woman that she is not to blame is often not enough to make a difference to her feelings of blame. They explained this, despite continuing to tell the woman she was not to blame. This constructed the woman as resistant to changing her beliefs about blame in sexual violence and in some cases, positioned their own roles and influence as futile. Notably, this is in stark contrast with the second theme in which women were positioned as passive and helpless to absorbing new discourses into their own.

Extract 26:

MADDY: *Rather than when they're not ready to hear it and you're kind of – and you then keep saying it, "No, no, no, yeah." Cos sometimes it is – because it's – it's so traumatic, what we're talking about, that it can take a long time for people to really digest things.*

RESEARCHER: *Yeah.*

MADDY: *And start challenging I guess also their own beliefs.*

Extract 27:

SAMANTHA: *Um, but I don't think that goes in straight away, I don't think that's – I don't think that that person feels when they walk out of their first meeting with me – 'oh great, I wasn't to blame'.*

RESEARCHER: *Yeah.*

SAMANTHA: *And 'I'm okay now'. No way. I think that takes time and I think that takes support and I think that takes almost that the person needs to be, um, supported to almost rebuild their like sense of self, you know, and how they maybe see themselves.*

Extract 28:

CHARLOTTE: *So, some just cry because they do recognise that what I'm saying is true, actually, um, and others will kind of, they'll say, 'Yes I know,' but they're still holding the belief.*

All professionals in this study presented two discourses in tandem, the first being that they always tried to challenge victim blaming and self-blame, and the second being that even though they continued to challenge, it often didn't result in the woman blaming herself any less than before. Professionals also frequently positioned knowledge as different from feeling. Therefore, they felt that the women with whom they worked could have the knowledge that they were not to blame; but, could still feel to blame, as is evident in the extract from Charlotte, above. She positions her counternarrative as 'true' and her role as trying to get the woman to believe the 'truth' that she was not to blame; but, she also knows that even when women told her they knew they were not to blame, they still held beliefs that they were to blame.

Some professionals also discussed a feeling that if they were to continue to tell the woman she was not to blame when she was not ready to gain a new belief or change her own beliefs, this would be the same as imposing new views on her in the same way that the victim blaming views were imposed on her. Tara and Rob both presented dilemmatic constructions of challenging self-blame, in which they were committed to challenging self-blame, but were simultaneously concerned that challenging self-blame could cause more harm to the woman and disempower her further.

Extract 29:

TARA: *But actually, if I do try and, you know, do the kind of the exploring and unpicking, the reframing, that could do her more harm than good. And I kind of got to a point where I thought, you know, in a way I felt like I was sort of putting forward my sort of, you know, apportioning of blame and responsibility and where it lies. But in some ways, was it not more important to respect that's how she wanted and needed, that's how she needed to see it, that's how she needed to look at it.*

Extract 30:

ROB: *But fundamentally, it's right in that, if you just impose another – another view, it is, if you like – because often these messages are deep seated, so it's just a societal message that women are often to blame, or always to blame... Then, just to say, 'no, you're – you're talking nonsense, it is just – you know, all of the messages you've had are plain wrong,' I think is just imposing another view, and not – not overly helpful.*

This ideological dilemma has strong links with one of the findings from the previous study, 'Knowing logically that she is not to blame but still feeling to blame'. As one of the ideological dilemmas discussed by the women themselves, it is of interest that this was replicated in this study with professionals working with women. They talked in similar terms, using similar words to construct a feeling in which women 'know' they are not really to blame for sexual violence, but deeper down, still feel they are. Out of eleven professionals, six explained this ideological dilemma between knowing and feeling, with Georgia explaining it in almost the exact same way as the women in the previous study.

Extract 31:

GEORGIA: *I say, "At some level it feels to me that you know you're not to blame."*

RESEARCHER: *Hmm.*

GEORGIA: *"However, feeling that you're not to blame is completely different." So, a hundred people can probably say, you know, "You were – you were six years old. There's no way you can be to blame; that – that's just not possible. But actually feeling that is completely different." So, we – we'd be working with, you know, getting from the knowing to the feeling. If you see what I mean?*

RESEARCHER: *Yeah.*

GEORGIA: *Yeah. And – and at a logical level there's that knowledge and everything out there, the media, whatever and – and – and if you think of it in an obvious way, it's in a practical way, then you couldn't be to blame.*

Just like the women in the previous study, professionals often used words like logical and rational, which constructed the self-blame

and victim blaming as irrational or illogical. However, they all agreed that women did 'know' at a logical level, that they were not to blame but 'felt' at a deeper level that they were to blame for sexual violence. This dichotomy continued throughout both studies.

Direct versus indirect challenge of self-blame

The final theme from the data was another ideological dilemma which was constructed by the professionals when considering how to challenge self-blame of women who had been blamed for sexual violence. This theme was specifically about the techniques and approaches used by the professionals when working with women to help them to understand victim blaming and self-blame. Professionals working with the women described themselves as 'direct' but also showed concern about being direct in their approaches about blame.

Every participant discussed this issue, with some professionals describing their approach as very direct or 'head on', constructing their challenge of the woman's beliefs as necessary and in pursuit of a better understanding for the woman. Others were more cautious and discussed the process of challenging self-blame and victim blaming as being a sensitive and tentative process, in which they worried about harming the woman by challenging deeply held beliefs, even when they didn't agree with them.

Extract 32:

TARA: *Because I think you have got to be very – absolutely I, I challenge and, and I have done over the years and I think it's important that sometimes that I have been more directive with some people than I would be with others. But I think you have got to be careful that it isn't done because somebody has got to be at a point that actually they are ready and open to receive that challenge and actually be ready to start to kind of take that on board and explore it.*

Extract 33:

CHARLOTTE: *I usually just challenge that thinking. So, in the example you just gave, I'd would say, but is that really the case? You know, was it the fact that you got a ta – you didn't get a taxi home or was it that actually that person's a rapist? So, I challenge it quite head-on, really, um.*

Samantha expressed a fear that she could traumatise women by challenging their narratives of self-blame or belief in victim blaming.

Extract 34:

SAMANTHA: *I would say that, but I wouldn't labour the point probably. But if I – once – once I've built up a relationship with somebody and I feel that I can challenge them in a way that they – they know me by now and they respect, you know, that I'm not trying to hurt them, 'cos you've got to be careful. Well, I think – I think sometimes you've got to be careful not to re-kind of traumatise somebody.*

Several professionals, including Sara below, discussed an ideological dilemma in which they want to challenge self-blame and victim blaming, but were worried about disempowering women by telling them that their beliefs are wrong. In the extract below, Sara describes the process as 'holding back what I think but obviously not agreeing'. She also described offering what she thought with aggressive terms such as 'jumping in' and 'shutting people down', which led her to avoid that approach and to focus more on providing space for women to consider and think about self-blame and victim blaming themselves rather than being 'told' not to believe rape myths and victim blaming narratives about themselves.

Extract 35:

SARA: *And I think what I find, erm, difficult and I sort of go back and forth about this a lot is that people hold really deep-seated beliefs about, erm, the fact that it is their fault and they're to blame and they're responsible. And I think as a therapist countering that can also just shut people down...*

RESEARCHER: *Yes, yeah.*

SARA: *...erm, and leave them feeling more isolated with these feelings that are so, just so difficult to articulate and so so so painful, erm, that no, as, as a therapist I just want to say, "No, this is wrong," like, "It's not like that." Like, "Please don't feel like that." But I think that that can, like it really sort of shakes people off. Erm, so I think, erm, part of my job is to let people explore those feelings and for me to hold back, erm, in some cases from saying what I think, erm, obviously not agreeing. But in part giving them space* *to talk about how that is for them to feel like that, what their experience is rather than jumping in and saying, "No, that's not how you should be feeling."*

Tara also explained why she was not able to be direct, positioning women as being more comfortable with self-blame and victim blaming than having to confront the reality of sexual violence being uncontrollable; something which Janoff-Bulman theorised in 1979. In the extract below, Tara appears concerned that by being too direct when women were not ready to hear that it was not their fault, she presents them with constructions of sexual violence and perpetrators that they may not be ready to accept. She discusses working with a woman who she had attempted to directly challenge about self-blame and victim blaming and had learned that attempting to deconstruct the self-blame narrative would leave the woman feeling more exposed, lacking in perceived control and would potentially make her feel worse.

Extract 36:

TARA: *Because she felt that that made it, she said, easier and safer for her to go forward knowing that it is preventable, it needn't happen again, because I will, I, I can take responsibility for it. Because she said, if I think that wasn't my fault, that was the perpetrators fault, she said to me that means it could happen again and that's less safe and I don't feel like I will – probably not those exact words but almost that I won't recover as well if I think it wasn't my, it wasn't my fault. Because it makes me feel like that could happen again at any point. She said I'd rather think, I'll take responsibility for what happened and then I feel more in control going forward. So that was an interesting one.*

This final theme presents some dilemmas for professionals supporting women, in which they continue to try to convince women that they are not to blame for sexual violence perpetrated against them, but also worry that they should not be too direct or challenging in case this damages the therapeutic relationship, retraumatises the woman or makes the woman feel as though she is being told that she is 'wrong'. At some points, professionals constructed self-blame in a similar manner to Janoff-Bulman (1979), that self-blame is an attempt at adaptation and can in some cases, help women to feel more in control of what happened so they can prevent it from happening to them again. Tara also gives an example of a woman saying to her 'I'd rather think, I'll take responsibility for what happened and then I feel more in control going forward' which is a clear example of counterfactual thinking (Miller et al., 2010).

The findings from this study present a complicated and dilemmatic construction of victim blaming and self-blame of women who have been subjected to sexual violence from the perspective of the professionals who support them.

Women were often discussed in disconnected dichotomies, in which professionals would describe women or blame in one way, but then later, describe them in the opposite way without connecting the two perspectives. They employed narratives and repertoires about blame and about women, that were at times, contradictory. Women were constructed as helpless, powerless and passive to beliefs about self-blame and victim blaming of women; but they were later constructed as resistant and challenging to new counternarratives about self-blame and victim blaming of women. This can be discussed in several ways. It is possible that women are both passive and active in the beliefs of victim blaming and self-blame – the ideological dilemma being caused by two competing interpretative repertoires and subject positions of women. It is interesting that women are positioned as passive to beliefs of society, their families and support network – but highly resistant to the professional supporting them.

It is also possible that the professionals construct women as passive to self-blame and victim blaming erroneously, and that the resistance they describe to alternatives to self-blame is also present in self-blame, but they assume that the woman is passive due to benevolent sexism or because they have constructed the woman as vulnerable. It is also of interest that the woman was only constructed as resistant, difficult or challenging when she was rejecting the narratives or challenges presented by the professional, but in all other terms, she was positioned as vulnerable and powerless.

This possible explanation of the dichotomy could link to the frequently used interpretative repertoire about women being unable to deconstruct self-blame and victim blaming narratives due to being abused in childhood. A lot of the times this was used in talk, the participant appeared to be assuming that the reason women may struggle to challenge self-blame is because she must have been abused in childhood which causes them to be powerless to the belief that they are to blame. This may present a circular discourse in which women are constructed as abused because they were powerless, and then powerless because they were abused. This finding could also relate to the way professionals in sexual violence are trained and to the research which suggests that women abused in childhood are more likely to blame themselves and are more likely to be continually revictimized in adulthood (Mason et al., 2008; Messman-Moore and Long, 2003). Again, the origins of the interpretative repertoire used by professionals is unclear but may be representative of several associated factors. It could be that over the years of their role, professionals have come to notice that women who were abused in childhood are more likely to blame themselves leading to a confirmation bias – or it could be that they hold stereotypes and beliefs that women who were abused in childhood are more vulnerable, have lower self-worth and low self-esteem. A combination of those of these things could cause confirmation bias, and indeed the data was lacking in talk that constructed women as empowered, confident, assertive or capable (except for when professionals were discussing their own concerns about women not believing their self-blame counternarrative).

In line with the existing literature (Campbell et al., 2001; Ullman, 1996; 1999), the family was positioned by professionals as being the most important factor in the support of a woman who has been subjected to sexual violence. However, in the talk, all professionals constructed the family in a dilemmatic way: as being vital to the woman but also being the main source of victim blaming and cause of self-blame. Even when professionals talked about how harmful the support network had been towards the woman, they still described them as being the most important 'safety net' a woman has.

The concept of 'knowing she is not to blame but still feeling to blame' arose in this study as it did in the previous study with women. There were two interpretative repertoires competing within the talk, with professionals explaining that they continued to challenge victim blaming and self-blame with women, but they also knew that their approach would be unlikely to reduce victim blaming or self-blame. Despite the two competing approaches, all professionals continued to use them in practice, perhaps representative of the hope that over long periods of time, women would eventually 'believe' them that they were not to blame for sexual violence. However, over half of the professional professionals described blame as something deeper than knowledge and logic; they constructed self-blame of women as being something different to logical thinking. There were frequent discussions about blame being not being about 'knowing' but about 'feeling', in which women could 'know' they were not really to blame for rape or sexual abuse, but still felt to blame. It was this irrational feeling of blame that professionals described as being difficult to shift. Professionals described the blame as being comforting in some cases, or as a way to retain control of their understanding of sexual violence. This has clear links to the way Janoff-Bulman (1979) constructed self-blame which has long been contested. It is of interest that so many current professionals working with women in sexual violence construct self-blame and victim blaming much in the same way as Janoff-Bulman (1979) despite self-blame and victim blaming being rejected as adaptive and comforting in more contemporary research (Frazier, 2005; Donde, 2016). Despite the similarities in discourses, professionals in this study appeared to be more nuanced than the theory suggested by Janoff-Bulman (1979). Self-blame was described as an attempt to regain control but was also framed as maladaptive and harmful by all professionals.

Reflexive comment

This study was interesting to analyse, as I hadn't recognised the dichotomies until I really started to explore the data. In the interviews, I had noticed the developing trend of professionals constructing the women as passive, vulnerable and helpless to victim blaming narratives in society – but I had not yet noticed the contradictions in the talk in which the women were then also constructed as resistant and difficult to influence. It made me rethink my own perceptions of victim blaming narratives and the way they are 'absorbed'. I realised I had used words like 'absorbed' and 'internalised' that positioned women as empty receptacles of beliefs and ideas without any interrogation or thought. This triggered a consideration as to whether I had also assumed that women and girls were passively absorbing victim blaming messages from an abstract concept ('society') without giving them (myself included) any credit for their own arguments and dilemmas. I have lectured and written articles in which I have described women and girls as passively absorbing beliefs from society, which runs the risk of oversimplifying complex processes and ignores the agency of the people at the heart of matter.

The discussion with professionals about how they were trying to deconstruct and challenge victim blaming and self-blame in their roles with women was also of interest to me as I had a genuine curiosity about how others were doing this – and ultimately – whether they thought it was working. Whilst it didn't surprise me that professionals didn't think they were having much effect on self-blame and victim blaming, I was surprised that I felt a little hopeless after analysing the data and writing up this chapter. It left me with a feeling of not knowing how to help women with feelings of self-blame and the harm done to them by victim blaming, if current efforts were not viewed as effective.

Professionals working with women subjected to sexual violence constructed self-blame and victim blaming as complex and dichotomous, with many of the key themes being dilemmatic. Professionals constructed victim blaming and self-blame as coming primarily from rape myths and the family network, and positioned women as passively accepting these victim blaming beliefs from external sources as a process of accepting or absorbing others' perceptions of them, their blame and the sexual violence. However, much of the way professionals talked about women and blame was contradictory which appeared to influence their practice with women who blamed themselves, resulting in professionals potentially viewing self-blame as impossible to change for some women.

17.

Discussions and considerations

This discussion chapter contains nine sections. The first section will explore the findings about language use in victim blaming and self-blame that have emerged from all three studies. The second section will discuss the learning from the literature review about the origins and mechanisms of victim blaming in society using the ecological systems model (Bronfenbrenner, 1979;1986). The third section examines the victim blaming of women by members of the general public and the findings from the BOWSVA study. In the fourth and fifth section, findings about victim blaming of women and self-blame of women are explored, respectively, from both the perspective of women themselves and the professionals who support them. In the seventh section, the relationship between rape myths, victim blaming, and self-blame is examined in light of the new findings. The eighth section of this chapter discusses and reflects upon the methodological approach taken to this research, including its strengths and limitations. The ninth section completes the chapter by discussing the practical implications of the research and ideas for future directions.

The use of language to construct victim blaming and self-blame

Language was found to be central to victim blaming and self-blame throughout my studies. In the literature reviewed, language use was found to have influenced or affected the methodology and findings in previous studies about sexual violence, victim blaming and self-blame. When studies used the word 'rape', responses from participants decreased, even if all participants had been raped (Donde et al., 2018).

This was an important finding for the current research about victim blaming and self-blame of women subjected to sexual violence, because it meant that there were methodological problems to avoid, purely based on the selection of language in interview questions, study descriptions and questionnaire items. It also confirms that the accepted language to describe forced sex: 'rape' and 'assault' or 'abuse' (Heath et al., 2011) still appear to affect research findings and their interpretation.

Similarly, the language that is used to describe blame was found to be both flawed and complex. Studies exploring victim blaming have included questions, items, interpretations and discussions that use 'cause', 'blame', 'responsibility' and 'fault' as synonyms (Anderson and Bissell, 2011; Sleath, 2011; Shaver and Drown, 1986). Throughout articles and study materials, the words are conflated or used interchangeably. This influenced the decision to deliberately only use the word 'blame' consistently to conduct all studies in this research, even if this word itself may have influenced findings.

It would be useful to conduct a set of parallel studies or one study with parallel items that use the words 'blame', 'cause', 'responsibility' and 'fault' separately to explore whether attribution of blame in sexual violence changes based on the language used.

This would also go some way to exploring how much language can influence socially desirable responding in studies about victim blaming in sexual violence, especially if participants prefer one word over another, or feel that they mean different things about women's blame, fault, cause or responsibility for sexual violence perpetrated against her.

Similarly, in the quantitative chapter, language was shown to have an important impact on the way psychometric measurements of RMA and victim blaming are developed, conducted and interpreted. Researchers (e.g. Sleath, 2011; McMahon and Farmer, 2011) have previously critiqued RMA scales for item language and phrases, which led to the withdrawal of the RMAS and the evolution of the IRMAS, AMMSA, U-IRMAS and the BOWSVA presented in this book.

An exploration of language is crucial if psychometric measures are to be valid and consistent, and so the current research focused on the effect of language in item development and in the interpretation of statistical results. Results from the BOWSVA study suggest that the language used to construct the offence, the woman and the man in each item influenced victim blaming.

The sexual offence was deliberately described in different ways across the items, to consider arguments about the impact of conflating or employing language that could impact the way participants responded (Heath et al., 2011; Shaver & Drown, 1986; Sleath, 2011).

In some items, the sexual offence was described with overt language such as 'rape', 'attack', 'force', 'assault' and 'abuse' and when this occurred, the items grouped together, meaning that participants tended to answer the same way. These items did appear to result in some of the lowest levels of victim blaming of the women, possibly because violent descriptions of offences may conform to the classic rape (Williams, 1984).

Conversely, when more subtle language such as 'touched', 'made to', 'had to', 'groped' or 'performed sex acts' was used to describe sexual offences in the items, victim blaming increased. This finding had important implications for the qualitative studies and influenced the language used in interview questions and used during discussions with women and professionals. For example, at the beginning of each interview, the participant was read some information about what constituted sexual violence to ensure they were able to talk about all forms of sexual violence rather than just 'rape' or 'sexual assault' which have narrow socially accepted definitions (Heath et al., 2011).

Outside of this research, these results suggest that the way academics construct sexual offence types in scenarios, case studies, experiment stimuli and psychometric items will have a significant impact on the outcomes of the study. These findings are only part of the issues around language, as this observation was also found for the way the woman was described and the words used to position the man committing the sexual offence. For example, when the woman was described as being sexually active, enjoying sex or being sexually liberal, victim blaming of the woman increased, which not only demonstrates the issues with language, but is also in line with Ringrose (2013), who argues that women are constructed in dichotomous terms when it comes to their sexuality.

In both qualitative interview chapters, critical discourse analysis focussed on the way language was used to construct victim blaming and self-blame of women subjected to sexual violence. Findings from the interviews with women and professionals suggested that analysis of the language use revealed nuanced, complex and contradictory ways women talk about themselves, victim blaming, and self-blame and the way professionals talk about the women they support. Language was explored as a set of tools that enabled and/or inhibited both the women and the professionals to construct, position and discuss blame in sexual violence.

The present research has demonstrated how language is constructing, empowering, disempowering and positioning the issue of blame in sexual violence. A relativist, social constructionist approach to victim blaming and self-blame of women subjected to sexual violence prioritises the language and narratives, which has been done throughout this book. However, as the overall research approach in this book was critical realism, whilst the language was shown to be instrumental in the construction of understandings of victim blaming and self-blame, there is more to both issues than only language construction and employment.

A critical realist approach to the issue of victim blaming of women in society proposes that whilst language is a tool to construct and seemingly maintain victim blaming and self-blame, these issues are not only socially constructed in language and have effects outside of language. The act of blaming women for sexual violence, the discrimination they face, the lack of justice in the legal system, the way they are treated by family and friends, the way they are treated by social care and the health system all continue, whether we perceive it or experience it ourselves, or not.

Victim blaming in society

Ecological model of factors contributing to victim blaming of women subjected to sexual violence

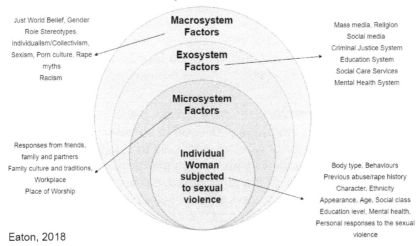

Just World Belief, Gender Role Stereotypes, Individualism/Collectivism, Sexism, Porn culture, Rape myths Racism

Macrosystem Factors

Exosystem Factors

Microsystem Factors

Individual Woman subjected to sexual violence

Mass media, Religion Social media Criminal Justice System Education System Social Care Services Mental Health System

Responses from friends, family and partners Family culture and traditions, Workplace Place of Worship

Body type, Behaviours Previous abuse/rape history Character, Ethnicity Appearance, Age, Social class Education level, Mental health, Personal responses to the sexual violence

Eaton, 2018

Drawing upon the ecological systems model (Bronfenbrenner, 1979;1986), this book explored findings and theories from new and existing studies about victim blaming and self-blame. Together, the chapters and the findings from the three studies presented here provide further evidence that victim blaming of women and girls cannot be explained by a single-factor theory or model, and that victim blaming is not located in only one source or system. Whilst victim blaming has often been explained using theories such as BJW (Lerner, 1980), hostile sexism (Lee, Fiske, & Glick, 2010) or cognitive theories such as attribution theory (Shaver, 1970), the current research suggests that any one theory is unable to be able to effectively explain victim blaming of women in society.

Almost every factor included in this book was discussed by participants in the two qualitative studies and both groups of participants had considerable knowledge of the systems in society that were identified as encouraging, maintaining and reinforcing victim blaming of women.

Women talked about the way the media portrayed them, the way the police treated them, the way the court system problematised them, the way their families blamed them, the way their religions led them to believe they were being punished by God, the way their cultures and communities shamed and silenced them, the way rape myths had made them second guess what had happened to them and the way sexist values made them believe that their female bodies caused sexual violence. Women and professionals had a thorough understanding of the different levels and systems within society and were aware that victim blaming of women was present in many different forms of media at once.

All three studies offered insight into why we might blame women for sexual violence perpetrated against them. The quantitative study provided a seven-factor solution to victim blaming, which whilst in its infancy, is more nuanced than the assumption that victim blaming is caused by RMA or BJW.

The solution suggests a complex mix of misogyny, rape myths, gender role stereotypes, relationship norms, male entitlement to the female body and the rejection of women as an independent sexual being.

When women were interviewed in the first qualitative study, they explained victim blaming of women from their own perspective – both as a woman who had been blamed for sexual violence and also as a woman who observes victim blaming of other women in her society and community. Women constructed victim blaming of them and other women as being behavioural and characterological in nature, often citing multiple rape myths. When professionals were asked the same question, they also cited the same myths for why they thought women were blamed for sexual violence.

For women and professionals, the rape myth still appears to have significant impact on them, despite both groups recognising that the beliefs are untrue and harmful to women. Both groups constructed these messages as coming from 'society'. The word 'society' was used by both groups to describe a large, influential force that was external to them. Whilst describing victim blaming, both women and professionals talked about society as if it was not connected to them or as if they were outside of it, but nonetheless impacted by it. They constructed society as misogynistic, victim-blaming, violent, and judgmental; often including the media, members of the general public, religions, cultures, communities, authorities and institutions within the concept of 'society'.

Victim blaming in society has been theorised to be linked to, or caused by, a number of different factors or explanations (Sleath, 2011). The most commonly cited explanations for victim blaming of women include the BJW (Lerner, 1980), RMA (Burt, 1980; Payne et al., 1999), hostile sexism, gender role stereotypes and attribution bias theories (Shaver, 1970). Whilst studies have shown inconsistent connections between these theories and the victim blaming of women (Grubb and Turner, 2012; Sleath, 2011), there has been little research to qualitatively understand these beliefs and biases against women (Maier, 2013).

Existing theories of victim blaming provide some clues about underlying mechanisms and motivations. Lerner (1980) theorised that BJW came from a need for control, personal safety and a belief in fairness and justice in an unsafe and uncertain environment. Burt (1980) and Brownmiller (1975) argued from a feminist perspective that victim blaming comes from a place of misogyny and hostile sexism, thereby suggesting that there is a hierarchy they identified as the patriarchy.

Theories of attribution bias and defensive attribution from cognitive psychology (Shaver, 1970; Mason et al., 2004) theorise that victim blaming is caused by faulty logic and cognitive biases in the brain of the individual which affect the information processing of causality.

Researchers have also argued that victim blaming is related to individualism and self-preservation, in which the underlying motivation is to convince the self that they are safe and able to control their environment (Anderson, 2001; Kalra & Bhugra, 2013).

Finally, much has been written about the way women are constructed and perceived based on religious and cultural norms all over the world (Franiuk & Shain, 2011; Heggen, 1996; Khuankaew, 2007; Turrell & Thomas, 2008).

Religion also has strong links with Lerner's BJW (1980), which theorises that there is a universal, cosmic force that can balance the justice in the world. In most major world religions, this takes the form of a God or concepts of reward and punishment such as judgement day, heaven and hell. However, in Hinduism and Buddhism this takes the form of karma, a cosmic force that causes consequences for one's actions to influence the good and bad things that happen to people in their current, previous and next lives (Franiuk & Shain, 2011; Khuankaew, 2007).

In addition to the links to blame, cause and justice, there was evidence in the literature that religion and cultural norms communicated and reinforced sexism and misogyny (Franiuk & Shain, 2011; Turrell & Thomas, 2008; Weaver, 2007). This overview of the explanations, theories and factors contributing to victim blaming of women suggests that one singular explanation, or even the culmination of a number of key theories is still unlikely to fully explain why others blame women for sexual violence perpetrated against them – and how and why this transfers to women as beliefs about self-blame.

Having examined the evidence from the existing literature and the findings from the new studies presented here, my diagram below is presented to illustrate just how complex a solution to explaining the victim blaming of women subjected to sexual violence could be. The model is based on all the literature evidence examined as part of this book and my PhD thesis, the findings from the quantitative study and the findings from the two qualitative studies.

The framework presents five levels of factors that contribute to the victim blaming and self-blame of women subjected to sexual violence. Inspired by the ecological systems model by Bronfenbrenner (1979;1986), this diagram proposes an integrated explanation of the motivations, systems, beliefs and methods of communication that lead to women being blamed and blaming themselves for sexual violence.

(Overleaf) Proposing an integrated framework of victim blaming of women subjected to sexual violence (Taylor, 2020)

FRAMEWORK OF VICTIM BLAMING OF WOMEN SUBJECTED TO SEXUAL VIOLENCE

EATON (2019)

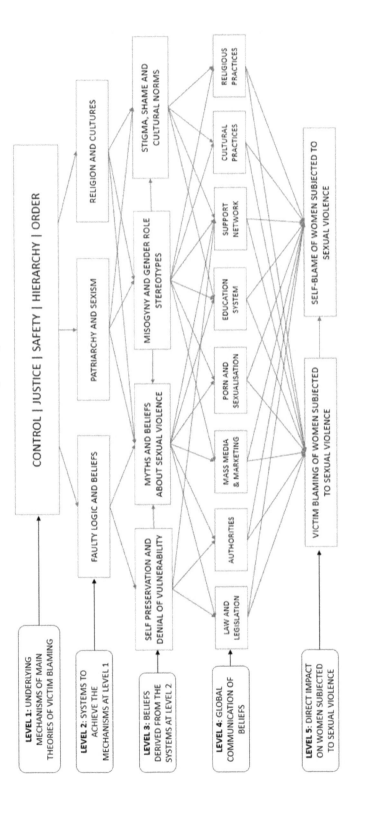

At level 1, the underlying mechanisms for victim blaming are broad concepts underpinning the key theories of victim blaming and represent qualities that humans seek from the world. Victim blaming is not specific only to sexual violence, and therefore there must be higher-order mechanisms that underpin the need to blame the victim of a distressing event. Existing literature and theories propose that people blame the victim because they are seeking control, safety, justice, order and hierarchy in the world (Lerner, 1980; Montada & Lerner, 1998). This level is the only level that is not specific to victim blaming of women in sexual violence but appears to be common to much of the literature around blame, attribution and justice.

At level 2, the model presents three main systems that support the five key mechanisms. These mechanisms are human-made. They are belief systems, values, norms, hierarchies, control strategies and approaches to reasoning that help people to feel that they have achieved safety, control, justice, order and hierarchy in their lives and in their communities. All main theories of victim blaming of women subjected to sexual violence can fit into the three systems, some fit into multiple categories at once. Faulty logic and beliefs can relate to attribution errors, BJW, RMA and individualism.

Patriarchy and sexism contribute to RMA, misogynistic values about women, rape-supportive beliefs, the sexualisation of women and girls as objects and gender role stereotypes used to blame women (Brownmiller, 1975; Burt, 1980). It is argued that religions and cultures were developed to maintain order, hierarchy, justice, control and feelings of safety, and therefore contribute to theories of BJW, cultural norms about women, relationships and sexual activity, religious beliefs about women, sex, abuse, gender roles and justice (Lerner, 1980; Turrell & Thomas, 2008). All these resulting beliefs are presented at level 3. Level 3 therefore presents the culmination of all the harmful beliefs that appear to contribute to the victim blaming of women subjected to sexual violence.

Level 4 presents the methods of global communication of the beliefs from level 3, based on the existing and current research. This level proposes that beliefs are communicated through a wide range of mediums, networks and authorities. Level 4 therefore illustrates the many angles from which women and the people around them receive harmful messages about women who are subjected to sexual violence, leading to level 5: the victim blaming of women and/or the self-blame of women.

Level 5 presents victim blaming and self-blame as parallel outcomes from the same systems, but links victim blaming to self-blame, due to the evidence that suggests that women who are blamed for sexual violence are likely to blame themselves (Peterson & Muehlenhard, 2004; Ullman, 2010). However, the current research did not support a reciprocal arrow back between self-blame and victim blaming, as whilst all of the women who took part in this research did blame themselves for sexual violence, none of them blamed other women for being subjected to sexual violence. Whilst experiencing victim blaming is related to feeling self-blame for sexual violence, it cannot be said that experiencing self-blame is related to victim blaming other women subjected to sexual violence.

The connections between and within the levels on the model are multiple and overlapping. Systems to achieve the five factors at level 1 influence many beliefs that contribute to victim blaming of women. Those beliefs are then communicated via a wide range of sources, which was evidenced in the two qualitative studies.

Therefore, women are likely to experience victim blaming narratives and repertoires from multiple sources throughout the lifespan, whether or not they are subjected to sexual violence themselves.

For the general public, this also means a lifetime of harmful victim blaming messages that become part of the interpretative repertoire about women's position in sexual violence and in the world. The multiple and overlapping connections between the systems, beliefs and communication methods means that challenging victim blaming of women cannot be achieved by siloed, single-explanation approaches such as challenging hostile sexism or educating people about rape myths.

The overlapping and interconnected nature of the factors contributing to the victim blaming of women presented in this model may also go some way to explaining why findings from studies relying on psychometric measurement of RMA, hostile sexism and BJW to draw conclusions about victim blaming have become inconsistent over the years (Sleath, 2011). The cause of victim blaming is multi-faceted and interlinked therefore the solutions to or approaches to understanding victim blaming of women in society must be multi-faceted, interlinked and consider the historical, cultural and hierarchical situatedness of victim blaming of women.

Findings about victim blaming of women

This section will discuss new findings about the victim blaming of women from all three empirical studies, and how evidence from each chapter supports the findings from others.

My BOWSVA scale chapter (Ch. 5) presented a new seven-factor solution to victim blaming of women: (1) She was asking for it, (2) She was in a dangerous situation, (3) She should have been more assertive, (4) He was entitled to her body, (5) The non-stereotypical sex offender, (6) The stereotypical rape myth and (7) She was a sexually active woman.

'She was asking for it' was one of the subscales and contained items that resulted in some of the highest levels of victim blaming. It positively correlated with the U-IRMAS and positively correlated with the 'she asked for it' subscale of the U-IRMAS. This form of victim blaming is common in the literature, with much written about this from a feminist perspective (Burt, 1980; Brownmiller, 1975).

The concept of women 'asking for it' positions women as wanting to be raped, enjoying sexual violence or at the very least, doing something that leads to being sexually attacked. It was no surprise that this came out in the principle components analysis for the BOWSVA, but it does solidify an explanation of victim blaming of women that argues that the general public do endorse attitudes towards women that suggest they believe that women can do or say things that 'ask for it'.

This is now the fourth psychometric measure that has contained a set of items that relate to the woman wanting it or asking for sexual violence (Gerger et al., 2007; McMahon and Farmer, 2011; Lonsway et al., 1999). This positioning of women as 'asking to be raped' also has strong links to pornography (Dines, 2011; Long, 2012).

'She was in a dangerous situation' subscale positioned all the women as being violently or forcibly assaulted in dangerous or risky situations, using overt language about the offence. This means that it is likely that this subscale needs further exploration, as it could have been the use of overt language such as 'violent', 'raped', 'forced', 'pushed' and 'attacked' that led to participants reducing the blame of the women in the items, or it could have been the description of the situations as dangerous or risky.

Equally, the use of such overt language could have communicated to the participants that the situation was dangerous and volatile and therefore they may not have expected her to be able to do anything differently to protect herself or stop the sexual violence. Previous evidence suggested that participants would blame a woman more if she was described as being in a dangerous or risky situation, but the new findings contradict previous work (Miller et al., 2010).

'She should have been more assertive' resulted in some of the highest victim blaming of the woman in the items. This subscale presented items that were not only worded in more subtle language but positioned women as unable to stop, escape or challenge the perpetrator of the offence. This appears to elicit increased victim blaming from participants. This could be related to the concept of sexual refusal assertiveness in which some researchers and theorists argued that women could avoid sexual violence if they were more assertive in the way they tried to avoid or refuse unwanted sexual advances (Greene & Navarro, 1998).

However, the assertion that women are not assertive enough or did not try hard enough to stop the sexual violence is a form of victim blaming, as it places blame on the woman to stop an offender, whilst not expecting the offender to stop themselves, or to never attack women in the first place.

It is possible that this subscale could relate to rape myths and stereotypes that women who do not fight off an offender secretly want to be assaulted or raped or even enjoy sexual violence. Despite recent research arguing that the majority of sexual violence victims freeze during and assault and are very unlikely to try to fight or escape (Moller et al., 2017; Moor et al., 2013), participants were more likely to blame women for sexual violence when they perceived them to be not assertive enough. Further to this, it was concerning to see that this subscale resulted in the lowest blame of the man committing the sexual offence, with only 25.8% of participants blaming the man overall.

This may have links to previous feminist work on token resistance, in which authors have argued that women are expected to engage in resistance to all sexual contact so as not to appear easy, but that due to their resistance being perceived as tokenistic, men were likely to ignore any kind of resistance from women they were sexually pursuing (Frese et al., 2004; Garcia, 1998).

'He was entitled to her body' was a small set of items that appeared to present scenarios in which men were 'taking sex' from very ill, sleeping or non-consenting women. All men in these scenarios were husbands or boyfriends and had continued or initiated sexual contact with the woman when she was not physically able to consent or had withdrawn her consent. None of the items were described as violent offences, but the woman was clearly positioned as ill, asleep or not aroused enough to have sex. Due to the presence in the items of both the relationship with the woman, and the fact that the men were described as sexually assaulting or raping the women whilst they were asleep or after withdrawing consent, this raises questions about whether victim blaming increases when the woman is seen as property of the man, or the man is perceived as entitled to sex with his female partner because they are in a long term relationship. There is also the possibility that a general public sample did not have an adequate understanding of consent or thought that their partners having sex with them whilst they were asleep or even if they were not sexually aroused, was normal or doesn't count as sexual violence (Donde et al., 2018). Further research on this specific topic would be useful.

'He was a non-stereotypical offender' was a component that grouped together items that described a male offender who was deliberately positioned as vulnerable or non-stereotypical. This meant describing him as handsome, friendly, troubled or seeking support before or during the offence. These items did not result in high levels of victim blaming and so further exploration was needed.

After closer analysis, it appears that the language in the items may have influenced the way participants responded. Whilst the man was positioned as non-stereotypical, all offences were still described as rapes, attacks and assaults. Therefore, it could be that the emotive language used to describe the offence was more of a cue to blame than the personal descriptions of the man himself.

Another possible explanation could be that the general public are less susceptible to non-stereotypical descriptions of offenders, and are more focussed on what the offender did, especially if it was violent or overt. If this is correct, it would be useful to explore whether scenarios of sexual violence in which the man was non-stereotypical and the offence was not described as overtly violent (avoiding emotive words such a raped, attacked, assaulted, forced) would result in higher blaming of the woman.

'The stereotypical rape myth' was a set of items that grouped together in the component analysis that resulted in very low blaming of the woman. This subscale positively correlated with U-IRMAS overall, although only moderately. Analysis of the items showed them to be conforming with the classic rape stereotype described by Williams (1984), which may explain why these particular items produced these results. Previous research has shown that when rape events conform to the classic rape stereotype, women are less likely to be blamed, more likely to be believed, more likely to be seen as credible and less likely to blame themselves (Campbell, 2005, 2006; Campbell & Raja, 2005; Fisher et al., 2003). This finding confirms that there is still a set of sexual offences and a set of norms that a general public sample deemed to be 'real', which resulted in very low blame towards the woman.

'She was a sexually active woman' was the final component presented in the pattern matrix and resulted in the second highest levels of blame of the woman. All items positioned the woman as sexualised, enjoying sex or having frequent sex, which resulted in over 63% of participants assigning blame to the woman in this subscale.

These findings relate to a myriad of previous research including findings that have suggested that women are constantly walking a tightrope of being either considered a slut or frigid (Ringrose, 2013); in a dichotomous and contradictory role in which women are expected to be sexy and attractive, but not to engage in sex, otherwise they risk being perceived as easy (Garcia, 1998). This finding was also supported by the later qualitative study with women, who recognised that their sexual activity or sexual relationships were used to blame them for sexual violence.

Women and men were reasonably equally represented in the BOWSVA study sample and statistical analysis showed that there were no significant differences in the way men and women blamed women subjected to sexual violence. The same conclusion was drawn, even when subscales were explored separately. This is in line with previous research that did not find a difference in victim blaming between the sex of participants (e.g., Sleath, 2011).

The data from the general public samples was abnormally distributed, which was anticipated. The topic is sensitive and the responses from participants would have been affected by socially desirable responding. However, despite these issues, many items resulted in anywhere between a quarter and a half of participants blaming the woman for sexual violence perpetrated against her, even when they had also assigned full blame to the man who was described as committing the offence.

As all items were descriptions of sexual offences that had been validated by experts in sexual violence, the ideal answers to every item would be that none of the women were to blame and all the men were to blame for choosing to commit a sexual offence against a non-consenting woman. However, as shown in Chapter 5, none of the subscales or items resulted in the woman being assigned zero blame and none of the subscales or items resulted in the man being assigned full blame for the offence. This means that, even with socially desirable responding and the central tendency in the data suggesting that the average response did not blame the woman, this disguised the large number of participants who did assign blame to the woman on each item.

This study also asked participants how much they blamed the man in each scenario, as an additional way of using the BOWSVA measure. The findings were complex and would benefit from much further analysis and an additional literature review of the act of blaming perpetrators of sexual violence against women, before any conclusions are drawn from the data. The analysis of this secondary part of the data will continue but was not included in the thesis, as the thesis focussed on the blaming of women subjected to sexual violence rather than the blaming of perpetrators, as written about by Sleath (2011).

Relationships between quantitative and qualitative study findings

Women and professionals in the interviews talked about every component that was suggested in the BOWSVA, but more importantly, they added depth and nuance to concepts of victim blaming and self-blame that have been discussed in the literature or have mainly been tested using questionnaires (Maier, 2013).

Related to the findings from Chapter 5, in the interviews women discussed their awareness of measuring themselves up to rape myth and beliefs about victim blaming that they had learned from all levels of the ecological systems. Participants were very aware of the stereotype of the victim they were expected to be and constructed their experiences as being in a victimhood hierarchy, in which some women and some rapes or sexual assaults were at the top, taken seriously and seen as a violent act against a woman – and some women and some rapes or assaults were dismissed or completely ignored. Women talked about feeling lucky or grateful if their rape or sexual assault fitted the accepted norm of the 'classic rape' and talked about feeling hopeless or uncertain if they knew that they, as a woman, or their experience did not fit the strict criteria of a 'real rape'.

However, the hierarchy went further than a concept of a 'real rape', and included all forms of sexual violence, the woman herself and the perpetrator. One woman talked about feeling as though her rape was 'as good as its gonna get' in terms of the way the police and her family were going to perceive what happened to her, because she was attacked by a stranger in a street with multiple witnesses. These discussions bear significant similarity to the work of Christie (1986) who theorised the 'ideal victim'. However, the 'ideal victim' notion was general to all crime.

The discussions with women and professionals, in conjunction with the existing literature about hierarchies of victimhood and victim blaming led to the development of the model shown below.

From interviews with women and professionals, victim blaming of women does appear to be based on salient factors about the woman, the offence and the offender (this is in addition to the larger cultural, societal, cognitive and religious norms, values, beliefs and attitudes discussed in the integrated model of victim blaming of women).

It could be argued that this hierarchy of victimhood is based on the minutiae known only to those with full details of what happened, possibly the police, local authorities, health professionals or the close support network.

It appeared that participants felt that they were measuring themselves against an invisible set of standards that they must conform to, that the offence and the offender must conform to, if they hoped to be taken seriously or supported. Women were aware of what would happen if they did not conform to all required criteria and used this knowledge to make decisions as to whether they would report to the police or tell family and friends.

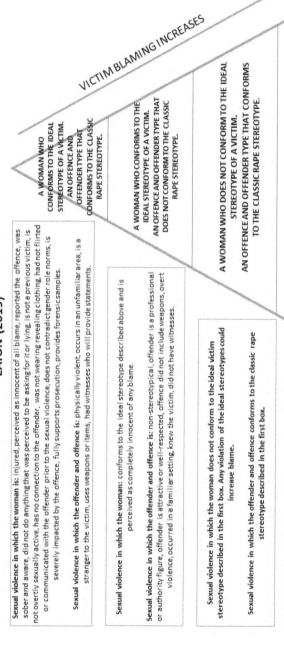

This echoes findings from Kahn et al. (1994) and Ryan, (1988) who found that women would measure their experiences against the classic rape before making a decision to report to police; with women rarely reporting to police if they felt the rape did not conform and there was a chance they would be blamed.

Once women had been blamed for sexual violence, professionals found that challenging or reducing belief in victim blaming and rape myths was difficult to achieve. Professionals constructed the challenge of beliefs about victim blaming and self-blame as futile in some cases.

Professionals constructed their own work as difficult and dilemmatic; often employing two competing discourses that women needed to know they were not to blame for sexual violence and that even when they tell women they are not to blame, it would not reduce her feelings of blame or her experiences of being blamed. This appeared to result in professionals who positioned themselves as less powerful than the other discourses in society that were blaming the woman for sexual violence.

This feeling of not being able to deconstruct victim blaming and self-blame resulted in talk that positioned women as too traumatised to be helped. This was a common interpretative repertoire and subject position, in which professionals explained that if the women could not challenge victim blaming or challenge their own self-blame, they must have been harmed in childhood.

This was an unexpected finding, as none of the professionals discussed evidence for this but constructed women who were struggling to challenge victim blaming as vulnerable and assumed that they must have significant childhood traumas that have led them to be unable to challenge victim blaming narratives. This positioning of the women could be presented as a form of victim blaming, in which professionals are blaming the women's inability to challenge difficult and harmful narratives about sexual violence on their assumed trauma histories. However, there is evidence in the literature that would suggest that women who were abused in childhood are more likely to blame themselves and be subjected to revictimisation following sexual violence (Ullman & Vasquez, 2015). Therefore, this point needs further exploration as to whether professionals are assuming that the women were abused in childhood, whether they have been taught that women who struggle with narratives about victim blaming have childhood traumas or whether this interpretative repertoire about women is coming from a collective feeling of powerlessness within the professionals.

Women experienced significant victim blaming from their family or close support network, and professionals told stories of women they supported who had been blamed by their families, friends or partners. However, it was the dilemmatic talk that was of most interest, in which both women and professionals talked about family as being the most important source of support, the first people they turned to with an expectation they would be unconditionally supportive and understanding. Whilst professionals did this much more often than women, families were constructed as the first port of call and the safety net for the woman. Simultaneously, the family were constructed as the most harmful, judgmental, isolating and intimidating response women could get. Both women and professionals talked about families isolating, disbelieving, ridiculing, blaming, shaming, attacking and silencing women when they disclosed sexual violence.

Despite this, the two discourses about the family were deployed concurrently, in which women and professionals recognised that the family was likely to blame the women, but that the family was still the first group of people they would go to after sexual violence (Ullman, 1996;1999; White & Rollins, 1981).

Findings about self-blame of women

Discussions of victim blaming and self-blame were closely intertwined, but some important findings come from the way professionals and women constructed self-blame in their talk. Self-blame was almost always presented in the talk as an ideological dilemma between two competing narratives.

The first key finding was about the way women adapt or take on victim blaming narratives as their own self-blame. Previous literature has not clearly explained how women might begin to blame themselves for sexual violence (Anderson, 1999) but the language used in previous studies tends to construct women as passively absorbing blame beliefs from society, their close support network and the media. However, there were clear differences between the way women and professionals constructed self-blame after sexual violence.

Whilst women discussed self-blame in complex, dilemmatic, challenging language, professionals discussed women as passively absorbing self-blame beliefs without any interrogation or challenge. Words such as 'absorb', 'take on', 'accept' and 'adopt', served to construct women as passive and powerless to accepting self-blame after sexual violence. This positioned women as simplistic in their thinking about themselves, the sexual violence and blame; in which they would take on the beliefs of anyone who blamed them and accept them into their own narrative without hesitation.

However, when contrasted with the way women constructed their feelings of self-blame, the studies revealed a difference. Whilst professionals constructed women as passive absorbers of new beliefs about blame, women constructed themselves as challenging, interrogating, confused, inquisitive and constantly unsure of their self-blame. Women frequently described a feeling of 'over-analysis' or 'over-thinking' in which they would replay the events in their minds whilst questioning or blaming everything they did or said.

However, this was not the end of the process for them. All women discussed a feeling of knowing they were not to blame for any of the sexual violence; having a counternarrative that they could not possibly be to blame, and that the perpetrator of the offence chose to hurt them. They talked about moving back and forth between blaming themselves and blaming the perpetrator – often resulting in both.

To add to this feeling of unease and challenge, women also talked about a difference between logically knowing they were not to blame and feeling to blame. This difference inspired the title of my PhD thesis, because every woman and almost every professional said those words during interviews. Women described it as a deep feeling that they 'knew' they were not to blame for any sexual violence (from a place of logic, reasoning and knowledge), but that they still 'felt' to blame (from a place of emotion or deeper).

This was reiterated by professionals who said that they could change the knowledge of the woman so that she understood that she was not to blame for sexual violence, but they felt it was very difficult for her to truly 'feel' she was not to blame.

Clearly, this discourse is different from the one that constructs women as passively accepting victim blaming, leading to self-blame. Women were fighting the narratives, challenging them and holding them at the same time as beliefs that they were not to blame at all. This positions women as having more agency and power than the narrative that constructs women as a passive sponge that absorbs everyone else's beliefs about herself.

Interestingly, professionals constructed women in a dilemmatic way when it came to helping them with self-blame beliefs, too. As already discussed, professionals positioned women as passive absorbers of new narratives and beliefs about victim blaming and self-blame, but when professionals were asked about how they helped women to understand that they were not to blame for sexual violence, they constructed the women as difficult to influence, difficult to change their beliefs and very resistant.

Therefore, professionals presented two constructions of women as simultaneously passive to societal beliefs about self-blame and victim blaming – but challenging and difficult in the counselling room when the professional was attempting to give the woman a new, positive narrative about victim blaming and self-blame. This suggests that professionals position women as both easily accepting and staunchly rejecting new victim blaming and self-blame beliefs.

One explanation for this could be that this represents a stereotype of women who have been assaulted as being submissive and passive in the world, but this then leads to frustration when this submissive and passive woman does not take on the new beliefs about self-blame being given to them by the professional. Perhaps there is an expectation that a woman so easily influenced by victim blaming and self-blame can easily be influenced to reject those beliefs about blame.

This is especially important because women did not construct themselves as passive or submissive to victim blaming or self-blame beliefs and provided examples of them challenging or questioning blame. Some women also discussed how they didn't believe they were to blame for sexual violence at all until many people (support network, police, other professionals) had told them that they were to blame – and even then, they were able to construct the blame as being a feeling, not a belief. As such, it may be that professionals working in sexual violence position women as having no agency, no power to challenge and therefore become frustrated when those same women do not accept new narratives.

A second explanation for this dilemmatic talk could be that women are more likely to use negative, blaming discourses about women but find it more difficult to use or access positive, empowering, non-blaming narratives about women. Evidence from previous studies has found that when women experience victim blaming or other negative responses to their disclosure of sexual violence, this has a much bigger impact on the woman than if they were to receive positive and supportive responses to their disclosure (Ullman, 2010).

If this finding was explored further, it may suggest that negative impacts on women may be more influential than positive impacts, therefore supporting the argument that a woman might be influenced or impacted more by victim blaming and self-blame than by a professional reassuring her that she is not to blame.

There could be a third explanation for the dilemmas about the two dichotomies: women as passive versus active and women as thinking versus feeling self-blame. It could be that women and professionals are constructing victim blaming and self-blame in their individual contexts and spaces, knowing that no matter how they construct or deconstruct victim blaming and self-blame, there is a larger, more powerful societal structure of victim blaming beliefs and millions of people who endorse those beliefs.

Professionals often constructed the process of helping a woman who blames herself for sexual violence as long, difficult and sometimes futile. They discussed how useful their weekly, singular narrative would be against a whole lifetime of messages, a support network, a legal system, the media and the larger societal misogynistic belief systems that continually position the woman as to blame for sexual violence.

The self is always constructed in a social context and women do not exist in a vacuum or silo (Gergen, 2011; Hood, 2012). Even when a woman constructs herself as not to blame for sexual violence, others are still able to construct her as to blame. Therefore, there could be a possibility that the dilemmas and dichotomies presented here are caused by the difference between the way the woman constructs herself and the way society continues to construct her, regardless of her own perspective (Hood, 2012). This could mean that even when women 'know' they are not to blame, they are still made to 'feel' to blame for sexual violence – and they remain aware that their own construction of themselves and what happens is different from the way others are constructing her and the sexual violence.

It is interesting to consider this explanation from the critical realist perspective, because this dilemma is precisely why a critical realist perspective argues that regardless of how an individual may perceive or construct an event, other systems and structures exist external to the mind of the individual perceiver (Bhaskar, 1975). Women could therefore construct themselves as being blameless for sexual violence, but this would not reduce their experience of societal victim blaming or the chances of discrimination, injustice or maltreatment when she discloses sexual violence.

This theme of dichotomy and dilemmatic talk continues into the final key finding about self-blame: that self-blame during and after sexual violence caused women to make significant changes to their lives in the name of 'staying safe', even when they knew, or learned that it wouldn't or didn't keep them safe. They constructed those changes as feeling necessary to protect themselves, but also useless or misguided. Women described changing their hair, appearance, jobs, hobbies, clothing, behaviour, attitudes, relationships, friendships and even their character or communication style to protect themselves.

This final finding is important because of how many campaigns about sexual violence encourage women to make changes to their lives, their actions, behaviours and decisions to avoid or protect themselves from sexual violence (e.g. London Metropolitan Police advised women to stop wearing headphones or looking at their phones when walking to avoid being raped (BBC, 2017)). Women said were aware of this and in most cases thought they followed that advice.

Those who were not directly advised to change something about themselves did so following counterfactual thinking or the need for perceived control (Branscombe et al., 2003; Frazier, 1990; Miller et al., 2010;) in which they sought out what they thought had caused the sexual violence and then changed something so that it would not happen to them again.

This also links to Janoff-Bulman's work (1979) and Pat Frazier's rebuttal (1990) who argued about the purpose and impact of self-blame and perceived past or future control over sexual violence. However, rather than women constructing these changes as adaptive and helpful, women constructed them as making them feel worse and affecting their mental health. Women reported that they tried to make changes to themselves and their lives but eventually realised that this hadn't or wouldn't protect them from sexual violence.

This was especially true for the women who were subjected to sexual violence again, even after they had made substantial changes to their appearance or lives. This realisation was profound and scary for most women, who had been led to believe that they could make simple changes that would protect them from a sex offender.

When women switched their narrative from changes being to protect herself to changes being useless or futile in protecting herself, they sometimes began to self-blame personal characteristics or internal reasons such as 'being a bad person' or 'being punished by God', which is supported by Janoff-Bulman (1979) and Lerner (1980).

Women are frequently told to change their behaviour, attire, character, decisions and lifestyle to avoid sexual violence, which positions those factors as to blame for sexual violence. This can be explained by rape myths, by misogyny, by self-preservation theories (Furnham, 2003) or by individualism theories (Jago & Christenfield, 2018). But when women then make those changes and are still subjected to sexual violence, this contradicts the belief that women can stop sexual violence by changing themselves, resulting in a realisation that the change didn't work. Women then shifted the blame to questioning their character or questioning whether there was some larger force at play; relating more to BJW as an explanation for self-blame (Janoff-Bulman, 1979; Lerner, 1980).

The reality is that the changes women make do not influence or change the actions, motivations or histories of the sex offender, hence why sex offender theory has long focussed on the integrated factors that explain why and how sex offenders commit offences against victims, which do not include a list of things that a victim may have done wrong or could have done better (Beech & Ward, 2006).

Often the changes women are encouraged to make to avoid sexual violence only pertain to the classic rape. Women are often told not to walk home alone, not to go anywhere alone after dark, not to wear headphones, not to drink in bars, not to meet men alone, not to go to certain areas and not to wear certain clothing. Whilst these changes are positioned as 'safety advice' for women, they do not protect women from the majority of sexual violence which occurs in a relationship with someone known to them (Sleath & Woodhams, 2014). In fact, these types of offences are the most likely to be seen as 'not a real victimisation' (Donde et al., 2018), as shown by the entitlement subscale in the BOWSVA.

They also lead women to ask, 'what did I do wrong?' when they are subjected to sexual violence, leading to them making changes to themselves or their lives. This is even more confusing for women who know they did not contravene the 'rules' to stay safe from sexual violence, who then consider whether it is something internal about them that attracts sex offenders or abusive relationships. This level of self-blame is pervasive. All women and professionals talked about women either being directly told to change something about themselves or feeling as though they should – but women were the only group to construct these changes as useless.

The relationship between rape myth acceptance and victim blaming of women

Throughout the three studies, RMA played an important role. It was not the sole explanation for victim blaming by the general public, the victim blaming women and professionals discussed, or the self-blame that women experienced – but it did frequently feature as a connected concept across all three studies.

In the quantitative study, the BOWSVA items and subscales were shown to have positive relationships with the U-IRMAS items and subscales. People who assigned more blame to women subjected to sexual violence in the BOWSVA items were also likely to agree with the rape myths in the U-IRMAS items.

The relationship was moderate and needs further exploration as the BOWSVA is tested further. However, the items that were constructed to conform to the classic rape did result in the lowest victim blaming of women, which suggests that the classic rape and the rape myths that underpin it are still influential in the attribution of blame to women (McMahon and Farmer, 2011; Sleath, 2011; Williams, 1984).

In interviews with women, they were able to identify all of the most common rape myths with details and examples. Women both accepted and rejected rape myths in complicated talk in which they would measure themselves against rape myths and the classic rape, whilst also rejecting rape myths as 'just myths'. The most common rape myths used to measure themselves against were those that were about assertiveness and about their bodies or appearance.

Women wrestled with whether they 'did enough' to escape, fight off or resist the offender and even though they all talked repeatedly about how many times they said 'no' or tried different strategies to stop the offence, they constructed themselves as lacking in confidence and unable to assert themselves. This is dilemmatic, as they would describe all the things they said and did to try to stop the offender but then chastise themselves for not being assertive enough.

This is likely to be related to the rape myth that 'real' rape victims physically fight off an offender and means that women might position themselves as 'not assertive enough' because they didn't physically fight the offender (Donde et al., 2018; Moller et al., 2017).

The second most common rape myth that women employed to measure their experiences against seemed to be the misogynistic beliefs and myths about their bodies and their appearance. Women talked frequently in the interviews about what they were wearing or what their body shape, body size, bra size or clothing style was at the time they were subjected to sexual violence. They talked assertively about their rejection of this myth and did not apply it to themselves; instead they gave counter examples about how they were wearing jeans and a jumper when they were attacked – or that their breast size was out of their control.

One woman said that she used to think it was because she developed breasts earlier than her peers and her body was naturally curvaceous, but she caveated that statement with her rejection of the myth and argued that she could do nothing about the shape of her body in adolescence or adulthood.

Even the women who had originally blamed themselves for sexual violence based on her body type or clothing, rejected this reasoning in the interviews and concluded that her body type or clothing could not have been to blame for sexual violence. This outcome contrasts with the other, in which women continued to wrestle with the rape myth that she was not assertive enough or should have fought off the offender better. With this rape myth, women rejected it and refused to blame themselves for their bodies or clothing. This suggests that RMA, victim blaming and self-blame may be connected but not causally – and the connection is likely to be more complicated than RMA simply leading to self-blame.

In interviews with professionals, they described themselves as constantly coming up against the power of the rape myth and the classic rape in their work with police and other professionals. They positioned rape myths as all encompassing, powerful forces that 'infected' society like a disease.

Unlike the women, the professionals had ample experience of the rape myths being used to blame women in the court of law, in police investigations, in social care proceedings and in mental health settings. They positioned themselves as defenders or challengers of the rape myths in which they took other professionals to task over their belief or use of rape myths to blame women subjected to sexual violence.

Rape myths did play a role in the victim blaming and self-blame of women, but according to the findings from the current research it was not a linear or causal relationship, and the use of rape myths in victim blaming and self-blame varied considerably.

Points about methodology and approach

There are a number of strengths to this research that arise from methodological and philosophical approaches to the work. There are also some important limitations. This section will discuss strengths and limitations of the research presented in this book.

One of the first strengths of this work was the depth and size of the literature review that was carried out in the first year of the academic research. Exploring, reading and gaining an understanding from the existing literature which included over 200 academic journals, books, PhD theses, national and international reports undoubtedly had a positive effect on the strength of the work presented here.

Drawing evidence from multiple disciplines and sources also meant that broader societal mechanisms and explanations could be considered or interrogated. The learning from the existing literature enabled a more nuanced and integrated understanding of victim blaming and self-blame of women, influenced the methods and materials and informed the interpretation of findings.

The critical realist approach to this research has facilitated a conjunction between realist and relativist philosophy, meaning that rather than constructing victim blaming and self-blame of women as wholly relative and socially constructed, it is possible to construct both issues as independent, impactful problems in the world that harm women – whilst also exploring the way language constructs the beliefs and norms that influence and reinforce those harms. The work was informed by feminist standpoint theory and sought to centre the voices of women, and to learn from women's thoughts, experiences and position in the world.

This mixed-methods research also sought to explore the issues of victim blaming and self-blame from three different angles in order to inform the research and to consider different positions, as many of the studies in victim blaming have tended to rely on self-report questionnaires only. However, the methodological approach in this book has presented the amount of nuanced learning that can come from combining quantitative and qualitative research on one specific topic.

This is especially true for how useful the discursive approach and focus on language has been, throughout the book. This focus improved the critique, development of the BOWSVA scale, influenced the wording of the interview questions and the analytic approach to the data. The discussion of language flows throughout the work as a tool to construct victim blaming and self-blame, whilst the critical realist element ensured that a focus on the real impact, harm and discrimination women was not lost in abstract discussions about language.

The methodology employed here sought to work alongside women and not to treat them just as sources of information or data. It is imperative that women subjected to sexual violence, who are consulted about issues that affect them, do not then experience silence from the researchers, or never find out what their thoughts were used for.

Women were therefore consulted throughout the work and were offered the opportunity to comment on and interpret the data analysis and study findings, including further work coming from my PhD thesis and their interviews.

There was parallel activism and campaigning, as I did not conduct the research in a vacuum and my personal activism with women and girls subjected to sexual violence continued throughout the four years of writing this book. Due to this, research was communicated repeatedly at all stages, not only at professional conferences or with other academics but to the general public and to thousands of women subjected to sexual violence. The work presented in this book has already influenced the development of free resources for women and professionals working with women and will continue to do so.

The research aimed to be as authentic and transparent as possible. The quantitative data in the BOWSVA study has been presented thoroughly, including each item response, which is not consistently presented in other studies (Anthoine et al., 2014).

Data was not heavily edited, transformed or changed to seek a desired outcome, with the only data cleaning undertaken being the deletion of non-complete responses that could not be analysed clearly. Outliers were not deleted as this would have ignored the real beliefs and responses of participants that did not 'fit' the norm, and abnormal distributions were not changed or improved to get better outcomes from the data. Instead, the data was explored using parametric and non-parametric approaches and conclusions were suggested tentatively. It is important to frame these approaches to the research as strengths, where they could be perceived as weaknesses.

All studies in this book have benefitted from thorough analysis with checking and re-checking of findings and interpretations with second coders, supervisors, alternative statistical tests and personal feedback from participants in all three studies.

Further strengths of this research include the decision to position myself as an active agent in the research – and not an objective psychologist.

As a woman who was subjected to sexual violence, as an activist and volunteer in feminist causes, as a professional working in the psychology of sexual abuse and violence towards women and girls and as a PhD researcher, I chose to adopt a highly reflective practice throughout the work – and to include critical reflexive comments at the end of each study and chapter – including the quantitative chapter (Ch.5) in which we rarely see the use of critical reflexivity as this is perceived as a 'qualitative' concept.

As discussed by Ortlipp (2008) and Bhaskar (1975), it is important to remain present and visible in the work that we do and to acknowledge our own experiences, upbringing, decisions, values, beliefs, assumptions and goals.

Finally, a key strength of this work is the potential for real world impact for women subjected to sexual violence and professionals working with those women affected. Victim blaming uniquely impacts women subjected to sexual violence and continues to be prevalent (Gravelin et al., 2019).

Whilst quantitative studies exploring prevalence and attitudes have been plentiful over the years, research that explores the experiences of being blamed, blaming the self and how to help women to stop blaming themselves for sexual violence has been less so. This work addresses an important gap in the research and pulls together theories, factors, frameworks and new evidence to suggest more nuanced ways of understanding and explaining victim blaming of women.

Limitations of the work have been discussed within each chapter but will be discussed more broadly here. The quantitative study providing an account of the development and testing of the BOWSVA must be considered as an initial development study and not a full validation of the measure. The factor structure and findings from the study need further exploration with different samples to confirm or reject the solution presented here, and to build understanding of attribution of blame. The data generated from the secondary scale in the BOWSVA which asked participants how much blame they assigned to the man in each scenario also needs further exploration before conclusions can be drawn, both about the blaming of perpetrators of sexual violence and the relationship this has with the blaming of their female victims described in the items.

The qualitative chapters (Ch. 15 & 16) utilised a critical discursive analysis approach to the data, which did yield important results, but the focus on language instead of experience may have been a limitation. The data from interviews could be analysed again using a complementary approach to focus on the experiences and feelings presented by participants (such as Interpretative Phenomenological Analysis), to explore additional experiential components less relevant to a Critical Discursive Analysis.

Each study also had a small sample size which prevents generalisation of results. However, generalisation was not a goal sought after by this work. Further, where most participants were interviewed face-to-face, a small number chose to take part over the phone, which may have an impact on the findings due to the difference in environment or experience of taking part without a face-to-face context.

Implications for practice and research

The research presented here has several implications for practitioners working with women subjected to sexual violence and for broader campaigns and interventions to tackle victim blaming of women. First, this book presents victim blaming and self-blame as a battleground of beliefs in which women fight to understand, accept or reject common narratives in society, beliefs about themselves, myths about sexual violence, blame from support networks and the positioning of women in a sexist society.

This means that future research and practice would benefit from adopting a feminist standpoint and opting to see women as active and challenging in their experiences of victim blaming and self-blame, rather than positioning them as passively absorbing beliefs. Adopting this position in practice would mean working with women as active agents who have their own individual thoughts, feelings and power to exert regarding victim blaming and self-blame, as opposed to working with them as naïve victims who accept others' beliefs without question and need teaching or leading to a better understanding of self.

The findings from this research present victim blaming as multi-faceted with many origins and motivations, which could be useful for practitioners working directly with women subjected to victim blaming. Rather than potentially explaining victim blaming as being solely down to RMA or misogyny, it may be helpful for practitioners to understand the layers and interlinking factors that influence so many people to blame women for sexual violence perpetrated against them.

Gaining this knowledge may improve awareness raising campaigns, training of professionals and support work with women which could become more holistic and contextual once all factors and theories of victim blaming were integrated. However, one possible negative consequence of realising how complex and multi-faceted victim blaming of women is, is that professionals could feel hopeless or powerless in their roles to reduce victim blaming and self-blame. As seen in Chapter 16 feedback, this was a concern raised by two of the professionals who wrote to me.

However, this does suggest that the professionals who read the chapter and gave feedback were also not aware of how multi-faceted and complex victim blaming was and gave them much to think about in their own approaches at work. This included one professional organisation which changed their training programme to include wider explanations of victim blaming after reading the draft chapter.

In terms of public influence, this research could also be used to influence the way the mass media, criminal justice system, education system and public awareness campaigns depict, position or describe sexual violence against women. With both professionals and women describing how the mass media and the criminal justice system were the most common authoritative sources of victim blaming of women, the findings here could be used to lobby both agencies to change the way they talk about women subjected to sexual violence. Public awareness campaigns could stop blaming the actions, decisions and appearance of women and focus more on the actions, decisions and motivations of perpetrators – and on the support provided by families and support networks. Therefore, national and regional campaigns and interventions focussing on the improvement of support and responses to women when they disclose could useful.

Recommendations for improving sexual violence prevention

This final section will suggest changes that could be made to improve prevention campaigns and media portrayal of sexual violence committed against women and girls.

- Journalists, news presenters, talk show hosts and media editors could engage in training and further education to improve the language they use to describe sexual violence, victims and offenders

- More responsibility could be placed on production companies and TV channels to ensure that they do not encourage misogyny and blaming of women and girls subjected to sexual violence

- Wider education on the harms of pornography should be implemented for both adults and children, including information about the ways sexual acts in porn do not reflect sexual acts in real life and the way sex is staged for film

- Prevention campaigns by authorities could be aimed at offenders, potential offenders and bystanders – rather than being aimed at women and girls to change their behaviours and appearance

- Prevention campaigns should seek to prevent sexual violence from being perpetrated at all and should not seek to encourage individual women to protect themselves from inevitable sexual violence

- Prevention campaigns should not position sexual violence, exploitation and abuse as 'poor choices' of women or children

- Prevention campaigns should be developed and piloted in conjunction with a group of diverse victims of sexual violence and experts in the field to ensure that messages are thoroughly researched and tested before use

- Women and girls should not be encouraged to change something about themselves to prevent sexual violence

- Prevention campaigns should name the problem and name the perpetrators of the problem clearly, rather than using metaphorical language about 'being a victim' which omits the choices and actions of the offender(s)

The research also has further implications for academic and social research. The focus on discourse in this book resulted in significant learning about the way language is used to describe or construct sexual violence, women, male perpetrators and blame can change the outcomes and interpretations of research materials, data and findings.

Future research with the general public to explore attitudes towards sexual violence against women needs to carefully consider the words, phrases and power of interpretative repertoires surrounding blame, sexual violence, gender roles and social norms when developing and conducting studies.

This book also presents a more nuanced and complex view of victim blaming of women subjected to sexual violence, in which multiple mechanisms work together at different levels of society to reinforce and encourage victim blaming of women. As previous research has tended to focus on RMA, BJW or hostile sexism as the explanation of victim blaming of women, the findings in this book may influence future theories or studies to look at this issue in a more integrated and holistic way, as opposed to looking for correlations with singular explanations or factors. The framework presented in my new model may be a good starting point for researchers to explore relationships between the influences in society that appear to be contributing to, maintaining or communicating victim blaming messages to, and about, women subjected to sexual violence.

One of the most under researched areas in the victim blaming literature seems to be the individualistic approach to responsibility and blame, in which women are told they are responsible for their own behaviours, experiences and safety – but the men who commit sex offences against them are not held responsible to the same extent. In a society in which individual responsibility and 'free choice' is championed, it is strange that women subjected to sexual violence should be seen as responsible and making choices that lead to sexual violence, but men committing sexual violence are seen as being 'led on' by women – especially as this would mean he had no responsibility and no free choice.

Second, it would be useful to perform more exploratory, qualitative studies about BJW in sexual violence against women. Whilst quantitative studies have shown inconsistent results, language use containing concepts from BJW are still commonly used in every day speech (karma will get you in the end, what goes around comes around, you get what you deserve, good things happen to good people). This may mean that when directly asked, participants of questionnaires do not endorse BJW items but do use these discourses and interpretative repertoires in discussion about women subjected to sexual violence.

Future research and campaigns building on this book

Planned research and campaigns building on the learning from this book include the further exploration and validation of the BOWSVA scale. The development and testing of peer reviewed resources for professionals, free resources for women to understand victim blaming and feelings of self-blame, a large dissemination event for professionals, free videos and blogs discussing the findings.

Further to this, the research has suggested several possibilities for future research into the implication of language in victim blaming and self-blame of women. Practice research also needs to be conducted to explore the process of coming to accept victim blaming as a belief about self, challenging that self-blame and then rejecting the belief. At present, the explanations of victim blaming, and self-blame do not suitably explain how this process occurs or how practitioners and support network members can help women to challenge victim blaming from others, or self-blame beliefs they hold about the sexual violence they were subjected to.

18.
Final thoughts

I would like to thank you for reading what feels like everything I can possibly cram into this book on the psychology of victim blaming of women and girls subjected to male violence and trauma.

If there is anything to take from this book, it is the understanding that women and girls exist in a complex, oppressive, patriarchal system which encourages and celebrates the victim blaming of women and girls every time they are subjected to male violence.

We have much work to do to dismantle the hundreds of systems and narratives that prop up the immense woman blaming we have in society.

We have to stop using 'prevention' programmes that are aimed at women and girls making their lives smaller and smaller. We have to stop using 'interventions' which convince women and girls they are to blame for male violence. We need to challenge and end the psychiatric diagnosis and treatment of women and girls who disclose abuse, trauma and sexual violence. We have to reform the criminal justice system and explore the pathetic prosecution and conviction rates against violent men who abuse women and girls. We have to upskill and mobilise workforces, media outlets and activist groups to change the discourse around male violence and female oppression.

We need to challenge victim blaming every single time it happens.

Men are 100% responsible for male violence.

Women and girls carry 0% of the blame. Ever.

None.

Nada.

Zero.

Reference List

Abrams, D., Viki, G.T., Masser, B., & Bohner, G. (2003). Perceptions of stranger and acquaintance rape: The role of benevolent and hostile sexism in victim blame and rape proclivity. Journal of Personality and Social Psychology, 84, 111-125. doi: 10.1037/0022-3514.84.1.111

Adams-Curtis, L. E., & Forbes, G. B. (2004). College Women's Experiences of Sexual Coercion: A Review of Cultural, Perpetrator, Victim, and Situational Variables. Trauma, Violence, & Abuse, 5(2), 91–122. https://doi.org/10.1177/1524838003262331

Alicke, M.D., & Yurak, T.J. (1995). Perpetrator responsibility and judgements of acquaintance rape. Journal of Applied Social Psychology, 25, 1900-1921. doi: 10.1111/j.1559-1816.1995.tb01823.x

Alsop, R., Fitzsimons, A., & Lennon, K. (2002). Theorizing gender. Bodmin: MPG Books, Ltd.

Amnesty International UK. (2005). Sexual assault research summary report. Retrieved from http://www.amnesty.org.uk/news_details.asp?NewsID=16618 Accessed: 21/02/2017

American Psychological Association, Task Force on the Sexualization of Girls (2007) Report of the APA Task Force on the Sexualization of Girls. Retrieved from: http://www.apa.org/pi/women/programs/girls/report-full.pdf

Andersen, M. L., & Renzetti, C. M. (1980). Rape crisis counselling and the culture of individualism. Contemporary Crises, 4, 323-339.

Anderson, I. (2001). Perceived motivation for rape: Gender differences in beliefs about female and male rape. Current Research in Social Psychology, 6, 1-12. Retrieved from http://www.uiowa.edu/~grpproc/crisp/crisp.html

Anderson, I. (1999) Characterological and behavioral blame in conversations about female and male rape. Journal of Language and Social Psychology, Vol. 18 No. 4, December 1999 377-394, Sage Publications

Anderson, I. and Bissell, H. (2011) Blame and fault attributions in sexual violence: are these distinct? Journal of Aggression, Conflict and Peace Research, Vol. 3, No.4, pp. 222-229, Emerald Group Publishing Limited, ISSN 1759-6599 DOI 10.1108/17596591111187747

Anthoine, E., Moret, L, Regnault, A., Sebille, V. and Harduin, JB. (2014) Sample size used to validate a scale: a review of publications on newly-developed patient reported outcomes measures, Health Qual Life Outcomes, 12:2, doi: 10.1186/s12955-014-0176-2

Balzarotti, S., Biassoni, F., Villani, D., Prunas, A., & Velotti, P. (2016). Individual differences in cognitive emotion regulation: Implications for subjective and psychological well-being. Journal of Happiness Studies, 17(1), 125-143. doi:10.1007s12144-016-9421-7

Bareket, O., Kahalon, R., Shnabel, N., & Glick, P. (2018). The Madonna-Whore dichotomy: Men who perceive women's nurturance and sexuality as mutually exclusive endorse patriarchy and show lower relationship satisfaction. Sex Roles. doi:10.1007/s11199-23 018-0895-7

Branscombe, N. R., Wohl, M. J. A., Owen, S., Allison, J. A., & N'gbala, A. (2003). Counterfactual thinking, blame assignment, and well-being in rape victims. Basic and Applied Social Psychology, 25(4), 265-273. DOI: 10.1207/S15324834BASP2504_1

Ben-David, S., & Schneider, O. (2005). Rape perceptions, gender role attitudes, and victim-perpetrator acquaintance. Sex Roles, 53, 385-399. doi: 10.1007/s11199-005-6761-4

Bentall, R. (2003) Madness Explained: Psychosis and human nature, Penguin Books

Bentall, R. (2009) Doctoring the mind: Why psychiatric treatments fail, Penguin Books

Bem, S. L. (1993). The lenses of gender: Transforming the debate on sexual inequality. New Haven, CT: Yale University Press.

Bhaskar, R. (1975). A realist theory of science. Brighton: Harvester.

Bhaskar, R. (1989). Reclaiming reality. London: Verso

Billig, M., Condor, S., Edwards, D., Gane, M., Middleton, D., & Radley, A. (1988). Ideological dilemmas: A social psychology of everyday thinking. London: SAGE

Bows, H. (2016) 'Age and Victimisation'. In Corteen, K., Morley, S., Taylor, P., & Turner, J. (Eds.) A Companion to Crime, Harm and Victimisation. Bristol, United Kingdom: Policy Press.

Bronfenbrenner, U. (1979). The ecology of human development: Experiments by nature and design. Cambridge, MA: Harvard University Press.

Bronfenbrenner, U. (1986). Ecology of the family as a context for human development: Research perspectives. Developmental Psychology, 22, 723-742.

Bronfenbrenner, U. (1995). Developmental ecology through space and time: A future perspective. In P. Moen, G. H. Elder, Jr., and K. Luscher (Eds.), Examining lives in context: Perspectives on the ecology of human development (pp. 619-647). Washington, DC: APA Books.

Brown, J.D. (2009) Choosing the Right Type of Rotation in PCA and EFA, Statistics Corner: Questions and answers about language testing statistics

Brownmiller, S. (1975) Against our Wills: Men, Women and Rape. New York, NY: The Ballentine Publishing Group

Browne, A. (1991). The victim's experience: Pathways to disclosure [Special issue]. Psychotherapy: Theory, Research, Practice, Training, 28, 150–156. doi: 10.1037/0033-3204.28.1.150

Bucher, J. & Manasse, M. (2011) When Screams Are Not Released: A Study of Communication and Consent in Acquaintance Rape Situations, Women & Criminal Justice 21(2):123-140 DOI: 10.1080/08974454.2011.558801

Bucholtz, M. (2000) p. 1440, 'The Politics of Transcription', Journal of Pragmatics 32: 1439–65

Buddie, A. M., & Miller, A. G. (2001). Beyond rape myths: A more complex view of the perceptions of rape victims. Sex Roles, 45, 139-160. doi: 10.1023/A:1013575209803

Burgess, A.W. and Holmstrom, L.L. (1979) Adaptive Strategies and Recovery from Rape. American Journal of Psychiatry, 136, 1278-1282.

Burt, M. (1980) Cultural Myths and Support for Rape, Journal of Personality and Social Psychology, Vol. 38, No. 2, 217-230

Bryant-Davis, T., Ullman, S.E., Tsong, Y. and Gobin, R. (2011) Surviving the Storm: The Role of Social Support and Religious Coping in Sexual Assault Recovery of African American Women, Violence Against Women, 17(12) 1601–1618, DOI: 10.1177/1077801211436138

Campbell, R. (1998). The community response to rape: Victims' experiences with the legal, medical, and mental health systems. American Journal of Community Psychology, 26, 355-378. doi: 10.1023/A:1022155003633

Campbell, R., Wasco, S.M., Ahrens, C.E., Sefl, T., & Barnes, H.E. (2001). Preventing the "Second Rape": Rape survivors' experiences with community services providers. Journal of Interpersonal Violence, 16, 1239-1259. doi: 10.1177/088626001016012002

Campbell, R., Dworkin, E. & Cabral, G. (2009) An ecological model of the impact of sexual assault on women's mental health, Trauma, Violence, & Abuse, Vol. 10, No. 3, July 2009 225-246, DOI: 10.1177/1524838009334456

Campbell, R. (2005). What really happened? A validation study of rape survivors' help-seeking experiences with the legal and medical systems. Violence & Victims, 20, 55-68.

Campbell, R. (2006). Rape survivors' experiences with the legal and medical systems: Do rape victim advocates make a difference? Violence Against Women, 12, 1-16.

Campbell, R., & Raja, S. (2005). The sexual assault and secondary victimization of female veterans: Help seeking experiences in military and civilian social systems. Psychology of Women Quarterly, 29, 97-106.

Carmody, D. C., & Washington, L. M. (2001). Rape myth acceptance among college women: The impact of race and prior victimization. Journal of Interpersonal Violence, 16, 424-436.

Cattell, R. (1978) The scientific use of factor analysis, New York

Chapman, A. (2015) Gender Bias in Education, EdChange

Christie, N. (1986) The Ideal Victim. From Crime Policy to Victim Policy, P 17-30, Palgrave Macmillan (Ezzat A Fattah, ed.) DOI: 10.1007/978-1-349-08305-3_2

Clarke, A. & Lawson, K. (2009) Women's Judgments of a Sexual Assault Scenario: The Role of Prejudicial Attitudes and Victim Weight, Violence and Victims 24(2):248-64, DOI: 10.1891/0886-6708.24.2.248

Clarke, A. & Stermac, L. (2011). The influence of stereotypical beliefs, participant gender, and survivor weight on sexual assault response. Journal of Interpersonal Violence, 26(11), 2285-2302.

Classen, C. C., Palesh, O. G., & Aggarwal, R. (2005). Sexual revictimization: A review of the empirical literature. Trauma, Violence, and Abuse, 6, 103-129.

Clay-Warner, J., & Burt, C.H. (2005). Rape reporting after reforms: Have times really changed? Violence Against Women, 11, 150-176. doi: 10.1177/1077801204271566

Clegg, S. (2006) The problem of agency in feminism: a critical realist approach, Gender and Education, 18:3, 309-324, DOI: 10.1080/09540250600667892

Coates, L. & Wade, A. (2004) Telling it like it isn't: obscuring perpetrator responsibility for violent crime, Discourse and Society, Vol 15(5): 499–526

Coople (2018) One in five millennials have more than two jobs, Retrieved from: https://www.coople.com/uk/coople-stories/one-five-millennials-two-jobs/ Accessed on 14/02/2019

Correia, I., & Vala, J. (2003). When will a victim be secondarily victimized? The effect of observers' belief in a just world, victim's innocence and persistence of suffering. Social Justice Research, 16, 379-400. doi: 10.1023/A:1026313716185

Correia, I., Vala, J., & Aguiar, P. (2001). The effects of belief in a just world and victim's innocence on secondary victimisation, judgements of justice and deservingness. Social Justice Research, 14, 327-342. doi: 10.1023/A:1014324125095

Coker, A.L., Smith, P.H., Thompson, M.P., Mckeown, R.E., Bethea, L. Davis, K.E. (2002) Social support protects against the negative effects of partner violence on mental health, Journal of Women's Health & Gender-Based Medicine 11(5):465-76, DOI: 10.1089/15246090260137644

Costello, A. & Osborne, J. (2005) Best Practices in Exploratory Factor Analysis: Four Recommendations for Getting the Most From Your Analysis, Vol. 10

Cowan, G. & Quinton, W. (1997) Cognitive Style And Attitudinal Correlates Of The Perceived Causes Of Rape Scale, Psychology of Women Quarterly, 21 (1997), 227-245

Creswell, J. W., & Plano Clark, V. L. (2011). Designing and conducting mixed methods research (2nd ed.). Thousand Oaks, CA: Sage.

Crome, S. & McCabe, M. (1995) The Impact of Rape on Individual, Interpersonal, and Family Functioning, Journal of Family Studies, 1:1, 58-70, DOI: 10.5172/jfs.1.1.58

Cuklanz, L.M. (2000). Rape on prime time. Philadelphia: University of Pennsylvania Press

Dawtry, R., Cozzolino, P and Callan, M. (2019) I blame therefore it was: Rape myth acceptance, victim blaming and memory reconstruction, Personality and Social Psychology Bulletin, pp.1-14, Sage Publications

Deitz, M. F., Williams, S. L., Rife, S. C., & Cantrell, P. (2015). Examining Cultural, Social, and Self-Related Aspects of Stigma in Relation to Sexual Assault and Trauma Symptoms. Violence Against Women, 21(5), 598–615. https://doi.org/10.1177/1077801215573330

Donde, S., Ragsdale, S., Koss, M. & Zucker, A. (2018) If It Wasn't Rape, Was It Sexual Assault? Comparing Rape and Sexual Assault Acknowledgment in College Women Who Have Experienced Rape. Violence Against Women Vol. 24(14) 1718–1738. DOI: 10.1177/1077801217743339

Dong, Y., & Peng, C. Y. (2013). Principled missing data methods for researchers. SpringerPlus, 2(1), 222. doi:10.1186/2193-1801-2-222

Donovan, R. A. (2007). To Blame or Not To Blame: Influences of Target Race and Observer Sex on Rape Blame Attribution. Journal of Interpersonal Violence, 22(6), 722–736. https://doi.org/10.1177/0886260507300754

Du Mont, J., Miller, K-.L., & Myhr, T.L. (2003). The role of "real rape" and "real victim" stereotypes in the police reporting practices of sexually assaulted women. Violence Against Women, 9, 466-486. doi: 10.1177/1077801202250960

Dunn, J. (2005) 'Victims' and 'Survivors': Emerging Vocabularies of Motive for 'Battered Women Who Stay', Sociological Inquiry 75 (1): 1 – 30

Duschinsky, R. (2013) What does sexualisation mean? Feminist Theory, 14(3) 255–264. DOI: 10.1177/1464700113499842

Eaton, J. (2019) 'Logically, I know I am not to blame, but I still feel to blame': Exploring and measuring victim blaming and self-blame of women subjected to sexual violence and abuse, University of Birmingham

Eaton, J. (2018) Sexual Exploitation and Mental Health of Adults, Research in Practice, Dartington Press

Eaton, J. & Holmes, D. (2017) Child Sexual Exploitation: An Evidence Scope, Research in Practice, Dartington Press

Edley, N. (2001). Conversation Analysis, Discursive Psychology and the Study of Ideology: A Response to Susan Speer. Feminism & Psychology, 11(1), 136–140. https://doi.org/10.1177/0959353501011001007

Egan, V. (2017) Rape patterns reported to the police, Conference Paper: New Directions in Sex Offender Practice, 2017

Fairclough, N. (2001). Critical discourse analysis as a method in social scientific research. In R. Wodak, & M. Meyer (Eds.), Methods in critical discourse analysis (pp. 121-138). London: Sage.

Feild, H.S. (1978). Attitudes toward rape: A comparative analysis of police, rapists, crisis counselors, and citizens. Journal of Personality and Social Psychology 36, 156–179. doi: 10.1037/0022-3514.36.2.156

Field, H.S., Bienen, L.B. (1980). Jurors and Rape: A Study in Psychology and Law. Lexington Books; Lexington, Mass.

Fileborn, B. (2017) Sexual Assault and Justice for Older Women: A Critical Review of the Literature, Trauma, Violence and Abuse, 1-12, DOI: 10.1177/1524838016641666

Filipas, H.H., & Ullman, S.E. (2001). Social reactions to sexual assault victims from various support sources. Violence and Victims, 16, 673-392. Retrieved from http://www.springerpub.com/product/08866708

Filipas, H.H & Ullman, S.E. (2006) Child Sexual Abuse, Coping Responses, Self-Blame, Posttraumatic Stress Disorder, and Adult Sexual Revictimization. Journal of Interpersonal Violence, Vol. 21, No. 5, pp.652-672, Sage Publications

Fisher, B. S., Daigle, L. E., Cullen, F. T., & Turner, M. G. (2003). Reporting sexual victimization to the police and others: Results from a national-level study of college women. Criminal Justice and Behavior, 30, 6–38. doi: 10.1177/0093854802239161

Flood, M. (2007) International encyclopedia of men and masculinities. London New York: Routledge. ISBN 9780415333436. ISBN 9780415333436

Foley L. A., Evancic C., Karnik K., King J., Parks A. (1995). Date rape: effects of race of assailant and victim and gender of subjects on perceptions. J. Black Psychol. 21 6–18. 10.1177/00957984950211002

Frazier, P.A., & Haney, B. (1996). Sexual assault cases in the legal system: Police, prosecutor, and victim perspectives. Law and Human Behavior, 20, 607-628. doi: 10.1007/BF01499234

Fredrickson, B. L., & Roberts, T.-A. (1997). Objectification Theory: Toward Understanding Women's Lived Experiences and Mental Health Risks. Psychology of Women Quarterly, 21(2), 173–206. https://doi.org/10.1111/j.1471-6402.1997.tb00108.x

Franiuk, R., Seefelt, J. L., Cepress, S. L., & Vandello, J. A. (2008). Prevalence and effects of rape myths in the media: The Kobe Bryant case. Violence Against Women, 14, 287–309.

Franiuk, R., Seefelt, J. L., & Vandello, J. A. (2008). Prevalence of rape myths in headlines and their effects on attitudes toward rape. Sex Roles, 58, 11-12, 790-801

Franiuk, R & Shain, A. (2011) Beyond Christianity: The Status of Women and Rape Myths, Sex Roles (2011) 65:783–791, DOI 10.1007/s11199-011-9974-8

Frazier, P. A., Mortensen, H., & Steward, J. (2005). Coping strategies as mediators of the relations among perceived control and distress in sexual assault survivors. Journal of Counselling Psychology, 52(3), 267-78.

Frese, B., Moya, M., & Megias, J. L. (2004). Social perception of rape: How rape myth acceptance modulates the influence of situational factors. Journal of Interpersonal Violence, 19, 143-161. doi: 10.1177/0886260503260245

Fowers, A. F., & Fowers, B. (2010). Social dominance and sexual self-schema as moderators of sexist reactions to female subtypes. Sex Roles, 62(7-8), 468-480. https://doi.org/10.1007/s11199-009-9607-7

Freud, S. 1913 The claims of psycho-analysis to scientific interest S.E. 13 165–190

Fulero, S. M., & DeLara, C. (1976). Rape victims and attributed responsibility: A defensive attribution approach. Victimology, 1(4), 551-563

Furnham, A. (2003). Belief in a just world: Research progress over the past decade. Personality and Individual Differences, 34, 795-817. doi:10.1016/S0191-8869(02)00072-7

Garcia, L.T (1998) Perceptions of Resistance to Unwanted Sexual Advances, Journal of Psychology & Human Sexuality, 10:1, 43-52, DOI: 10.1300/J056v10n01_03

George W. H., Martinez L. J. (2002). Victim blaming in rape: effects of victim and perpetrator race, type of rape, and participant racism. Psychol. Women Q. 26 110–119. 10.1111/1471-6402.00049

Gergen, K. (2011) The self as a social construction, Psychological Studies 56(1):108-116, DOI: 10.1007/s12646-011-0066-1

Gerber, G.L., Cronin, J.M., & Steigman, H.J. (2004). Attributions of blame in sexual assault to perpetrators and victims of both genders. Journal of Applied Social Psychology, 34, 2149-2165. doi: 10.1111/j.1559-1816.2004.tb02694.x

Gerger, H., Kley, H., Bohner, G., & Siebler, F. (2007). The acceptance of modern myths about sexual aggression scale: development and validation in German and English. Aggressive Behavior, 33, 422–440.

Glick, P., & Fiske, S. T. (1996). The ambivalent sexism inventory: Differentiating hostile and benevolent sexism. Journal of Personality and Social Psychology, 70(3), 491-512. doi:10.1037/0022-3514.70.3.491

Gorsuch, R. (1983) Factor Anaylsis (2nd Ed), Hillsdale

Gotovac, S. & Towson, S. (2015) Perceptions of sexual assault victims/survivors: the influence of sexual history and body weight, Violence Vict, 30(1): 66-80.

Grant, M. J., & Booth, A. (2009). A typology of reviews: an analysis of 14 review types and associated methodologies. Health Information & Libraries Journal, 26(2), 91-108. http://doi.org/10.1111/j.1471-1842.2009.00848.x

Grauerholz, L. (2000). An ecological approach to understanding sexual revictimization: Linking personal, interpersonal and sociocultural factors and processes. Child Maltreatment, 5, 5-17

Gravelin, C., Biernat, M & Bucher, C. (2019) Blaming the Victim of Acquaintance Rape: Individual, Situational, and Sociocultural Factors, Front. Psychol., https://doi.org/10.3389/fpsyg.2018.02422

Greene, D., & Navarro, R.L. (1998). Situation-specific assertiveness in the epidemiology of sexual victimization among university women: A prospective path analysis. Psychology of Women Quarterly, 22, 589–604.

Gross, R. M. (1994). Buddhism. In J. Holm & J. Bowker (Eds.), Women in religion (pp. 1–29). London: Continuum.

Grubb, A., & Harrower, J. (2008). Attribution of blame in cases of rape: An analysis of participant gender, type of rape and perceived similarity to the victim. Aggression and Violent Behavior, 13, 396-405. doi:10.1016/j.avb.2008.06.006

Grubb, A. & Turner (2012). Attribution of blame in rape cases: A review of the impact of rape myth acceptance, gender role conformity and substance use on victim blaming

Hafer C. L. (2000). Do innocent victims threaten the belief in a just world? Evidence from a modified stroop task. J. Pers. Soc. Psychol. 79 165–173. 10.1037/0022-3514.79.2.165

Harned, M. (2005). Understanding women's labeling of unwanted sexual experiences with dating partners, Violence Against Women. 11, 374-413.

Harrison, J., MacGibbon, L., & Morton, M. (2001). Regimes of trustworthiness in qualitative research: The rigors of reciprocity. Qualitative Inquiry, 7(3), 323-345.

Harrison, L., Howerton, D., Secarea, A., & Nguyen, C. (2008). Effects of ingroup bias and gender role violations on acquaintance rape attributions. Sex Roles, 59, 713-725. doi: 10.1007/s11199-008-9472-9

Heath, N., Lynch, S., Fritch, A., McArthur, L. & Smith, S. (2011) Silent Survivors: Rape Myth Acceptance in Incarcerated Women's Narratives of Disclosure and Reporting of Rape, Psychology of Women Quarterly, 35(4) 596-610 DOI: 10.1177/0361684311407870

Heggen, C. (1996). Religious beliefs and abuse. In C. Kroeger & J. Beck (Eds.), Women, Abuse and the Bible (pp. 15-27). Grand Rapids: Baker Books.

Heider, F. (1958). The Psychology of Interpersonal Relations. Wiley, New York

Hockett, J. & Saucier, D. (2015) A systematic literature review of "rape victims" versus "rape survivors": Implications for theory, research, and practice, Aggression and Violent Behaviour, 25, 1-14, Elsevier

Hood, B. (2012) The Self Illusion: Why there is no 'you' inside your head, Constable

Horsley, R. A & Horsley, R. J. (1987) On the trail of 'witches': Wise women, midwives and the European witch hunts, Women in German Yearbook, Vol. 3, pp. 1-28, University of Nebraska Press

Inglehart, R. (1997). Modernization and postmodernization. Princeton, NJ: Princeton University Press.

Jago, C. P., & Christenfeld, N. (2018). The Impact of Sexual Assault Prevention Information on Perceived Control and Victim Blaming. https://doi.org/10.31234/osf.io/m8qwc

Janoff-Bulman, R. (1979) Characterological Versus Behavioural Self-Blame: Inquiries Into Depression and Rape, Journal of Personality and Social Psychology, Vol. 37, No. 10, 1798-1809

Jaycox, L., Zoellner, L. and Foa, E. (2002) Cognitive–Behavior Therapy for PTSD in Rape Survivors, JCLP/In Session: Psychotherapy in Practice, Vol. 58(8), 891–906, DOI: 10.1002/jclp.10065

Jimenez, J. & Abreu, J. (2003) Race and sex effects on attitudinal perceptions of acquaintance rape. Journal of Counselling Psychology 50: 252–256

Johnstone, L. & Boyle, M. (2018) The Power Threat Meaning Framework: Towards the identification of patterns in emotional distress, unusual experiences and troubled or troubling behaviour, as an alternative to functional psychiatric diagnosis, The British Psychological Society

Kalra, G. & Bhugra, D. (2013) Sexual violence against women: Understanding cross-cultural intersections, Indian J Psychiatry. 2013 Jul-Sep; 55(3): 244–249. doi: 10.4103/0019-5545.117139

Kalof, L. (2000) Vulnerability to sexual coercion among college women: A longitudinal study, Gender Issues 18(4):47-58 DOI: 10.1007/s12147-001-0023-8

Kahn, A., Jackson, J., Kully, C., Badger, K.& Halvorsen, J. (2003) Calling It Rape: Differences In Experiences Of Women Who Do Or Do Not Label Their Sexual Assault As Rape, Psychology of Women Quarterly, 27 (2003), 233–242

Kahn, A. S., Mathie, V. A., & Torgler, C. (1994). Rape scripts and rape acknowledgment. Psychology of Women Quarterly, 18, 53–66.

Kahneman, D., & Miller, D. T. (1986). Norm theory: Comparing reality to its alternatives. Psychological Review, 93, 136-153

Kang H. (2013). The prevention and handling of the missing data. Korean journal of anesthesiology, 64(5), 402-6.

Karson, M. (2014) Is so-called victim blaming always bad? Psychology Today, Retrieved from: https://www.psychologytoday.com/gb/blog/feeling-our-way/201409/is-so-called-victim-blaming-always-bad on 2nd February 2019

Kelly, L. (2010).The (in)credible words of women: False allegations in European rape research. Violence Against Women, 16, 1345-1355. doi:10.1177/1077801210387748

Klein, R. (Ed). (2013) Framing Sexual and Domestic Violence through Language, Palgrave Macmillan

Kline, P. (1979) Psychometrics and Psychology, London Academic Press

Khuankaew, O. (2007). Buddhism and violence against women. In D. C. Maguire & S. Shaikh (Eds.), Violence against women in contemporary world religion: Roots and Cures (pp. 174–191). Cleveland: Pilgrim Press.

Kitzinger, C. & Frith, H. (1999) Just say no? The use of conversation analysis in developing a feminist perspective on sexual refusal, Discourse and Society, Vol 10(3): 293–316

Kline, P. (1993) An Easy Guide to Factor Analysis, Routledge

Krahe, B. (1991). Police officers' definitions of rape: A prototype study. Journal of Community and Applied Social Psychology, 1, 223-244. doi:10.1002/casp.2450010305.

Koss, M. & Oros, C. (1982) Sexual experiences survey: A research instrument's investigation of sexual aggression and victimization. Journal of Consulting Psychology 50: 455–457.

Kunst, J., Bailey, A., Prendergast, C. & Gundersen, A. (2018) Sexism, Rape Myths and Feminist Identification Explain Gender Differences in

Attitudes Toward the #metoo Social Media Campaign in Two Countries, Media Psychology

Lea, S., Hunt, L. & Shaw, S. (2011) Sexual Assault of Older Women by Strangers, Journal of Interpersonal Violence, 26(11) 2303–2320, DOI: 10.1177/0886260510383036

Lee, T. L., Fiske, S. T., & Glick, P. (2010). Next gen ambivalent sexism: Converging correlates, causality in context, and converse causality, an introduction to the special issue. Sex Roles, 62(7), 395-404. doi:10.1007/s11199-010-9747-9

Lefley, H. P., Scott, C. S., Llabre, M., & Hicks, D. (1993). Cultural beliefs about rape and victims' response in three ethnic groups. American Journal of Orthopsychiatry, 63(4), 623-632. http://dx.doi.org/10.1037/h0079477

Lerner, M. J. (1980). The belief in a just world. New York: Plenum Press.

Lerner, M. J. (1997) What does the belief in a just world protect us from? The dread of death or the fear of undeserved suffering? New York, Plenum Press.

Levant, R.F.; Alto, K.M. (2017). "Gender Role Strain Paradigm". In Nadal, Kevin L. The SAGE Encyclopedia of Psychology and Gender. SAGE Publications. p. 718. ISBN 978-1-48-338427-6.

Littleton, H., Axsom, D., & Grills-Taquechel, A. (2009). Sexual Assault Victims' Acknowledgment Status and Revictimization Risk. Psychology of Women Quarterly, 33(1), 34–42. https://doi.org/10.1111/j.1471-6402.2008.01472.x

Livingston, J.A., Testa, M., & VanZile-Tamsen, C. (2007). The reciprocal relationship between sexual victimization and sexual assertiveness. Violence Against Women, 13, 1–16.

Long, J. (2012) Anti-porn: The resurgence of anti-pornography feminism. Zed Books, London

Lonsway, K. & Fitzgerald, L. (1995) Attitudinal antecedents of rape myth acceptance: A theoretical and empirical reexamination. Journal of Personality and Social Psychology 68: 704–711.

Loughlan, S., Pina, A., Vasquez, E. & Puvia, E. (2013) Sexual Objectification Increases Rape Victim Blame and Decreases Perceived Suffering, Psychology of Women Quarterly DOI: 10.1177/0361684313485718

Lyng, Stephen (1990). "Edgework: A Social Psychological Analysis of Voluntary Risk Taking". American Journal of Sociology. 95 (4): 851–886. doi:10.2307/2780644. JSTOR 2780644.

Macy, R., Nurius, P., & Norris, J. (2006). Responding in their best interests: Contextualizing women's coping with acquaintance sexual assault. Violence Against Women, 12, 478–500.

MacCallum, R., Widaman, K., Zhang, S. and Hong, S. (1999) Sample size in factor analysis, Psychological Methods, Vol. 4, No. 1, pp. 84-99

Magestro, M. (2015) Assault on the small screen: Representations of Sexual Violence on Prime Time Television, Rowman and LittleField Publishers, USA

Malle, B. (2006) The Actor–Observer Asymmetry in Attribution: A (Surprising) Meta-Analysis, Psychological Bulletin, Vol. 132, No. 6, 895–919

Maier, S.L. (2008). "I have heard horrible stories..." Rape victim advocates' perceptions of the revictimization of rape victims by the police and medical system. Violence Against Women, 14, 786-808. doi: 10.1177/1077801208320245

Maier, S. (2013) The Complexity of Victim Questioning Attitudes by Rape Victim Advocates: Exploring Some Gray Areas, Violence Against Women

Martin, P.Y. (2005) Rape Work: Victims, Gender, and Emotions in Organization and Community Context. New York: Routledge.

Mason, G. E., Riger, S., & Foley, L. C. (2004). The impact of past sexual experiences on attributions of responsibility for rape. Journal of Interpersonal Violence, 19, 1157-1171.

Maurer, T. & Robinson, D. (2008) Effects of Attire, Alcohol, and Gender on Perceptions of Date Rape, Sex Roles 58(5):423-434 DOI: 10.1007/s11199-007-9343-9

Markman, K. Gavanski. I., Sherman, S. & MNullen, M. (1993) The Mental Simulation of Better and Worse Possible Worlds, Journal of Experimental Social Psychology 29(1), DOI: 10.1006/jesp.1993.1005

Masser, B., Viki, G. T., & Power, C. (2006). Hostile sexism and rape proclivity amongst men. Sex Roles, 54(7), 565-574. doi:10.1007/s11199-006-9022-2

McGregor, M. J., Wiebe, E., Marion, S. A., & Livingstone, C. (2000). Why don't more women report sexual assault to the police? Can. Med. Assoc. J.162,659–660

McKenzie-Mohr, S. & Lafrance, M. (2011) Telling stories without the words: 'Tightrope talk' in women's accounts of coming to live well after rape or depression, Feminism & Psychology, 21(1) 49–73, DOI: 10.1177/0959353510371367

McMahon, S., & Farmer, G. L. (2011). An updated measure for assessing subtle rape myths. Social Work Research, 35, 71-81.

Messman-Moore, T.L., & Long, P.J. (2003). The role of childhood sexual abuse sequelae in the sexual revictimization of women: An empirical review and theoretical reformulation. Clinical Psychology Review, 23, 537–571.

Miller, A., Handley, I., Markman, K. & Miller, J. (2010) Deconstructing Self-Blame Following Sexual Assault: The Critical Roles of Cognitive Content and Process, Violence Against Women, 16(10), 1120-1137, DOI: 10.1177/1077801210382874

Miller, A., Markman, K. & Handley, I. (2007) Self-Blame Among Sexual Assault Victims Prospectively Predicts Revictimization: A Perceived Sociolegal Context Model of Risk, Basic and Applied Social Psychology, 29(2), 129–136

Miller, A. K., Amacker, A. M., & King, A. R. (2011). Sexual victimization history and perceived similarity to a sexual assault victim: A path model of perceiver variables predicting victim culpability attributions. Sex Roles, 64(5), 372-381. 6 doi:10.1007/s11199-010-9910-3

Moor, A., Ben-Meir, E., Golan-Shapira, D. & Farchi, M. (2013) Rape: A Trauma of Paralyzing Dehumanization, Journal of Aggression, Maltreatment & Trauma, 22:10, 1051-1069, DOI: 10.1080/10926771.2013.848965

Montada, L., & Lerner, M. J. (Eds.). (1998). Responses to victimizations and belief in a just world. New York, NY: Plenum Press.

Muganyizi, P. S., Nyström, L., Lindmark, G., Emmelin, M., Massawe, S., & Axemo, P. (2010). Effect of supporter characteristics on expressions of negative social reactions toward rape survivors in Dar Es Salaam, Tanzania. Health Care for Women International, 31, 668–685. doi:10.1080/07399331003629378.

Moller, A., Sondergaard, H.P., Helstrom L. (2017) Tonic immobility during sexual assault – a common reaction predicting post-traumatic stress disorder and severe depression. Acta Obstet Gynecol Scand 2017; DOI: 10.1111/aogs.13174

Muram, D., Miller, K., & Cutler, A. (1992). Sexual Assault of the Elderly Victim. Journal of Interpersonal Violence, 7(1), 70–76. https://doi.org/10.1177/088626092007001006

NSPCC, (2012) Ringrose, Jessica and Gill, Rosalind and Livingstone, Sonia and Harvey, Laura, A qualitative study of children, young people and 'sexting': a report prepared for the NSPCC. National Society for the Prevention of Cruelty to Children, London, UK.

Office for National Statistics, (2015)

O'Neill, M. L., & Kerig, P. K. (2000). Attributions of self-blame and perceived control as moderators of adjustment in battered women. Journal of Interpersonal Violence, 15(10), 1036-1049. doi: 10.1177/088626000015010002

Ortlipp, M. (2008). Keeping and Using Reflective Journals in the Qualitative Research Process. The Qualitative Report, 13(4), 695-705. Retrieved from https://nsuworks.nova.edu/tqr/vol13/iss4/8

Oyserman, D., Coon, H. and Kemmelmeir, M. (2002) Rethinking Individualism and Collectivism: Evaluation of Theoretical Assumptions and Meta-Analyses, Psychological Bulletin, American Psychological Association, 2002, Vol. 128, No. 1, 3–72

Page, T. E., Pina, A., & Giner-Sorolla, R. (2016). "It was only harmless banter!" The development and preliminary validation of the moral disengagement in sexual harassment scale. Aggressive Behavior, 42(3), 254-273. doi:10.1002/ab.21621

Parr, S. (2015) Integrating Critical Realist and Feminist Methodologies: Ethical and Analytical Dilemmas, Sheffield Hallam University

Payne, D.L., Lonsway, K.A., & Fitzgerald, L.F. (1999). Rape myth acceptance: exploration of its structure and its measurement using the Illinois Rape Myth Acceptance Scale. Journal of Research in Personality, 33, 27-68. doi: 10.1006/jrpe.1998.2238

Perilloux, C., Duntley, J. and Buss, D (2014) Blame attribution in sexual victimisation, Journal of personality and individual differences, http://dx.doi.org/10.1016/j.paid.2014.01.058

Peterson, Z. D., & Muehlenhard, C. L. (2004). Was it rape? The function of women's rape myth acceptance and definitions of sex in labelling their own experiences. Sex Roles, 51, 129-144. doi: 10.1023/B:SERS.0000037758.95376.00

Pinciotti, C. M., & Orcutt, H. K. (2017). Understanding Gender Differences in Rape Victim Blaming: The Power of Social Influence and Just World Beliefs. Journal of Interpersonal Violence. https://doi.org/10.1177/0886260517725736

Potter, J. and Wetherell, M. (1987). Discourse and Social Psychology: Beyond Attitudes and Behaviour. London: Sage.

Rayburn, N. R., Mendoza, M., & Davison, G. C. (2003). Bystanders' perceptions of perpetrators and victims of hate crime: An investigation using the person perception paradigm. Journal of Interpersonal Violence, 18, 1055-1074. doi:10.1177/0886260503254513

Relyea, M. & Ullman, S.E. (2015) Unsupported or Turned Against: Understanding How Two Types of Negative Social Reactions to Sexual Assault Relate to Post-assault Outcomes, Psychology of Women Quarterly, Vol 39(1), 37-52, DOI: 10.1177/0361684313512610

Ringrose, Jessica (2013) Postfeminist Education? Girls and the Sexual Politics of Schooling. London: Routledge.

Roese, N. J. (1997). Counterfactual thinking. Psychological Bulletin, 121, 133-148.

Romero-Sánchez, M., Krahé, B., Moya, M., & L., J. (2018). Alcohol-Related Victim Behavior and Rape Myth Acceptance as Predictors of Victim Blame in Sexual Assault Cases. Violence Against Women, 24(9), 1052–1069. https://doi.org/10.1177/1077801217727372

Ross, L. (1977) The intuitive psychologist and his shortcomings: Distortions in the attribution process. In Advances in experimental social psychology. Vol. 10. Edited by L. Berkowitz, 173–220. New York: Academic Press.

Russell, B.L. & Trigg, K.Y. (2004) Sex Roles 50: 565. https://doi.org/10.1023/B:SERS.0000023075.32252.fd

Ryan, W. (1971) Blaming the Victim, Penguin Randomhouse

Sakallı-Uğurlu, N. (2010). Ambivalent sexism, gender, and major as predictors of Turkish college students' attitudes toward women and men's atypical educational choices. Sex Roles, 62(7), 427-437. doi:10.1007/s11199-009-9673-x

Sampson, E. E. (2001). Reinterpreting individualism and collectivism: Their religious roots and monologic versus dialogic person-other relationship. American Psychologist, 55, 1425–1432.

Schacter, Daniel L. (2011). Psychology Second Edition. 41 Madison Avenue, New York, NY 10010: Worth Publishers. pp. 482–483. ISBN 978-1-4292-3719-2.

Simonson, K. & Subich, L. (1999) Rape perceptions as a function of gender-role traditionality and victim-perpetrator association, Sex Roles: A Journal of Research. (40) 7-8

Shaw, S., Nye, E., Jamel, J. & Flowe, H. (2009) The print media and rape, British Psychological Society

Shaver, K. G. (1970). Defensive attribution: Effects of severity and relevance on the responsibility assigned for an accident. Journal of Personality and Social Psychology, 14(2), 101-113.

Shaver, K.G. (1985). The attribution of blame: Causality, responsibility and blameworthiness. Springer: Verlag.

Shaver, K. G., & Drown, D. (1986). On causality, responsibility, and self-blame: A theoretical note. Journal of Personality and Social Psychology, 50(4), 697-702

Sigurvinsdottir, R., & Ullman, S. E. (2016). Sexual Assault in Bisexual and Heterosexual Women Survivors. Journal of bisexuality, 16(2), 163-180.

Sleath, E. (2011) Examining The Blaming Of Rape Victims And Perpetrators: Rape Myths, Belief In A Just World, Gender Role Beliefs, And Applied Findings, University of Leicester

Sleath, E. and Woodhams, J. (2014) Expectations about victim and offender behaviour during stranger rape. Psychology, Crime and Law, volume 20 (8): 798-820

Sollee, K. (2017) Witches, Sluts and Feminists: Conjuring the sex positive, ThreeL Media

Sudderth, L. K. (1998). "It'll come right back at me": The interactional context of discussing rape with others. Violence Against Women, 4, 572–594. doi: 10.1177/ 1077801298004005004

Tabachnick, B. G., & Fidell, L. S. (2007). Using multivariate statistics (5th ed.). Upper Saddle River, NJ: Pearson Allyn & Bacon

Turrell, S. & Thomas, C. (2008) Where Was God?, Women & Therapy, 24:3-4, 133-147, DOI: 10.1300/J015v24n03_08

Triandis, H. C. (1995). Individualism and collectivism. Boulder, CO: Westview Press

Ullman, S.E. (2007). A 10 year update of "review and critique of empirical studies of rape avoidance". Criminal Justice and Behavior, 34, 411-429. doi: 10.1177/0093854806297117

Ullman, S.E. (1996a). Social reactions, coping strategies, and self-blame attributions in adjustment to sexual assault. Psychology of Women Quarterly, 20, 505–526

Ullman, S. E. (1999). Social support and recovery from sexual assault: A review. Aggression and Violent Behavior, 4, 343-358.

Ullman, S. (2010) Talking about sexual assault: Society's response to survivors, American Psychological Association

Ullman, S. E. and Peter-Hagene, L. (2014), Social Reactions To Sexual Assault Disclosure, Coping, Perceived Control, And Ptsd Symptoms In Sexual Assault Victims. J. Community Psychol., 42: 495-508. doi:10.1002/jcop.21624

Ullman, S.E. & Vasquez, A.L. (2015) Mediators of Sexual Revictimization Risk in Adult Sexual Assault Victims, Journal of Child Sexual Abuse, 24:3, 300-314, DOI: 10.1080/10538712.2015.1006748

Ussher, J. (2013) Diagnosing difficult women and pathologising femininity: Gender bias in psychiatric nosology, Feminism and Psychology, 23 (1) 63-69, DOI: 10.1177/0959353512467968

Viki, G.T., & Abrams, D. (2002). But she was unfaithful: Benevolent sexism and reactions to rape victims who violate traditional gender role expectations. Sex Roles, 47, 289-293. doi: 10.1023/A:1021342912248

Vonderhaar, R. & Carmody, D. (2015) There Are No "Innocent Victims": The Influence of Just World Beliefs and Prior Victimization on Rape Myth Acceptance, Journal of Interpersonal Violence 2015, Vol. 30(10) 1615–1632, DOI: 10.1177/0886260514549196

Walby, S. & Allen, J. (2004) Domestic violence, sexual assault and stalking: Findings from the British Crime Survey, Home Office Research Study 276, HM Government

Ward, C.A. (1995). Attitudes toward rape: Feminist and social psychological perspectives. London: Sage.

Ward, C. (1988). The Attitudes towards Rape Victims Scale: Construction, validation and cross-cultural applicability. Psychology of Women Quarterly, 12, 127-146. doi:10.1111/j.1471-6402.1988.tb00932.x

Ward, T., & Beech, A. (2006). An integrated theory of sexual offending. Aggression and Violent Behavior, 11(1), 44-63. http://dx.doi.org/10.1016/j.avb.2005.05.002

Waterman, A. S. (1984). The psychology of individualism. New York: Praeger

Weaver, K.M. (2007).Women's rights and shari'a law: A workable reality? Duke Journal of Comparative & International Law, 17, 483–510.

Weaver B. & Maxwell, H. (2014) Exploratory factor analysis and reliability analysis with missing data: A simple method for SPSS users, The Quantitative Methods for Psychology, Vol 10, No. 2

West, Candace; Zimmerman, Don H. (2002). "Doing gender". In Fenstermaker, Sarah; West, Candace. Doing gender, doing difference: inequality, power, and institutional change. New York: Routledge. pp. 3–25. ISBN 9780415931793.

Wetherell, M., Taylor, S. & Yates, S. (2014) Discourse Theory and Practice, A Reader, Sage Publications

White, P. & Rollins, J. (1981) Rape: A Family Crisis, Family Relations, Vol. 30, No. 1, pp. 103-109

Williams, L. S. (1984). The classic rape: When do victims report? Social Problems, 31, 459–467. doi: 10.1525/sp.1984.31.4. 03a00070

Williams, G. (2003, p.463) Blame and responsibility. Ethical Theory and Moral Practice, 6, 427-445.

Williams, J. & Serna, K. (2017) Reconsidering Forced Labels: Outcomes of Sexual Assault Survivors Versus Victims (and Those Who Choose Neither), Violence Against Women, 1–16, DOI: 10.1177/1077801217711268

Women and Equalities Committee, (2016) Sexual harassment and sexual violence in schools, Third report of session 2016-17, House of Commons

Worell, J., & Remer, P. (2003). Feminist perspectives in therapy: Empowering diverse women (2nd ed.). Hoboken, NJ, US: John Wiley & Sons Inc.

Xue, J., Fang, G., Huang, H., Cui, N., Rhodes, K & Gelles, R. (2016) Rape Myths and the Cross-Cultural Adaptation of the Illinois Rape Myth Acceptance Scale in China, Journal of Interpersonal Violence, 34 (7):1428-1460. doi: 10.1177/0886260516651315.

Yardley, L. (2000). Dilemmas in qualitative health research. Psychology and health, 15(2), 215-228.

Zachariadis, M., Scott, S.V., & Barrett, M.I. (2013). Methodological Implications of Critical Realism for Mixed-Methods Research. MIS Quarterly, 37, 855-879.